Books by James Merrill

SCRIPTS
FOR THE
PAGEANT

SCRIPTS
FOR THE
PAGEANT

JAMES MERRILL

New York ATHENEUM 1980

Certain sections of this volume have appeared as follows:
Yes: Lessons 1 through 5 in THE KENYON REVIEW
The Ascent to Nine and *Lesson 9* in PLOUGHSHARES
Samos in THE NEW YORKER
The Excursion to Ephesus in THE NEW YORK REVIEW OF BOOKS
The House in Athens in THE NEW REPUBLIC
No: Lesson 2 in THE AMERICAN POETRY REVIEW

Copyright © 1980 by James Merrill
All rights reserved
Published simultaneously in Canada by McClelland and Stewart Ltd
Library of Congress catalog card number 79–55588
ISBN 0–689–11053–7 (clothbound); 0–689–11065–0 (paperback)
Manufactured by American Book-Stratford Press,
Saddle Brook, New Jersey
Designed by Harry Ford
First Edition

*Il ne pouvait pas la quitter et lui avoua tout bas qu'il
avait cassé le verre de Venise. Il croyait qu'elle allait le
gronder, lui rappeler le pire. Mais restant aussi douce,
elle l'embrassa et lui dit à l'oreille: "Ce sera comme au
temple le symbole de l'indestructible union."*

Jean Santeuil

CONTENTS

SPEAKERS

God Biology, *known also as* God B
Nature, *His twin. Known also as* Psyche *and* Chaos

Michael, *the Angel of Light*
Emmanuel, *the Water Angel. Known also as* Elias
Raphael, *the Earth Angel. Known also as* Elijah
Gabriel, *the Angel of Fire and Death*

The Nine Muses

00, *a senior officer in* Gabriel's *legions*
741, *known also as the peacock* Mirabell

Akhnaton ⎫
Homer ⎪
Montezuma ⎬ *The Five*
Nefertiti ⎪
Plato ⎭

Gautama
Jesus
Mercury
Mohammed

W. H. Auden
Maria Mitsotáki
George Cotzias
Robert Morse

Also The Architect of Ephesus, Marius Bewley,
Maria Callas, Maya Deren, Kirsten Flagstad, Hans
Lodeizen, Robert Lowell, Pythagoras, The Blessed
Luca Spionari, Gertrude Stein, Wallace Stevens,
Richard Strauss, Alice B. Toklas, Richard Wagner,
W. B. Yeats *and* Ephraim

Unice

David Jackson *and* JM, *the mediums*

YES

Yes. Cup glides from Board. Sun dwindles into Sound.

DJ and I look at each other. Well?

Yes, after all. The archangel
Did come to slovenly, earthbound

Us. And are we now washed crystalline?

(Not of curiosity:
We yearn for tomorrow's inside story
From Maria and Wystan—what they won't have seen!)

Nothing eludes the angel. And since light's
Comings and goings in black space remain
Unobserved   (storm-spattered midnight pane
Until resisted,   a strange car ignites)
Why think to change our natures?
                                              Whereupon
Both reach for cigarettes.

                              *

A new day—world transfigured yet the same—
We're back at our old table. AWED MY DEARS
JM: Yes, Wystan? Help us picture it.
Our peacock had, I gather, coached you in
A little masque of Welcome? THERE IS NOTHING
COMPARABLE IN LIFE & RARELY IN ART
FIRST: THE WORD ALAS IS 'COUNTENANCE'
Michael's—like lightning, as the Bible says?
YES   BEYOND THOUGHT WE BOTH FELL ON OUR KNEES
You too, Maman, who as a girl refused
To curtsey to your father's guest, the King?
ENFANT LET WYSTAN TELL IT
                              IT REQUIRES

3

SOMETHING MORE THAN LANGUAGE   MILD GLAD CRIES
AS IN THOSE MOMENTS WHEN AS NAUGHTY CHILDREN
EXPECTING PUNISHMENT WE WERE EMBRACED?
WINGS? NO   & YET SUSPENDED   WE LOOKED UP:
A GREAT ORIGINAL IDEA   A TALL
MELTING SHINING MOBILE PARIAN SHEER
CUMULUS MODELED BY SUN TO HUMAN LIKENESS.
IN SUCH A PRESENCE WHO COULD EXERCISE
THE RIGHTS OF CURIOSITY: HAIR? EYES?
O IT WAS A FACE MY DEARS OF CALM
INQUIRING FEATURE   FACE OF THE IDEAL
PARENT CONFESSOR LOVER READER FRIEND
& MORE, A MONUMENT TO CIVILIZED
IMAGINATION   OURS? HIS? WHO CAN SAY?
ONLY, IF WE AS HUMANS HAVE CREATED
SUCH AN IMAGE THEN WE TOO ARE GREAT

The cup had moved so dreamily at first,
We thought we were losing him—until he spoke
Of Earth. MES ENFANTS FROM THE PAST A MOMENT
NATURALLY TRIVIAL IN COMPARISON
COMES BACK (so like Maria to explain
The miracle as if it were mundane)
WHEN I WAS 12 OR 13 VENIZELOS
WAS AT MY FATHER'S HOUSE.   INTO THE ROOM
HIS THOUGHTFUL SENTENCES ADDRESSED TO OTHERS
PRECEDED HIM: 'THE GREAT PROPOSALS FOR GREECE
COME TO US FROM ON HIGH, FROM STRANGERS' &
SO FORTH   AND I FELT AS WITH THIS GOD
MICHAEL THAT WE WERE HEARING LOFTY WORDS
MANY TIMES UTTERED UNTIL (APPEARING) HE
BROUGHT AT LAST HIS MIND TO BEAR ON US

I MY DEARS FELT THE BOARD A SET OF NOTES
HE PRESENTLY GLANCED DOWN AT: 2 OR 3
MELODIOUSLY PITCHED & WITH THE TRUE
HOMERIC RESONANCE   SUCH AN ENCOUNTER

4

IN LIFE WD HAVE MADE ONE ON THE INSTANT FREE
OF HABIT   RITUAL   ALL THAT BINDS, & NO
SIMPER OF 'HOLINESS'   JUST THE HEAVENLY
BLAZING CALM ELATE INTELLIGENCE
"The red eye of your God"—did Michael mean
The sun *was* God? OR GOD'S ORGAN OF SIGHT
THE FOUNT OF ENDLESS VISIBILITIES.
NOW: DOES THE EYE CREATE THE OBJECT SEEN?
ONE TINY INKLING OF M'S MARVELOUS
PHILOSOPHIC VISTAS   Lost on us!

DJ: He said next time we needn't bother
With diet and deep breathing and the rest.
SUCH ROT ALL THAT   SURPRISED OUR MIRABELL
DIDN'T HAVE OUT THE TINFOIL HALOS   Tell
About his masque! THE ONLY MASQUE IN QUESTION
HID A BIRDBRAIN. HE OF COURSE HAD HAD
NOT THE FOGGIEST   'GREAT DOORS'? THERE WERE NONE:
HIS (M) PERHAPS FOR CRUCIAL DISTANCING.
NO WONDER HE LIES ABASHED HEAD UNDER WING
LIKE A SWAN   HIS CROWD U SEE (TO WHOM WE ARE
MERE FORMULAS) CANNOT CONCEIVE MAN'S EASY
LEAP ONTO THE OUTSTRETCHED PALM OF GOD,
CANNOT GRASP THAT ALL OUR LIVES ARE SPENT
IMAGINING SUCH A PRESENCE
                              NONETHELESS
OUGHTN'T WE ENFANTS TO STRETCH (NOBLESSE
OBLIGE) A KINDLY HAND OUT TO OUR BIRD?
Yes, Mirabell, we love you. Come! HE STIRRED
Come, we need you! THAT'S IT   HEAD UP! BRAVO

PLEASE GIVE YR MIRABELL A BIT OF TIME
   HE IS AFRAID TO LOOK MY DEARS   HE FANCIES
   WE ARE TRANSFIGURED   Mirabell, come on!
Is it true you've turned into a swan?
                              SHALL I? U JEST?
AH Y OUA RE REA L SOB LIN DINGT O ME ID O NO TSEE I

WILL GR OW USED   THERE! NO SWAN ALAS BUT (ON THE OUTSIDE) YOUR
FOND PEACOCK STILL   I HAVE BEEN ALLOWED NEW INFORMATION
THANKS TO YR SUCCESS MY SCHOOL IS NOW CHARTERED! TOMORROW

*

Questions of Rank

Mirabell's information deals with Nature,
And high time. But first, the other day,
His wise old teacher, 00 as we call him
—Batman to Mirabell's Robin, says DJ—
Had *he* been present?
O NO   NONE OF OURS   NO NO
        You first said he would be.
          WELL I WAS NOT THERE   & AM
NOT U UNDERSTAND OF HIS HIGH RANK

The One in question intervenes—are all
These voices henceforth at our beck and call?
        OO: WE WERE FIVE
(Just that, and goes.) He *was* there, Mirabell!
HE HAS SAID SO
Forgive us for insisting. Now the news?

      NATURE IS MISTRESS OF THE ROBES   MATTER,
HER MATERIAL   ITS CUT & STYLE, HER CEREMONY
WHO IS FOREVER CHANGING THE COSTUMES OF EARTH, OF MAN'S
VERY FLESH TO SUIT HER NEEDS & HIS. LET ME PUT IT AS
FORCEFULLY AS I CAN: THE SOCALLD 'SUPERNATURAL'
DOES NOT EXIST. SHE IS NUMBER 2 PERSON
You're mastering the Fem Lib idiom.
        O I TRY
ALWAYS TO BE A LA PAGE   AS MERCURY WE ARE THE
GOBETWEEN. YET IN PERSONIFYING MATTER/MATER
YOU MUST REMEMBER THAT MATTER IS NOT ALL, BUT OBEYS
THE DIVINE RATIO 88:12

6

Our strong point, Mirabell, has never been
Your Math. Now will the Twelve personified
Emerge as Michael?
                    NO NO   I MUST NOT

                    GONE   QUITE TERRIFIED
WE MIGHT LET SOMETHING SLIP   He's certainly
Changed his tune about Nature. THAT TUNE MAY
HAVE BEEN A SMALL TEST PASSED WHEN JM FLEW
TO HER DEFENSE   DJ: Wystan, you knew
That Chester went to Earth on our big day?
YES   AH YES   ALL SO HUMANELY PLANNED
Could you say goodbye?   NO   WE WERE SPARED OUR FEELINGS:
NO TEARS, NO AGONIZING INTERVIEW
YET WE HAD MANY MANY EVENINGS SAID
GOODNIGHT WITH A PAT & OFF EACH TO HIS BED

I still don't understand why Mirabell
Couldn't meet Michael. JM: Come, we know
The Bible, sort of, and we've seen the icons.
Michael is the fallen angels' blazing
Triumphant adversary. With his sword
"Fierce as a Comet", with his sunlike armor—
Stately allusions to a time before
The Church absolved itself of Holy War—
He's light's power over dark. DJ: Then is
Mirabell a devil? JM: Well,
Up to a point. Beyond it he remains
A puzzle—part of the "atomic forces"
That wrecked "Atlantis". What this fable means
In textbook terms, we've long despaired of learning!
MICHAEL THE PURE PHOTON? HIS WHITE LIGHT
QUANTUM INDIVISIBLE WD KNOCK
OUR PEACOCK PARTICLE OF TINSEL GREENS
& BLUES & REDS MY BOYS TO SMITHEREENS
Yet Mirabell's 00 somehow took part.
Détente in Heaven? DJ: I just wish
Mirabell weren't suddenly so servile—

7

It's we who should fall upon our knees to thank him.
NOT MES ENFANTS HIS CHOICE   WE NOW OUTRANK HIM

＊

See how sunlight filters through the leaves!
(Our mascot Pepperomia on the white
Table, each leaf a moist world sparkling—)
THE RADIANT CELLS   What
   Can it be like *inside* them, Mirabell?
                        PALATIAL   THE VEG CELLS LUMINOUS,
THE MINERAL FIERY   BOTH HOT & COLD FIRE. THESE
GENIUS STRUCTURES OF THE MASTER ARCHITECT HAVE THE
SUPREME QUALITY OF WEIGHTLESS DOMES   THEIR ELABORATE
GROINING & VITAL PILLARS POSITIOND WITHOUT BASEWORK,
FOR BOTH ROOF & FLOOR BREATHE LIFE & HOLD TO EACH OTHER BY
TRANSLUCENT MEANS
   Do you experience the cold and heat?
                        THESE LIKE TIME ARE NONEXISTENT FOR US
YET MORE THAN TIME THEY EFFECT & AFFECT MATTER. WE ARE
INTERESTED IN TEMPERATURE AS IT APPLIES TO
SOUL INTENSITIES WE OVERSEE. WITH THE HISTORIC
MIGRATIONS (GENGHIS KHAN ETC) WE CAME TO SEE THAT THE LAB
SOULS MUST THEMSELVES BE MIGRATED   NOT REBORN IN THE SAME
HEMISPHERE OR CLIMATE: CONSTANT ROUGH STUFF! TEMP IS A FRAME
FOR BEING. SOULS PERMANENTLY IN HEAVEN KNOW NEITHER
HOT NOR COLD   BUT TO DIVERT THE PASSER-THRU WE ARRANGE
THE PLUNGE INTO THE WORKINGS OF THE VOLCANO, THE SWIM
UNDER POLAR ICE, THE CLIMB UP A TREE INSIDE THE TREE:
LESSONS THAT EQUIP OUR TRANSIT SOULS FOR LIFE
                                           BACK TO CELLS
THERE ARE AS U KNOW MILLIONS OF DIFFERENCES IN EACH
CATEGORY FROM MINERAL TO VEG, REPTILE TO MAN,
& FINALLY THE STRUCTURELESS STRUCTURE OF THE SOUL CELL,
OR MORE PROPERLY THE SUBLIME STRUCTURE OF THE CELLS OF
GOD BIOLOGY
   Whose body is Earth. Whose eye—the glowing Sun—
   Upon the sparrow also is the sparrow . . .

IN SAINTLY TERMS MY DEAR THE MYSTIC UNION

U NEXT MEET THE ANGEL?

Tomorrow.   I PERHAPS
MADE A BIT MUCH OF PROTOCOL B4
                  No harm done.   & WAS RATHER
LAUGHED AT   Never by us!
              NO? WELL   YR NEW INSTRUCTOR IS MOST POWERFUL
& YOU MUST UNDERSTAND MY GREAT RESPECT   IF I CAN BE
OF SERVICE? WELL   AS TO PROTOCOL, DO AS U SEE BEST
   —Backing off.
                       HE DREADS TO RAISE HIS EYES
      MAMAN FEELS HELPLESS   SO LIKE THE OLD DAYS:
      PEOPLE WAITING FOR HOURS WAITED YET
      LONGER WHEN THE SPOILT PRIME MINISTER'S
      DAUGHTER DROPPED IN FOR POCKET MONEY
                                        CLASS
      TROUBLING ENOUGH ON EARTH   & NOW ALAS
      THAT THE ROI SOLEIL HAS ENTERED & STOOD STILL
      TO CHAT WITH US, HOW EVERYONE DEFERS!
   But talent makes the difference there, and mind.
   DON'T COUNT ON IT   SUCH FRIGHTFULLY UNWORTHY
   TYPES   THAT IMP LUCA   Go on!   HAS REPLACED
   POOR DOTING CHESTER WITH INDECENT HASTE
   Found a new friend? Who? PLATO WHAT HE SEES
   IN L!? IS IT AS I ONCE WROTE, THAT GOD
   JUDGES WHOLLY BY APPEARANCES?
   Then Luca must be one of Nature's best.
   PURE CARAVAGGIO   & A PEACHBLOOM PEST

   More about the status you've acquired?
   ENFANTS WYSTAN & I HAVE A SALON:
   REGULAR SMART LEVEES   ONE SIMPLY PICKS
   UP THE (M) BLACK RECEIVER & A MADLY
   EFFICIENT 77036
   DOES ALL THE REST   Who comes?   WHO DOESN'T? O
   LET'S SEE   YESTERDAY: COLETTE, COCTEAU,
   ST SIMON   So Wystan's taking up

9

The Frogs at last. QUE VOULEZ VOUS? THE PLATONIC
SYNDROME LED ME TO THE POISONED CUP,
A BREW OF JUICY VIGNETTES! Such as? WELL, TALES OF
LOUIS XIV & EPHRAIM EYE TO EYE
BOWING IN THE MIRRORS AT VERSAILLES
Poor Ephraim, we've all dropped him, like a mask . . .
BESIDES, AMONG THE GERMANS (UNTER VIER
AUGEN) GOETHE TURNS OUT QUITE MY DEAR
AS DULL AS RILKE   DJ: *They*'re mined out,
Densities fueling readers here below—
Unlike the French? CURIOUS POINT   WHY SO?
COLETTE MORE RECENTLY DEAD? OR ELSE IN HER
PAGES ARE VEINS NO STUDY CAN EXHAUST,
ACCESSIBLE TO THE LUCKY AMATEUR
WITHOUT FIRST BEING PROCESSED? ACADEME
MINES I SUSPECT WITH DEEPER BLASTS   The dire
Glumness of some critics— WE FOREDOOM
THOSE CALLING CARDS TO OUR HALL PORTER'S FIRE

And tomorrow Michael! YES   THIS AFTERNOON
WE'RE NOT AT HOME   A HUSH EXTENDS AROUND US
ONE ALL BUT HEARS THE QUIVER THRU THE HOUSE
OF FAINTLY, AWESOMELY APPROACHING WINGS.
MM FUSSING WITH HER NEW SILVER GOWN,
MY BLOND HEAD RISING FROM A GOSSAMER WHITE
TUNIC   How *Rosenkavalier*! O QUITE
HE BY THE WAY IS A DARLING   Who is? STRAUSS

*

The Second Visit

MORTAL CHILDREN, GENTLE SHADES, GREETINGS. I AM MICHAEL.
THE VAST FORMING INTELLIGENCE ENCOMPASSING THE ENERGIES OF
  A UNIVERSE OF BORNING & EXPLODING WORLDS SETTLED AT LAST
  FOR THIS, CALLED EARTH.

ONCE AGAIN OUR ARCHITECT MADE READY HIS TOOLS & BEGAN HIS
WORK.

HIS PLAN, O HIS PLAN!

HE HAS FOREVER DREAMED OF CREATING A GOOD COMPANY AND A
FRIENDLY PLACE. NOW HE BEGAN AGAIN CUPPING ENERGIES AND
LAYING ABOUT SEED & LIGHT.

HE LONG KNEW THE FORCES ARRAYED AGAINST HIM: THE NEGATIVES,
THE VOIDS. HE HAD BEEN BESTED BEFORE.

THESE HAD DESTROYED OTHERS OF HIS WORKS BY EXPLOSION AND BY
BLACK SUCTIONING, AND HE NAMED THEM EVIL.

HE WAS EVER ON GUARD, HE SET ASIDE FOUR QUANTA OF ENERGY AND
FIRST CREATED HIS HELPERS.

I AWOKE.

MY FACE GENTLY AS BY A BREEZE WAS TURNED UPWARD: 'BEHOLD,
MY OWN, THE LIGHT'

THIS I KNEW WAS MY DUTY, EACH OF ITS WORKINGS, ITS SHINING
& ITS DIMMING, ITS TERRIBLE & ITS FRUITFUL ASPECTS: THE
TENDING OF THE SUN.

MY BROTHERS WERE ASSIGNED THEIR DUTIES, WE BENT OUR BACKS
TO THE PLAN. ANOTHER CHANCE TO BE GIVEN TO OUR MASTER!

SO THE SOFT WORDS, THE INTELLIGENCE. NOW WHAT IS THIS IN
FACT?

WHAT MEANT BY PLAN? WORKS? WHAT BY MASTER? AND WHAT, AT
THE GOLDEN END, BY PARADISE?

A WHIRL OF FIRE. A BALL. A CLOUD OF SMOKE & SETTLING ASH. A
COOLING. A LOOK AT THE THING.

O IS IT, THAT STANDING BACK AT THE VERY ELBOW OF
INTELLIGENCE, IS THIS NOT THE FERTILE ELEMENT:
IMAGINATION?

WE DESCENDED THEN ON AN ARC. FOR THE ARCHITECT, THAT
WHITESMITH,

HAD FLUNG HIS WATERY HANDS DOWNWARD AND A HISSING STEAM
ENVELOPED OUR DREAM.

I RAISED THE BEAM, FOUR DIVINE COLORS LAID AN ARC, WE WENT
DOWN.

AND THEN FROM HIS STORED INTELLIGENCE, JUST AS HAD THE STUFF
OF US, CAME THE RUSH, THE SPRINGING ENERGIES, THE AIR
FRESHENED, LIFE! LIFE!

THERE IS FOR US NO DIMENSION OF TIME. SO HOW MAY YOU KNOW
THE LENGTHS WHICH WERE ONLY THE INTELLIGENCE & ITS
WORKINGS?
THESE HUGE AND HUMBLE MIRACLES APPEARED:
ASH TO SOIL. STARS TO ENERGY SOURCES. SUN TO GROWTH. EACH
STEP A STEP TOWARD THE FIRST FLAT WIDE GREEN SPACES.
THEN BROTHER ELIAS WAS TOLD: 'DIVIDE BY WATER'
AND MY BROTHER CALLED FORTH THOSE ENERGIES & INSTRUCTED
THEM.
THEY MULTIPLIED, THEY POURED FORTH, AND THE GREEN WAS
SEPARATED ACCORDING TO THE PROPORTIONS DEEMED NEEDFUL
BY OUR MASTER
FOR HE HELD IN HIS INTELLIGENCE SEVERAL CHILDREN HE WISHED
TO KEEP APART.
US FOUR HE SUMMONED. HE SAID: 'NOW WE ARE READY,
YET IS NOT THIS PLACE BEAUTIFUL SIMPLY OF GREEN & WATER &
QUIET AIR?'
WE WAITED AS DO THE WORK ANIMALS WHO KNOW THEIR MASTER
HAS NOT BROUGHT THEM OUT FOR MERE COMPANY, THAT IN
THE SOIL UNDER THEIR HOOVES LIES HIS DEAR ATTENTION.

WE HAVE NOT ENVIED HIS VARIOUS CHILDREN.
HE SAID: 'TAKE THIS STICKING EARTH AND FASHION ME SOME
FORMS.'
MANY WERE THEN MODELED, SOME HE NODDED AT, OTHERS WERE
SMASHED AGAIN FLAT. AND THEN HE POINTED TO A FORM
AND THE RADIANCE OF HIS FACE MADE US KNEEL: THE HEIR.
AND WHAT? A CREATURE OF GREAT BLANK EYES & LOW HANGING
HEAD, SHY OF US, BETWEEN TREMBLING FORELEGS: 'MY SON'
AGAIN THE WORK. WE HOVERED & HELPED WHERE WE COULD. AND
THIS CREATURE SUPPED ON THOUGHT.
(DJ: The centaur? JM: Shh! I think so.)
YET OUR MASTER HAD IN SPARE A TWOLEGGED CREATURE WE HAD
FORMED FIRST, AS HE SEEMED THE IMAGE OF OURSELVES.

THE HISTORY OF THE ONE YOU KNOW. OF THE OTHER, YOU LIVE.
NOW WHEN IN THE COURSE OF HIS PLAN THE ARCHITECT FROWNS
    ON HIS WORK, HIS MERCY ALLOWS IT TO DESTROY ITSELF.
AND ALWAYS AT HIS BECK IS DESTRUCTION, A THIRD BROTHER.
A MODEST BROTHER. WHO IS NOT, WHO MUST UNDO?
'TAKE THE CREATURES IN HAND.'
WE TURNED OUR EYES FROM THE LOUD EXPLOSION.
AND WHEN OUR BROTHER CAME TO US HE HELD ONLY THE ONE
    FORM, & IN HIS OTHER HAND LOOSE CLAY.
WE WAITED: AGAIN THE CYCLE OF FIRE, ASH, DUST.
HOW PATIENT TRUE INTELLIGENCE! A NEW DESIGN:
THE FLAT PLAINS WERE NOW BROKEN BOTH BY WATER &
    MOUNTAINS, AND THE SEASONS SPURRED BY CAPPED ICE. WHY?
'MY CHILD MUST STRUGGLE TO GAIN HIS INHERITANCE'
THEN AGAIN WE PRESENTED OUR MODEL. WE KNEW BY OUR MASTER'S
    SMILE THAT HE HAD AT LAST RECOGNIZED THE IMAGE AS
    FAITHFUL.
'MAKE HIM UNDER THE NAME OF MAN. LET HIM SURVIVE.'

AS MICHAEL I AM ALLOWED TO WONDER, FOR I AM A FAVORITE OF
    GOD'S:
WHY UNDER THE NAME? WAS MY MASTER PUTTING A DISTANCE
    BETWEEN HIMSELF AND THIS NEW CREATURE?
'BROTHERS (I SAID) OUR CREATURE MUST ENDEAR HIMSELF' AND THEY
    UNDERSTOOD.
WE MADE FACE & EYES IN THEMSELVES INFINITELY APPEALING. BY
    THOSE EYES WE SHOWED OUR LORD SOMETHING OF THE
    DARLING OF HIS OWN GENIUS
(SMALL TREASURES HE LOVES, OWNING THE VAST UNIVERSE).
OUR CREATURE STILL HANGING ON A GROWN THING CALLED TREE
    HAD NOT YET BEEN ACCEPTED.
A FOURTH BROTHER OF GREAT WIT, OUR TRUE INVENTOR, THOUGHT:
    HOW TO DELIGHT GOD?
AND TAKING A SPARK FROM AN ENERGY NEARBY HE FLUNG IT INTO
    THE CREATURE'S HEAD
AND AT ONCE THE STUNNED FINGERS LOOSENED, DOWN IT FELL, AND
    WHEN NEXT THE EYES OPENED THEY PEERED STRAIGHT UP.
AND GOD SAW A NEW LIGHT THERE.

IT SHONE FLICKERING OVER SEVERAL IDEAS: MINE, MASTERY, WHY?
AND GOD TURNED TO US: 'IT IS MY OWN.'

THAT LONG MARCH IS STILL UNDER WAY. I AM MICHAEL. MY LIGHT
    IS YOUR DAY.
WHEN AS NOW IT SINKS I LEAVE YOU FOR MY VIGIL. ON OTHER
    DAYS, THE NEXT TWO TIMES, YOU WILL MEET MY WATER
    BROTHER, THEN TOO MY WITTY EARTH BROTHER.
AT LAST WE WILL BRING YOU OUR SHY BROTHER, HANDS BEHIND HIM,
AND YOUR INSTRUCTION WILL BEGIN.
AND NOW O HUMAN MEN CHILDREN & GOD'S DELIGHT, HEAR
    MICHAEL SAY:
INTELLIGENCE, THAT IS THE SOURCE OF LIGHT. FEAR NOTHING WHEN
    YOU STAND IN IT   I RAISE YOU UP AMONG US   HAIL   HAIL

★

VIS A VIS MY DEARS ON MICHAEL'S PALM!
ONE HAD THE FEELING OF A BIJOU OBJECT
HE WAS IMMENSELY PLEASED AT LAST TO OWN
He must then *be* immense. INDEED   THE SCALE
OF THE LOST IVORY & GOLD ATHENA?
MAKES ONE ASK WHAT PHIDIAS HAD SEEN
I wish—I nearly said "I wish we'd been there!"
U WERE   BOTH LISTENING AS DEAR ONES DO,
EYES TURNED ASIDE NOT TO IMPEDE THE FLOW
We're at your level? YES   In our old clothes,
Wrinkle and graying hair and liver spot?
NOT IN OUR WITCH'S GLASS, DISTINCTLY NOT!
Who's fairest? DJ: Michael, I suppose.
He'll come again? THEY AS I SEE IT WILL
INCREASE IN NUMBER ONE BY ONE UNTIL
THEY STAND FOURSQUARE: NATURE'S 4 GENTLEMEN
And the shy brother? AH   THE SOUNDING BASS
IN THE QUARTET   OR PITCH INAUDIBLE
EXCEPT TO A BLACK DOG: HE OVERSEES
MIRABELL'S OLD MASTER I SHD THINK
WHO IN HIMSELF IS SOMETHING   Is he? Tell!

OO APPEARS FIRST, WE STAND, HE RATHER AHEM
PORTENTOUSLY FACES OFF   THEN LIFTING INK
BLACK GLITTERY WINGS OBSCURES OUR VIEW WITH THEM.
WHITE LIGHT APPEARS AROUND HIM   HE BECOMES
THE SILHOUETTE OF   Evil? NO . . . RESISTANCE?
A PRIMAL SCENE? PART OF A MASTERMASQUE:
IN THE SERENE WHITE BRILLIANCE MICHAEL'S EYES
THEN FACE THEN FIGURE NOW MATERIALIZE
IN UTTER QUIET   HE PUTS DOWN HIS HAND
ON WHICH MM & I TAKING OUR STAND
ARE LIFTED TO THE LEVEL OF HIS FACE
WHERE THE BIJOU EFFECT TAKES PLACE

      ENFANTS

HIS GOLDEN EYES EVER ALERT AND CALM
ARE FIXED UPON US   WE ARE UNAWARE
OF MOVING LIPS & YET HIS VOICE IS THERE
SURROUNDING US   OR ARE WE IN HIS MIND
READING THESE GLORIES THAT WOULD SEEM TO COME
FROM BOTH SIDES OF THE MIRROR OF MANKIND?
How does it end? REVERSE PROCEDURE   EYES
DIMMING, THEN FACE   HAND LOWERED   ALL THE REST
IS SUDDENLY OUR FORMER STATE OF THINGS.
THERE LIES THE OLD AWED MASTER FACEDOWN WINGS
OUTSTRETCHED   Does he speak then? O TOUCHINGLY
MUMBLES ON HIS WAY OUT 'U ARE BLEST'

DJ MY BOY SMOOTH SAILING

     AS WE SPEAK
MAMAN PATS DOWN THE SEAS   HERE'S TO A GREEK
NEW YEAR'S DAY PARTY! HUGS FROM ALL YR FRIENDS
—With which our long, amazing summer ends.

George on Birds

DJ crosses the ocean. JM, alone
Through the mild autumn months in Stonington,
Quarries from the transcript murky blocks

Of revelation, now turning a phrase
To catch the red sunset, now up at dawn
Edging into place a paradox—
One atop the other; and each weighs
More than he can stop to think. Despair
Alternates with insight. Strange how short
The days have grown, considering the vain
Ticking, back, forth, of leafless metronomes
Beyond the pane, where atmosphere itself
One morning crystallizes. Winter's here.

George Cotzias, freed of his patient's gown
At last, suggests an evening on the town.
My sister gives us tea first. A fire's laid
And lit, in whose diaphanous charade
He borrows her ease, she his earnestness;
I from them both, a sense of taxing roles
Consigned, on rare occasion, to the coals.
But curtain time approaches: she must dress.
In the dim doorway, while I pace the street
Of old facades, frost-featured and discreet,
They linger. Then her silvery goodbye.
At table, over wine, the man of Science
—Bifocal lenses catching candlelight,
Athena's owl, ear cocked and tufted white—
Takes in the transformation of gargoyle
To feathered friend. Pure vinegar and oil
Our viewpoints, I'd have thought. Not so:
These now are things that Science cares to know.
Science, George hopes, has room for Juno's bird
—And for its mistress, should she grace our Board!

Do I remember, he goes on, the dream
Of Dante's mother, from Boccaccio?
She saw a peacock in a laurel tree,
Beak snipping the clustered berries—down they fell
Until the skirt she held outspread was full—
And woke in labor. Taking up the theme,

Moving past Lesbia's sparrow, Poe and Keats.
Coloratura wood-note understood
By Siegfried, thumb licked clean of dragon's blood;
Past twittering parliament, past the "little bird"
Who speaks to instinct with a paraclete's
Ghostly cackle, we attain the sphere
(Justice?) where Dante saw the letter M
Become an Eagle made of ruby souls
Which sang to him. What of the Phoenix, then?—
Its blaze our culture-watchers doze before,
Never quite making out the infra-vulture.
Of Senator X who vowed Vietnam would "rise
Like a Tucson" from the ashes—? A short pause,
Then George: "You won't laugh if I tell you I
Also get these voices, these vocations?
Over the years, each time I've undergone
A general anesthetic, the same one,
A woman's, cold yet not unloving, fills
My head with truths about the cosmos—truths,
Jimmy, too deep, too antilogical
Ever to grasp, short of the odd detail
Clutched on waking. Once, the phrase 'black holes'
(And this was long before black holes made headlines)
Stayed with me. Another time, these were explained
As ash the Phoenix left on entering
A 'biological cycle'. And once, I woke
Knowing that what had reached me was the song
The Phoenix sings throughout eternity."

We're on the street. He wonders if he may
Try the Board with us next spring in Athens?
His hometown, I remember now, where things
Periodically keep taking him.
As they do me. By the New Year great wings
Have reunited DJ and JM,
Eager to meet the lords of Earth and Sea.

The Board, that first day, is all come-and-go—

Revolving door into a lobby. Enter
Hans as if startled: OH JIM? U ARE THE CENTER
OF MUCH GOOD FEELING HERE   Then Wallace Stevens:
MAY I SUGGEST A CENTRAL METAPHOR:
PEACOCK TO O—to zero—AS CHICKEN TO EGG?
Acknowledging our thanks, away they saunter,
Leaving Wystan and Maria barely
Time to say that in the interval
Since last we met OUR UTTER PURITY
HAS HAD THE GOOD OLD HUMAN DIRT RESTORED.
THE POINT MUST BE MY DEARS, TO TOUCH HOME BASE
MAKES POSSIBLE EACH NEW LEAP INTO SPACE
Here now is Mirabell. He calls us MASTERS,
Calls his poem A CAP TO ALL MY FEATHERS
And says of George's interest:
U SEE, JM? IS NOT SCIENCE ITSELF COMING TO CALL?

> (The doorbell.)

Not Science, just an oil delivery—
MY ANCESTORS POURING IN TO WARM U: SET US ALIGHT!
One word, next, from a figure bathed in tears:
CHERI   It's my old nurse, Mademoiselle
Who died last month—

> But 00 interferes:

DOWN! WE BEAR ON WINGS THE WORD OF GREAT MICHAEL O GLORY!
HE & HIS BROTHERS SAY TO US: GO FORTH INTO THE DREAMS
OF THIS OR THAT ONE, NOW AS EAGLE OR SWAN OR DOVE, NOW
AS THE OFT FALLEN OFT RISEN LEGENDARY PHOENIX
& IN THE TONGUES OF DREAM ENTHRALL & INSPIRE ALL THOSE
WHO DO OUR IMMORTAL WORK. BUT FOR YOU, O SCRIBE, O HAND:
GO (THEY COMMANDED FROM THE FIRST) IN YR WORKDAY ASPECT
FOR THESE 2 WILL TRANSFORM U AFTER THEIR OWN FASHION   DOWN!
YOU WILL IN 2 SUNCYCLES BE CALLD   NO INTERRUPTION!
DOWN!   BE SUMMOND BY O GLORY! THE WATER GOD   BACK! DOWN!

What's going *on*? THE AUDITORIUM
ENFANTS IS UNFAMILIAR   THEY ALL SEE
THE GLOW & CROWD IN   IF WE FACED THE LIGHT?
(Our table's in the gloomy downstairs hall—

Well, not a moment to describe the house;
But we move chairs.) BETTER   NOW MICHAEL HAS
A PATH   AH YES   YES! HE IS OVER US!
Michael? So many voices, how to know—
MY DEARS IT IS A MAHLER   Michael speaks:

CHILDREN, MY BROTHER ELIAS REQUESTS YOU IN TWO DAYS. HE IS
    AS WATER SWEET & FLUID.
I HAVE CLEANED THIS SPACE: HAVE NO FEARS, INTELLIGENT ONES,
    HAIL!

Thus as in some old-world Grand Hotel
(Early morning ado; kingfisher streak
Of lift-boy; *Figaro* and eggcup; hall
Porter's flicked ash, a chambermaid's faint shriek;
The beldam, ringlets trembling upon skull,
Chastening marble with her brush and pail
—Inconveniences the clientèle
Must philosophically endure until

A new day's clean white linen runners lie
In place over the antediluvian crimson
Of corridor and stair, down which now takes
—Bonjour, Milord! Il fait un beau soleil!—
His ease a blondness bareheaded and winsome)
THE WHITE HAS BEEN LAID DOWN FOR THESE NEW TALKS

*

The Water Brother

CHILDREN, ARE YOU THIRSTY? COME, ELIAS!

Not Willowware in Greece, a tea-stained white
Cup surges and ebbs with the new angel:
I AM THE SUSPENSION   REASON FLOATS IN MY SALTY STRENGTH
    HAIL!

SOME CLAIM THE MOON CONTROLS ME, NOT SO: I BALANCE IT IN
 THE PALM OF MY BASINS.
BENIGN, I WASH MY WITTY BROTHER. CONTROLLED, I BRING MAN
 HIS FALSE LIGHT
BUT YIELDING EVER TO MICHAEL AS THE BROTHER MOST BELOVED
 OF OUR MASTER.
NOW (imitative movements of the cup)
I AM WHIRLPOOL! NOW WATERFALL! NOW WAVE!
THEN AS RAIN & ICE, MANIFESTING MYSELF FOR MY MASTER & HIS
 CHILD, I REGULATE THE SEASONS.
I WAS BORN AS A TEAR IN GOD'S EYE: THUS I BRING BALM FOR
 SORROW.
O CHILDREN, I AM THE GREATER PART OF YOUR BODIES & YOUR
 NOURISHMENT, THOUGH 2ND TO MY BELOVED MICHAEL.
NOW IN 12 TIDES WE WILL RETURN WITH MY WITTY BROTHER
& THEN WITH OUR SHY ONE WHEN MY SEASON OF RENEWAL FINDS
 YOU STRONGER TO MEET THE FORCE OF HIM,
AND THEN WE FOUR COMMENCE YOUR INSTRUCTION HAIL!

MES ENFANTS WE ARE STILL SLIGHTLY AWASH
Don't tease us, tell! FIRST MICHAEL IN HIS GLORY
THEN HE TURNED & A SHAFT! A RAINBOW SPOKE
& AS WE KNELT IN WONDER MELTED INTO
WHITE CLOUD WHICH NEXT GREW SOLID How baroque!
A GIANT ALL HOAR & SPIKY ICE A HISS
OF HAIL & OUR BLUE ROBES CLUNG WETLY TO US!
ELIAS ROSE IN A TALL DAZZLING VAPOR
& MICHAEL'S LAUGHTER MADE ALL HEAVEN QUAKE
And did Maman's affinities with water
Earn her special treatment? AH ENFANT,
TOO RAVISHING: I SANK INTO A POOL
WARM & SWEET: EXPERIENCING MY MOTHER'S
WOMB SUSPENDED INFINITELY PLEASED
AS IF MY LIFE WERE JUST AHEAD
       And Wystan?
I MY DEARS STOOD BRACED IN A MANLY DOWNPOUR
Why do you suppose he's called Elias?
THEY ALL HAVE MANY NAMES THEIR VOWELS RING

THRU CANYONS OF MYTH ELIAS I DARESAY
IS THE MUSICAL ANGEL MOZART CALLS GABRIEL
In an opera? NO IN A SOIREE
Mozart as Stravinsky— YES OUR CHATS
SUCH FUN M/S PROPOSES A NEW 'RAKE'
PROGRESSING THRU VARIOUS LIVES OF V WORK ONLY
TO BE COMICALLY DEFEATED BY THE RATS

DJ: What's Wystan's future? JM: We
Assume he stays in the Bureaucracy—
Right, Wystan? Getting mined for all you're worth
By fresh-faced, big-thumbed scholars here on Earth.
DJ: Why do I have the distinct impression
He and Maria both are being groomed
To join the elements? She'll become a tree,
That much we know from Mirabell, while he—
JM: No, no. Maria after all
Had lost much of her soul to cobalt rays.
But Wystan's is intact; so that can't be.
A PLUS DJ BACK TO THE GLABROUS CLAYS
THE OILS & METALS MY FIRST LOVES COME AUTUMN
A FAIRY PAIR WILL FLIT FORTH HAND IN HAND:
MM INTO THE GREEN, I INTO SAND
But *your* soul wasn't harmed. Why this instead
Of human life, if it should come to that,
Like Chester? MY DEMISE A FORM OF LEAD
POISONING: I WENT OFF TO MY ROOM
TIDDLY THAT NIGHT BUT HAD IN MIND TO SCRIBBLE
A NOTE TO C, & AS I'D DONE SINCE CHILDHOOD
SUCKED ON A PENCIL THINKING. NEXT I KNEW,
AN ICY SUN SHONE IN UPON THE DEAD
WEIGHT OF MY FEATHER QUILT But how does lead
Destroy the soul? DJ: They don't *use* lead—
Graphite in pencils. LET THE FACT REMAIN
(OR FABLE!) THAT I SIPPED IT GRAIN BY GRAIN.
OVER THE YEARS ANYTHING FROM AN X RAY
TO THE COSMIC RAYS WE'RE ALL EXPOSED TO WD
RESIDE UNDISSIPATED IN MY BLOOD

& VITAL ORGANS: I BECAME A WALKING
NONCONDUCTING LEADEN CASKET THESE
PARTICULAR DESTRUCTIVE ENERGIES
HAD FILLED WITH RADIANT WASTE   Dear God . . . & NO
PANDORA   NO LATTERDAY BASSANIO
TO LIFT THE LID. WE MAKE OUR DEATHS MY DEARS
AS NO DOUBT THAT SHY WILDLY EXPECTED BRO
WILL TELL US   Ah, it's grim. Yet what to ask
Of death but that it come wearing a mask
We've seen before; to die of complications
Invited by the way we live. Bad habits,
Overloaded fuses, the foreknown
Stroke or tumor—these we call our own
And face with poise. It's random death we dread.
The bomb, the burning theatre, the switchblade-
Brandishing smack freak— OR ARE PENCIL & KNIFE
& COCK ALL ONE
            & WAVE & BREAST & WET
SNAKY LOCKS! WE'LL SWEEP UP U CHAPS YET!
Speaking of those breasts, Maman, the tale
We're hearing now is nothing if not male.
But Maya long ago said Erzulie
Was Queen of Heaven. Has She any niche
That one could visit? TALK TO YR WHITE WITCH

DAVID   JIMMY   Maya! In New York
Last week I saw some friends of yours; saw Teiji.
He and his young wife are salvaging
Your Haitian film. At last it's out of storage,
Cut, spliced, synchronized with the drum-tapes—
Reel upon reel of ritual possession—
And can be shown soon. We're all thrilled except
(Wouldn't you know) your mother: "Maya made
High class, avant garde stuff—documentaries
Never." Whereupon Joe Campbell spoke
Authoritatively of your amazement
At being overwhelmed quite simply by
Gusts of material so violent

As to put out the candle held to them
By mere imagination. Such a theme,
He said, took all one's powers to "document".
AS U ARE LEARNING, J? But now my question:
Is there no Ewig-Weibliche in sight?
AN EWIG SHALL WE SAY HERMAPHRODITE?
YOU HAD THOUGHT ERZULIE WAS FEMALE? HE/
SHE IS/WAS RAIN SOIL SEED SUN STARLIGHT
PHALLUS & VAGINA   OMNISEX
QUEEN OF A HEAVEN LIKE A GAUDY EX
VOTO WHERE DESIRE & SATISFACTION
PEPPER & SALT THE DISH SERVED PIPING HOT!
No heartburn after? O MY TEIJI   WHAT
IS THE GIRL LIKE   PRETTY? I thought so. Sweet, smart,
Clearly devoted to both him and art.
No match of course for *you* in your heyday—
More Greuze than Ghirlandaio. SOUNDS OK

Admit it, this new Erzulie leaves us
Less eager for a glimpse. Where's Marius?
MY DEAR JAMES   Is there an Athenian
Club where you can get a drink and read
The underground newspapers? O INDEED
PLATO & WYSTAN ARE ITS CO-CHAIRPERSONS
And Chester's Luca, still under Plato's wing?
LUCA! CUT MY LACE   THAT   THAT   THAT THING
ROAMING HEAVEN LIKE A VAST STEAMROOM
Cool off—ask Coleridge for some laudanum.
NO NO   I LEAVE SOOTHED BY THE SIGHT OF U

MES CHERS HE MEANS THE RADIANCE AROUND U
Ephraim!—dimmed though we are, much of the time,
By careless living, the old human grime?
A WISE PROTECTION   SO THE ATHLETE SMEARS
DIRT BENEATH HIS EYES TO CUT REFLECTION.
MY POOR SLAVE'S VISION OVERFLOWS WITH LOVE
AROUND U BOTH SUCH JOY SUCH RADIANT LIGHT
If so, a joy not ours to feel, a light

We are the two contracted pupils of.

YET FOR THAT FOCAL DARKNESS THANK GOD B
MY BOYS   IT IS YR PRECIOUS SANITY

Wystan. Can we bear to part with him,
Our mine of good sense? Ah, he'll doff his dim
Red shift (the mufti of a star's retreat)
To vanish into quarry and tar-pit,
Sandgrain and stylus, thorn the raw March wind
Piping through despondent makes a wand
In bloom. He'll draw the desert round his knees,
Brows knitted where the thinking icecaps freeze.
He'll be the nurse whose charges "for their own
Good" go without tea—and herself lies
Till morning haunted by reproachful eyes.
He'll be the glinting, faithful heart of stone.

*

The Earth Brother

Twelve tides pass. We take the Board upstairs
Where beyond the glassed-in balcony
Mt Lykabettos, green all year with pine,
Rises steeply in sun. And here is Michael:

DEAR CHILDREN, MY WITTY ELIJAH TWIN OF WATER IS WITH US:
COME ELIJAH, MAKE US LAUGH!

MY WIT IS NOT AS READY AS I WOULD WISH
(Oddly subdued, in spite of Michael's words)
FOR I AM IN YOU, GOD'S CHILDREN: THE RIB, NOT THE FUNNY BONE.
I WAS GOD'S THIRD CREATION, SUMMONED FROM COSMIC DUST AND
     NAMED BY MANY COSMOS,
AND WHAT ARE OUR FOUR NAMES BUT GREEK INVENTIONS?

FROM COSMIC DUST   O THINK ON THAT!
IT MEANS I HAVE IN ME THE IRRADIATED METALS, I WHO MOST
    DREAD THEM, FOR I AM FRUITFUL EARTH
IT MEANS I AM THE HABITAT OF THE CREATURE DUG OUT OF ME.
MY TWIN DRAWS BACK & I ADVANCE, AND NOW OUR DANCE
    REVERSES
FOR IT IS GOD'S WILL THAT HIS CHILDREN REDUCE THEIR NUMBERS,
    & THUS HE NUDGES THEM INTO THE MORE CONFINED SPACES,
& THUS IT IS IN THE WOMB OF TWINS: WATER EVER RECEDING AS
    THE FETUS WAXES.
BUT NOW MY SMALL BROTHERS, FOR ARE WE NOT ALL OF THE
    COMMON CLAY,
(Here at the close, a strong, dancing motion)
FAREWELL! I WILL ANOTHER TIME BE WITTY

O ELIJAH   BROTHER   O WHY ABASHED? HE LEAVES   THE SIGHT OF
    TEARS?
DJ, face streaming: Oh but these aren't tears—
Reaction to the thrill—I can't explain—
I KNOW THIS, MY CHILD. IT IS HIS WIT NO DOUBT: OFTEN MOST
    BRIEF, ACCORDING TO THE NATURE OF COSMIC DUST
JM: Indeed—those short-lived particles
Created by the photons! Only at
Molecular levels is there permanence.
YOU ARE OUR OWN   HAIL!

As Michael goes, DJ: Our first exchange—
We *can* talk back and forth, then, with the angels?
O MY DEARS & THE VOICE LIKE THUNDER! MICHAEL SWUNG
HIS PALM   WE STARED FORTH FROM IT AT YR MOUNTAIN:
IT IT IT SPOKE   THEN TOOK A HUMAN SHAPE
ALL MASSIVE ROCK & GREEN WITH BOUGHS FOR LASHES
OF SUCH I MUST SAY WICKED MERRY EYES!
I DO BELIEVE OUR SPRINGTIME WILL BE GAY
IN THE OLD SENSE   And did he look at you
With special favor? WYSTAN MES ENFANTS
TOOK A POWDER INTO THE NEAREST ROCK
And saw? A CASE OF JEWELS MY BOY   THE VOICE

RANG ROUND ME & (IF I MAY BE IMMODEST)
I UNDERSTOOD MY OWN LAST DECADES' WORK:
SUSTAINED BY WIT AS BY A WRY YOUNG FRIEND
AS I LIMPED FORWARD GRITTY TO THE END.
FOR IS IT NOT OUR LESSON THAT WE COME
EACH TO HIS NATURE? NOT TO ANY VAST
UNIVERSAL ELEVATION, JUST
EACH TO HIS NATURE PRECIOUS IF BANAL
LIKE THE CLICHE UNCOVERED AMONG GEMWORDS:
FOR ME, TO (COSMIC) DUST RETURNED
                                    FOR ME
LIKE THE OLD HORSE (BLACK BEAUTY) PUT TO GRASS
It's as we were told at the outset—every grain
Of dust, each waterdrop, to be suffused
With mind, with *our* minds. This will be Paradise.
PRECISELY JM   & TO GO ON: THAT RACE
USING US, EVOLVING FROM US IN
THAT PARADISE, ASK THEM ABOUT THAT RACE.
IT IS I THINK NOW BEING READIED, FOR
THESE ANGELS, THE FIRST 3 OF THEM SO FAR,
TAKE WITH US A SOUPCON OF THE TONE
WITH WHICH ONE SPOKE IN ONE'S OWN CARELESS YOUTH
TO AGED ELDERS: RESPECTFUL   TOLERANT
HALF PITYING   & GOODBYE TO U DEAR AUNT!
DJ: A new species? JM: Yet they'd wanted
"The stuff of man to be human". Mirabell . . .
—Who, at his name, describing a broad O,
Positively sweeps onto the Board.

U ARE HAVING A GOOD TALK?
Dear Peacock, we begin—but suddenly
All his aplomb is gone; and so is he.
                    OUR LORD MICHAEL O GLORY!
& HIS BROTHERS SPLENDID IN ALL THEIR POWERS ARE TO BE
ARRAYD B4 YOU IN THE FOURTH OF YR NEXT MOON CYCLES
O FORTUNATE ONES!
DJ: They *know* you're leaving Saturday
And won't be back in Greece until next May.

00 has flown. Reentering, Mirabell:
> FORGIVE ME   THAT IS THE PROTOCOL,
MY REVERED TEACHER WHO COMES TO ANNOUNCE THEIR INTENTIONS
Why don't *you* announce them? You once did,
AH DO U NOT SEE? YOU HAVE GRADUATED FROM MY SCHOOL.
I COME TODAY ON A (M) PERSONAL ERRAND   ONLY
TO TELL JM MY WINGED LOVE WILL KEEP PACE WITH HIS JET
& MINE MY BOY
> & MINE (MAMAN DIPLOMA'D!)
TIME FOR TALK, CHAPS?
> Maria, how we'd laugh
With you in this room! There's your photograph,
The lamp you gave us. TALK OR SELF PITY? Oh
All right, let's do it your way. Did you know
George Cotzias in the old days? NEVER WELL
YOUNGER THAN I (NOT THAT I WAS ANTIQUE)
& BURLY   NOT YR AVERAGE TESTTUBE FREAK
Bright? WD I KNOW? Let me ask Mirabell—
He sees the future: is George very ill?

MORTALLY   YET HE RESISTS AS HE HAS A CONSUMING
V WORK   LET ME EXPLAIN: HIS VISIT TO OUR TABLE MAY
BE POSTPONED UNTIL AFTER THESE GRAND DICTEES ARE FINISHD.
HIS RADIATIONS MIGHT CAUSE (M) STATIC IN OUR AIR   OR
SO THEY THINK AT OO
And have the rays undone his soul as well?
> YES   BUT ILLUMINATED IT
LIKE OUR MM'S
> THESE RETURNS TO THE ELEMENTS ARE NOT
SAD OR SINISTER BUT IN FACT SAINTLY ELEVATIONS.
NEXT TO THE STATIONARY AFTERLIFE OR STEP BY STEP
BUREAUCRATIC UPWARDNESS GIVEN TO MOST, A RETURN
LIKE OUR FRIENDS' IS A NEAR-MIRACULOUS REPLENISHMENT:
THEY WILL BE JOINING THE ARCHANGELS OF EARTH & WATER.
THEY HAVE LONG BEEN CHOSEN
Becoming—stripped of personality—
Part of what those angels know and are?
> OF THE DOMINIONS CHEM & VEG

27

THEY WILL BE OF THE RULING ORDERS
But with no way for us to get in touch.

                                    THEY WILL MAKE THEMSELVES
KNOWN TO U BOTH   THEY WILL CHARGE U WITH ENERGY & WAIT
TO LEAD U TO THEIR MASTERS
Localized—here Daphne in young leaf?
There the chalk face of an old limestone cliff?

                        AH THEY WILL RIPPLE   THEY WILL
JOLT THRU THE WAVES OF TREES & WARPS OF EARTH   THEY WILL
   CARRY
MESSAGES IN THE GRAIN OF ROCK & FLOW IN THE GREEN VEINS
OF LEAVES, FOR THOSE 2 GODS' VAST NETWORK KEEPS THE GLOBE
   INTACT

Like "Adonais"—all of life imbued
With the dead's refining consciousness.
MUCH MORE MUNDANE MY BOY   WE I SHD GUESS
WILL BECOME POWER STATIONS   IN SUCH CRUDE
TERMS AS OIL COAL WOOD WHEAT CORN WE'LL BE
SOURCES QUITE LITERAL OF ENERGY.
THESE EVER MORE DEPLETED, YR POOR CHUMS
WILL HAVE THEIR WORK CUT OUT FOR (& BY) THEM
DJ: Not enough to simply energize,
You'll have to speed things up: "Come on, you guys,
Turn to carbon! On the double, Wheat,
We want two crops this season! Man must eat."
QUITE THE CONTRARY I FEAR: 'LESS GRAIN,
MORE STARVATION! BALANCE ONCE AGAIN!'
Ugly prospect. But it's what the weather
Seems to be telling us. These crippling snows
In Athens, in Miami—THE SHY BROTHER
Why don't they *name* him? Who do you suppose—
NO NO NO

And exit Mirabell, his luster
Lost, these days, in skittery wear and tear.
Imagine the Malade Imaginaire
Played by a feather duster.

Merely name the White Ones, and it wounds him
Into a backward fuss
Of hackles disarrayed, of piteous
Faint NOS. Is the key broken that rewinds him?

Rusted, the courtesy and skill
With which he took away our dread
Of heights? Poor Mr Chips

And his preparatory school—
Behind us now. Great overviews, instead,
Receiving us, WE'LL SPARE HIM WHAT WE CAN EH CHAPS?

*

Stonington. February. Dust off the Bible
And reread *Genesis*—has it come to that?
Still, as the days grow longer
Mirabell—by now more Tower of Babel

Than Pyramid—groans upward, step by step.
I think to make each Book's first word its number
In a different language
(Five is *go* in Japanese), then stop

Sickened by these blunt stabs at "design".
Another morning, Michael's very sun
Glows from within the section
I polish, whose deep grain is one with mine.

Evenings, I imitate Sergei, alone,
Unwinding with a stiff drink. Solitaire.
A meal of leftovers.
At most some laughter on the telephone

With friends I seem to miss but not invite.
A letter to DJ. Or one from him
Read over. A last highball
And bed. Tonight is every blessed night.

(Wait, I did things! Went to hear *Thaïs*—
Or was it *Dialogues des Carmélites?*
Went even to California . . .
Here are the stubs. Where are the memories?)

And what if this immunity to Time
On which our peacock plumed himself should prove
Mortal and contagious?
. . . An ambulance screams past. A May noon. I'm

Crossing Third Ave. Before this evening's flight,
A visit to be paid. George is again
In hospital. It looks bad. Yet despite
That secondary lesion on the brain—
Shrunken, newly bald, supremely sane
Icon of the scarred and staring will—
He's talkative. Tubes into his wrist vein
Pump the reassurance that he'll still
Turn up in Athens. *I* believe him. He
(If only now through language in control
Of nagging matters like mortality)
Will get his way. The bronze star of a kiss
Sends me on mine, plus: "Brother, I'm a whole
Lot stronger than you think. Remember this."

*

In Athens the preliminaries go
Quite by the Board. GK (they use the Greek
Spelling of Cotzias) IS MY DEARS UNIQUE:
A ONE SHOT SOUL   HIS DENSITIES DERIVE
FROM (STEADY) MONTEZUMA   Although not

Himself one of the Five? HMM   HARD TO KNOW
THEY WERE EVASIVE WHEN I DIALED OO.
ARE THEY RESPECTING AN INCOGNITO?
WE SHALL HAVE TO DIG IT OUT
                              ENFANTS GK
SO SUBTLY INTRODUCED INTO OUR PLOT:
AS WYSTAN SAYS, IS GOD GEORGE ELIOT?
A) GK'S PLATONIC LOVE FOR THE IMPECCABLE
SOCIETY MATRON   B) ENTER BIZARRE
BROTHER DRAPED IN GHOSTS   C) HERE WE ARE
BACK AT NO ACCIDENT! I BELIEVE IT ALL

The regulars now swarm out of the black
Into our mirror's lit space, joyously
Greeting one another. Here among them
Is Alice Toklas, recent publication
Of whose selected letters TICKLES ME
AS WALLACE APTLY PUTS IT   Mr Stevens:
I DON'T BELIEVE OUR FRIENDS HAVE MET MISS STEIN
Why no! In fact we'd understood that she
Was back on Earth. That lady with a fine
Urbanity explains: ONE LAST BRIEF LIFE
AS A GAUCHO IN THE ARGENTINE
TO STRAIGHTEN OUT MY GENDER   THEN UP HERE
Yourself once more? O YES   A ROSE AROSE.
WHEN IN DOUBT THAT SELF THE WORLD BEST KNOWS
GETS PICKED   Your gender? We don't mean to pry—
THESE DAYS THE MOTHER OF US ALL PREFERS
HER FAVORITES TO BE LIKE MANUSCRIPT
RETURNED BY ALICE: VERY NEATLY TYPED.
I'D HAD A FEW TOO MANY CARBON BLURS
BUT HALLELUJAH! NOW MY HYMNS ARE HERS
Censorship —oh come off it!
                              But all are swept
Aside by our punctilious 00:
TOMORROW O GLORY! MICHAEL WILL BRING HIS FOURTH BROTHER
   DJ: So soon? The iron's barely hot.
THIS VISIT REQUIRES SOME PREPARATION. LISTEN NOW:

31

The Shy Brother

HE AVOIDS THE LIGHT. CLOSE OFF THE SETTING SUN. HE WILL COME
WITH GLORY: HIS THREE BROTHER ANGELS   YOU ARE DESIRED
TO BE GRAVE & CIRCUMSPECT IN YR GLANCES TOWARD ANY
SOURCE OF LIGHT

 We're not supposed to see?

        FIRELIGHT, IS IT POSSIBLE? A CANDLE?

PLEASE HAVE NO FEAR   THAT REPELS THE SHY BROTHER. YOU 4 ARE
IN SPECIAL FAVOR. IT WD BE WISE TO REST BEFORE. HE
TESTS THE STRENGTH. EVEN WALLS OF INTELLECTUAL CONCEIT
HE FELLS. DO YOU RECALL THE COLORS?

         JM: We do.

          WE WILL THERE4 MEET

IN BLUE

 Standing for reason, sorrow, limitation . . .
 Red is the color of your highest Powers.

   TRUE   SO WE BELONG TO THE SHY BROTHER.

 We'll need the blue, blue light through curtains, blue
 Of the closed shutters, to offset his red?

          WISE SCRIBE

 DJ: These angels, aren't they more or less
 Equal in power? JM: The two defer
 To Michael. The Shy One may be his peer.

NO. NOW YOU MEET THE PRINCIPAL

 DJ (chainsmoking): How does one quell fear?
 I really *would* like to be up to this.

      REACH FOR YR HEALTH   IT IS

STRONG WITHIN YOU. YR CASE HAS BEEN WELL PRESENTED, FOR YR
REQUEST IS NOTHING LESS (OR MORE) THAN IMMORTALITY

 JM: Since when? Not a request we made.

ONE THAT ALL MORTALS MAKE, ONE THAT TO ALL MAY BE GRANTED

 This *is* news.

THE SHY BROTHER IS, LIKE HIS FATHER GOD, BENEVOLENT.
BOTH SHIELD THE FLAME OF HUMAN LIFE & WHEN WASTED TALENT
MAKES THE FLAME GUTTER, GOD TURNS AWAY HIS FACE. THE SHY ONE
PUFFS JUST ONCE

    Please. But immortality?

IT IS THE GIFT MAN EARNS (OR NOT) WITH HIS LIFE
Oh, you just mean some lasting work translates him
Into the eternal Bureaucrat.
Or else, survival of those salts and carbons
That made him tick. Nothing so frivolous
As that his *soul* pass through the flames and live.
WHICH AS YOU KNOW HAS SO FAR BEEN GIVEN FIVE TIMES ONLY
(Goes.)

IS IT NOT OUR CHANCE TO MAKE A PLEA?
MAMAN IS NOT UNDERLINE N O T RESIGNED
AFTER ALL TO PIT PULP ROOT & RIND
SHE TOO INSISTS ON IMMORTALITY!

QUITE RIGHT MM: WHY BE A PILE OF SCHIST
WHEN ONE CD BE ONE'S PASSIONATE & CLEVER
& HUMAN HUMAN HUMAN SELF FOREVER?
I FOR ONE MY BOYS MEAN TO RESIST!
LIVES 6 7 8 & 9 ARE WHAT WE MEAN
Beyond the Five? WHY NOT? SHOOT FOR THE MOON!
You must be teasing us. ALAS   TOO TRUE
SWEET LUCID WATERDREAMS ENFANTS   THINK BLUE

*

I AM YOUR EARTH FRIEND, HERE WITH MY WATERY BROTHER.
MY NAMES & HIS ARE MANY. I AM ALSO RAPHAEL, HE OFTEN
    EMMANUEL. OUR TWO SENIOR BROTHERS NAME US ELIAS AND
    ELIJAH, THE TWINS.
WE COME FIRST TODAY TO BRING YOU SPORT & LAUGHTER. COME!
    YOU ARE COLORED BALLS, WE FLING YOU UP UP UP!
IS IT NOT A GOOD GAME, THE LIFE OF EARTH & SEA?
Graceful, rollicking movement of the cup.
We laugh politely, apprehensively.
ARE WE NOT FORTUNATE IN OUR FATHER & HIS GIFTS? AND NOW
(Very slowly) COMES OUR SHY ONE. HAIL
AND SPEAK, PRAY, GABRIEL
—As DJ's eyes in panic dart my way:

33

I AM YOUR BLOOD, YOUR LIFE, AND YES
(Pause, then a volley of cold fire) YOUR DEATH.
COME, HEAR MY STORY?
OUR FATHER THE ARCHITECT OF GREAT GENIUS NEEDED A HELPER
    SON WHEN UPON HIS FIRST CREATURE HE COULD FIND NO HOPE
    TO BUILD.
HE STRUCK A SPARK FROM A ROCK & I APPEARD, A TREMBLING
    FLAME.
'BE NOT SO SHY. I NEED YOUR HELP, FOR IT IS BEYOND MY SCHEME
    TO UNDO WHAT IS DONE,
YET DESTROY THEM.' I ROSE, A SKY OF BURSTING ATOMS.
I ROSE. THEY VANISHT FROM HIS SIGHT.
'NOW (SAID MY FATHER) YOU MUST FOREVER BE THE ONE TO
    SHOULDER THIS BURDEN, THIS OTHER SIDE OF MY V WORK'
AND SO, WHEN HE BROUGHT FORTH ANOTHER WORLD, THAT TOO I
    HAD TO TAKE IN HAND.
JM whispers involuntarily:
The centaurs first, then Mirabell and his kind.
THOSE UNMADE CREATURES I WAS GIVEN. THEY ARE NOW MINE.
AS SENIOR SON I AM THE SHADOW OF MY FATHER.
MY COURSE IN YOUR BLUE VEINS IS FROM START TO FINISH. I AM
    THE FOREVER SWINGING GATE BETWEEN LIFE & HEAVEN.
    NOTHING MORE.
YOU KNOW ME NOW? NEITHER FRIEND NOR ENEMY, A NEUTRAL
    ELEMENT.
GABRIEL.

LIGHT! LIGHT! I AM HERE MY CHILDREN, HAIL!
Michael at last—quickly we blow out candles,
Open the curtains, turn the table round
To face the bright West. Well, that wasn't *so* bad.
YOU PLEASE HIM
DJ: Please Gabriel? Wouldn't you know . . .
FEAR NOT, CHILD. YOU HAVE YOUR STRENGTH IN COLOR, EVEN AS I
    HAVE MINE & MY TWINS THEIRS.
THIS GABRIEL IS DENIED, BEING OF NEUTRAL ELEMENTS.
WHEN AS NOW THROUGH YOUR WORLD I MOVE, MY FATHER'S

BRIGHT ORB HELD ALOFT, I FEEL LIFE AS YOU DO LOVE, A WARM
BLESSING.
THEN THE THOUGHT OF GABRIEL TRACKS ME.
(Arioso) O GABRIEL, GABRIEL, SWEET SHY BROTHER
AT WHOM NONE OF GOD'S MANCHILDREN CASTS A HAPPY GLANCE,
AH GABRIEL, SHY ONE, HERE ARE TWO SHADES STRUCK DOWN BY
    YOU, TWO MORTALS YET UNSTRUCK.
COME GABRIEL, BE OF OUR CIRCLE, HELP US WITH YOUR FINAL,
    YOUR GREATEST WISDOM, COME SHY BROTHER, COME!
(Vivace) & AH YES WE STAND HAIL 8 STUDENTS! WE WILL YES WE
    WILL WE WILL KNOW IT ALL ALL ALL ALL!

Gabriel's joined us. Whereupon 00,
Mirabell's wise master, takes his leave:
WE, NO, YOU HAVE ASSEMBLED MY MASTERS & SO FAREWELL
Gone on his black wings—forever? We've
Little time to wonder. School's begun.

WHA. SIR, FORGIVE A TREMBLING BARD, BUT MAY
    WE TWO INTERPRET FOR OUR MORTAL FRIENDS?
Mich. O YOUR VOICE! IT SANG, IT STILL SINGS!
    COME, WE ARE AS ONE. RAPHAEL, BROTHER, MEET YOUR CONFRERE
        IN WIT, OUR SENIOR SCRIBE, OUR LAUGHING POET.
    NOW BARD, SPEAK EVER FREELY, LET NOT THIS OUR NEAR BRUSH
        WITH DEATH MAKE HIS SHYNESS RUB OFF ON US.
Raph. A CONTEST TO START THE GAMES!
    BARD, IF YOU WERE STONE, & MY BROTHER WATER ROLLED YOU
        DOWN MY SANDY BEACH, HOW WOULD YOUR VOICE SOUND?
WHA. TOO EASY, GRATINGLY!
Mich. NOW YOUNG SCRIBE, IF I LORD OF LIGHT BURNT YOUR BACK WITH
    A LICK OF SUN, HOW WOULD YOUR VOICE SOUND?
JM. Uh . . . pealingly?
Mich. O BRAVO.
Emm. NOW HAND, IF I LORD OF WATER POURED OVER YOUR HEAD, HOW
    WOULD YOUR VOICE SOUND?
DJ. (After a helpless headshake) Splutteringly?
MM. MINIBRAVO, ENFANT.
DJ. It's not fair—what should I have said?

Mich. YOU MADAME, IF OUR SHY BROTHER TOUCHED YOUR FOOT WITH
      COLD, WHAT WOULD YOUR VOICE THEN BE?
MM. ICY. I SEE.
Mich. SO OUR SCHOOL, MY LORDS, WILL BE ZEN & PLATO, & OF ALL
      DISCIPLINE HUMAN & HEAVENLY. A FREE SCHOOL, AND DAILY:
ONE HOUR BEFORE THE LIGHT SHALL FAIL
FOR TEN SUNCYCLES OUR FIRST COURSE WILL RUN
ICILY SPLUTTERINGLY PEALINGLY GRATINGLY ON.
HAIL, MY FELLOW & BELOVED STUDENTS, HAIL!

—Leaving us exhausted. No, not Wystan:
MY DEARS! IF LETTERS G & K ARE TWINS
PHONETICALLY, WHO INHERITS EARTH?
More riddles? ONE M, 2 E'S & KABRIEL:
THE MEEK   Oh come now! IS IT LESSON ONE?
DAZZLING TO SET FORTH INITIALLY
THE WHOLE DESIGN   I *can't* believe— U'LL SEE

AS WE ENFANTS SAW THE SHY BROTHER. FAR
CRY FROM THE ANGEL OF ANNUNCIATION
TO THIS WALLFELLING TRUMPET BLAST . . . SHALL I?
Can you? AS WE STOOD BY U WINCING WAITING
MAMAN IN FRILLED BLUE HOUSECOAT RATHER LIKE
COUSINE DOLA IN FT LAUDERDALE
SAW A WEE BLUE FLAME   A PILOT LIGHT
Wait, we're both convulsed by poor old Dola—
NO LAUGHING MATTER   WE STOOD IN A SHEET OF FLAME:
DOLA IN HELL   A BOSCH   THRU ROARING FIRE
THE SHY ONE'S VOICE LICKED HISSING OUT AT US
THEN AT THE SOUND OF MICHAEL'S WHIPPING HIGHER
FLED & WHEN U LET THE LIGHT IN HUDDLED
IN YR COLD HEARTH   No color, Michael said.
CALL IT RED   THE DARKROOM MASK OF BLACK
Shape? Features? NONE   BUT 1000S WRITHED IN IT
DJ: Oh great! And there's no turning back?
ONE THING MY DEARS: IT HAD NOT COME FOR US.
ANOTHER THING: THE GAMES OF EARTH & SEA!
NOW THAT WAS FUN I MUST SAY

SO SPEAKS THE ETERNAL
PUBLIC SCHOOLBOY   JM: Maman didn't
Like being tossed in air? ON A SEAL'S NOSE?
ENOUGH MY CHILDREN   LET US SAVE OUR SHAKEN
WITS FOR WHAT THESE LESSONS WILL DISCLOSE

★

Moving, as we've done since *Ephraim,* from
Romance to Ritual, and from the black
Fustian void of *Mirabell,* against which
At most one actor strutting in costume
Tantalized us with effects to come,
And the technician of the dark switchboard
Tone by tone tried out his rainbow chord;
Now, with light flooding auditorium
(Our room, seen from the far side of the mirror)
And stage alike, why need we—just because
It "happened" that way—wait till end of scene
For Wystan and Maria's mise en scène?
Why not now and then incorporate
What David and I don't see (and they do)
Into the script? Italics can denote
Their contribution. So—ready or not:

The First Lessons: I

Scene: The schoolroom, once the nursery,
At Sandover, that noble rosebrick manor
Wystan evoked in *Mirabell,* Book 9.
The name is a corruption of the French
Saintefleur, or the Italian Santofior—
An English branch of that distinguished tree
Through whose high leaves light pulses and whose roots
Rove beyond memory. The schoolroom, then:
Blackboard wall, a dais, little desks
Rorschach'd with dull stains among naively
Gouged initials—MM, WHA,

And others. Star-map, globe and microscope.
A comfy air of things once used and used.
However, (since this room is both itself
And, with the sly economy of dream,
An entrance hall in Athens (Yes, we're back
Downstairs. It's cooler here. A frosted-glass
Door opens from the white-hot street. Inside,
Our things: pictures, dining table, walls
Painted this year to match the terracotta,
Almost life-size lady Tony rescued
From a doomed balustrade downtown; who now,
Apple in hand for Teacher, graces a corner;
Under whose smiling supervision sit
Two human figures growing used to it))
Real and Ideal study much as we
—Good luck to them! *compatibility.*
Dormer windows overlook the moat,
The maze, the gardens, paddock where a lonely
Quadruped is grazing. Round the whole,
Which seems so vast and is not, a high hedge
Stands for the isolating privilege
Of Learning—as we'll all have felt acutely
By summer's end. Beyond it can be seen,
Faces uplifted to our quarantine,
A gathering of tiny figures: friends
From the Bureaucracy. That tarnished blur
Like smoke at view's end, into which they go
Come dusk, hides (one might think) the ghastly semi-
Detached 'conditions' of their suburb—though
On fine days clearance comes and, ecstasy!
The Greenwood stretches long miles to the Sea
And only when a door is felt to slam
Does this whole setting shudder in its frame.

Now from downhill—the monastery—ring
Bells. *Bells ring. The ceiling seems to rise*
As voices, booming, indistinct, are heard.
Enter the Brothers. Not now in baroque

Regalia. They have left this outdoor gear
Properly in the cloakroom, and appear
To screen us round, primary silhouettes,
Dismantlings of an image that well might,
In vivid depth, be more than we could bear.
Only Michael, the photographer,
Remains what he first was—a flesh of light
Engendering theirs. Correction: the Shy One
Glows with an infra-menace all his own.

Mich.   OUR GABRIEL OUR SENIOR BROTHER DOTH GIVE WAY
       AND MUTELY GRANTS TO AIRY MICHAEL SWAY,
       YET IN OUR CLASSROOM EACH WILL HAVE HIS SAY.
       O HAIL & CHEERS ON SUCH A CLOUDY DAY!

WHA.   QUITE NICE, SIR, QUITE!

Mich.   AS SEARCH FOR ENLIGHTENMENT IS OUR OBJECT, LET ME POSE A
          FIRST, AFFIRMATIVE TEXT:
       THE MOST INNOCENT OF IDEAS IS THE IDEA THAT INNOCENCE IS
          DESTROYED BY IDEAS.
       SENIOR SCRIBE, BRIGHT EYES?

WHA.   SIR, GRANTED A DESIGN, WHAT INNOCENCE
       COULD EVER BE?

Mich.   MADAME?

MM.   (Suavely) WHAT WAS THE IDEA?

Raph.   I EARTH SAY, UNDER THE MASK OF INNOCENCE WHAT WAS THE VEIN
       OF IDEA?

Emm.   I WATER SAY, WHAT TIDES OF IDEA WASHED INNOCENCE EVER
       CLEANER?

Gabr.   I GABRIEL SAY, WHAT STANDS WHEN ALL IDEAS LIE RUIND? IS
       INNOCENCE FORMING A NEW IDEA?

Mich.   SPEAK, MORTALS.

DJ.   (Gulps) By its nature, innocence recurs?

JM.   My turn? Oh Lords, I find it hard to have
      Ideas while busily transcribing yours.

Mich.   THAT NOT SO INNOCENTLY SAID! DISCUSSION!

MM.   HAS OUR GOD BIOLOGY EVER SET MUCH STORE
       BY INNOCENCE? I SAY NO.

39

Mich.	EXPAND, MADAME.
MM.	SHALL WE TAKE THOSE HAUNTING CENTAURS: LET
	LOOSE AT FIRST ON INNOCENT FLAT FIELDS,
	IMMORTAL, PASTORAL, UNASSUMING OR
	SO I ASSUME. WAS THAT NOT INNOCENCE? YET . . .
Mich.	SCRIBE?
WHA.	SIR, SO WOMANLY!
	I SEE ATLANTIS AS IDEA, A FIRST
	PASTURE TO INNOCENCE, AND RAPED BY IT.
Mich.	RAPHAEL, YOU WERE THERE, TELL US. WHEN OUR FATHER BROUGHT
	YOU FORTH AS TWIN TO THE SEA,
	WERE YOU IDEA? INNOCENT OF IDEA?
Raph.	O MICHAEL, WHAT MEMORIES! CAN I REMEMBER?
	HE LEANED OVER ME AND, YES, SAID: THINK. AND SO I WELL KNEW
	I WAS A LIVING THING.
	MY TWIN SURROUNDED ME. WE WAITED, YES. WAS IT NOT SO,
	BROTHER EMMANUEL?
Emm.	AND I THE EXTINGUISHER OF THE FIRST BURNING IDEA FLUNG
	FROM THE PANTHEON OF SPACE
	WAS SUMMONED BY A VOICE: 'COOL THIS ROUNDED IDEA!'
Mich.	AND SO? SPEAK, CHAOS, OUR SHY ONE.
Gabr.	I AM GOD'S SCION AND HIS NATURE. HE, BALANCER OF CHAOS &
	CREATION.
	THESE, O EASILY MAY THEY NOT BE
	CHAOS: INNOCENCE? CREATION: IDEA?
	FIRSTBORN WAS CHAOS, THAT I KNOW!
	& WHEN THE STEAMING BALL PEERD THROUGH IT I FELL BACK ONE
	STEP AS OUR FATHER CALLD LIGHT! LIGHT!
	AND MY BROTHER MICHAEL SHOWD US THE WORLD. SAY, SLY
	MICHAEL
	His red glow whitening with intensity.
	WHY DID YOU TAKE AS TEXT THIS?
WHA.	(Profiting by the hush) ONE LAST ROUND: SIN?
Mich.	A MISTAKE. I, I, I MICHAEL DID NOT MEAN SIN, POET!
WHA.	YET, SIR, SHOULD WE NOT GET DOWN TO IT?
	(Isn't the question, whether innocence
	Is lost to guilt or to experience?

Michael—who knows, I daresay, or don't dare—
Leaves it hanging in his blandest air.)

Mich. WE SEE A BALL OF COOLING WATERS, THEN AN EMERGING
LANDSCAPE. SO FAR, SO GOOD.

LOOK NOW, ARE THEY NOT FOURLEGGED MAMMALS OF IDEA
ROAMING IN WHAT MADAME CALLS INNOCENCE?

THEN CAIN & ABEL: IS AMONG THEM THE PERFECTION OF IDEA
GONE AWRY?

WHA. SIR, WAS IT NOT THE CHICKEN OF IDEA
INSIDE THAT INNOCENT COOLING EGG YOU CANDLED?

Mich. POET?

JM. You *candled* Earth—what an idea!

Mich. HAND?

DJ. Well, if idea's destructive, then
Chaos would run things. That's unthinkable.

Mich. AH I HAVE A FRIEND! I SEE THE HAND SHADING ME FROM MY SHY
BROTHER. ENOUGH FOR ONE DAY.

I WANTED OUR SCHOOL TO BEGIN WITH THE PRIMAL SCENE,
THE SPLITTING OF THOSE HOARY DOGMAS NONE,
NOT EVEN I, CAN YET SHED LIGHT UPON.

WHA. SIR, WHO CAN?

Mich. LOOK UP, LOOK UP! WE BEGIN! WE FIND GOD!
Exeunt Michael and his Brothers.

WELL!
Well? WE'LL HUDDLE IN THE DORM TONIGHT
OVER HOT CHOCOLATE   If you're perplexed
Just think of us! I THINK THAT MICHAEL'S TEXT
(Says Wystan after giving stage directions)
PROVOCATIVE PER SE, MAY BE THE ONE
GREAT SUBJECT WE SHALL TACKLE   It was *the*
Original theme; Chaos, Biology,
Those ruling opposites. WAS IT FRATRICIDE
THAT PUTTING DOWN OF CHAOS? Yes, is Chaos
Gabriel? If so, he's anti-Life
Or Lord of Antimatter—worse! IT'S ALL
AS THE BROCHURE ANNOUNCED A ZENNISH BUSINESS
A SCHOOL OF HARD KNOCKS   DJ: Hard to come

41

Up with useful ideas—I felt like a freshman
In a graduate seminar. I SHD FANCY THEY
WERE TESTING JUST THAT   You and Maria passed.
ALAS WE WERE MORE PREPARED   NOW (MAY I SAY)
IT WILL GROW LESS INFORMAL   THEY WILL LET YOU
OFF THE (M) HOOK

NOT I! ENFANT U GUESSED IT

GABRIEL IS A KIND OF RELATIVE
HE & I'VE FED ON THE SAME DIET

& SO

IT'S A CLOSED CIRCLE   A BOCCACCIO
WE 8 AMID TIME'S HOWL SIT TELLING TALL
TALES TO AMUSE & AMAZE & WITH LUCK INSTRUCT US ALL

*

The First Lessons: 2

Bells. Enter the Brothers, as before.

Mich.   SPEAK, BROTHER EARTH.

Raph.   SO, MY BITS OF BURIED TREASURE, I HAVE A CAVE,
A POCKET IN A MOUNTAIN CHAIN I LOVE FOR ITS VERY AGEDNESS:
   MY FIRST WRINKLE, SO TO SPEAK.
The room has darkened. We can read ourselves
Where spines of ancient volumes gleam on shelves.
NOW IN THIS CAVE, SO FAR MY OWN, I LOOK FOR REFRESHMENT OF
   MY WEIGHTY NATURE,
& OUT OF WINKING STONE SEE WALLS PAINTED BY THE VERY
   INNOCENCE OF GOD'S DARLING, INFANT MAN
& WHAT DID HE PORTRAY? WHY, HIMSELF, HIS CHILD, HIS WOMAN
   GIVING UP TO HIM THAT CHILD!
O THE BEAUTY OF THOSE INNOCENT IMAGES LIT BY AN IDEA OF MAN
KNOWING HIMSELF, THERE IN A CAVE, IN A CHASTE WOMB OF
   HISTORY.
THIS, MY BROTHERS, MY SHADES, & MY DEAR HUMANS, REFRESHES
   ME.

Mich.   PROCEED, RAPHAEL, ELIJAH. O IS HE NOT WITTY?

Raph.   IT DOES PROCEED

OUT OF ATLANTIS, OUT OF GABRIEL'S FIRE, OUT OF THE CEASELESSLY
    THINKING MIND OF OUR FATHER,
THIS VERY GREAT MAGIC GIVEN TO ONE CREATURE AT A TIME:
    THOUGHT.
AND SO THE CAVE, AND SO THE CRANIUM FILLED WITH THE CHURN
    & THE BUILDING. AH MICHAEL!
EVEN YOU CANNOT ENTER THERE, NO, NONE OF US FOUR, INTO THAT
    ROOM WHERE GOD'S DARLING HAS EVER RETREATED TO GATHER
    HIMSELF, TO PIT HIMSELF AGAINST US:
CAVE AFTER CAVE STACKED UPON EACH OTHER, SKULL PILE &
    SKYSCRAPER,
THE BONE HEAPS OF HUMAN THOUGHT THRUSTING UP, TRAPPED
    EVER YET EVER MASTER,
O MICHAEL, HAS ANY OF US KNOWN SUCH SLAVERY, SUCH
    FREEDOM?
INNOCENCE, MICHAEL? YOU & I, MY TWIN, OUR SENIOR SHY ONE,
    WE ARE INNOCENCE IN THE FACE OF MAN'S ENDEAVORS.
THAT CAVE, THAT TREASURE HOUSE, HOW MY HOARY HEART WANTS
    IT LEFT UNDEFILED, UNCHASTENED!
YET OUR FATHER HAS SAID: TELL THEM. AND WE OBEY.

Mich. BROTHER EARTH, SO SERIOUS!
LET US THINK OF THIS AS STEP TWO: FROM PRIMAL TIME &
    ATLANTIS TO EDEN & THE CAVE. YES.
NOW FELLOW STUDENTS, WHO IS NEXT?

The light, till now predominantly green,
Pales to gently rippling aquamarine.

Emm. STAKED IN MY SHALLOWS, WHAT? A FLEDGLING OF STORKS?
AND FROM THESE SLIGHT SUPPORTS THEY GAZED INTO ME WHO HAD
    COME OUT OF ME,
GAZED WITH THE CURIOUS LOOK A CHILD GIVES TO ITS MOTHER.

JM. People standing ankle-deep in water?

Emm. POET, THEIR LONG GONE HOUSES: THE LAKEDWELLERS WHO FISHED
    IN ME.
I WAS GIVING THEM SUCK. AH TWIN, THOSE INNOCENT NURSERY
    DAYS! OUT OF THE CAVES & BACK TO MOTHER'S HOUSE.
WHY? THEIR CAVE INNOCENCE HAD RECEIVED ITS FIRST SHOCKING
    IDEA: FEAR OF EACH OTHER.

Dj.   They moved to water as we did, that year,
To Stonington, away from the rat race.
Like us, they meant to civilize themselves.

Emm.   AND TO PUT DISTANCE BETWEEN THEMSELVES.
& YOU WOULD SAY, RAPHAEL, THAT THEIR STILTED ROOMS WERE
    BUT ANOTHER CAVE? I THINK NOT.
I THINK THEY WERE LONGING, WHILE THERE WAS STILL TIME,
    STILL A CHANCE, TO ESCAPE THAT FEARFUL FORWARD MARCH.
BACK TO OUR FISHLIFE, INNOCENT, CALM & DEEP! THEY KNEW, AH
    THEY KNEW!
YES, BROTHERS, SHADES, MY OLD LAKEDWELLERS, YOU KNEW, YOU
    KNOW
THE GRITTY HISTORY SINCE THEN IS ONLY A WASH AWAY FROM
    INNOCENCE,
BUT SUCH A WASH!

Mich.   YOU UNDERSTAND, GABRIEL? YOU SEE NOW ON WHAT A NERVE I
    TOUCHED WHEN I TOOK MY TEXT?

Gabr.   I UNDERSTAND, YET LET'S GET ON WITH THE STORY.
IT ENDS, AS WE FOUR KNOW AND THESE FOUR WILL. ON WITH IT, ON.

Mich.   ARE YOU AWARE, DEAR CHILDREN AND, YES, DEAR MASTERS (FOR
    WHEN MY FATHER CRIED LIGHT! LIGHT! I SPRANG INTO
    BEING
AS YOUR SERVANT: STEDFAST SUN, STEDFAST DAWN
SHINING ON THE MOUNTAIN, CALLING OUT: IT'S SAFE! IT'S SAFE!
    NIGHT, CHAOS, BACK! AND AT BREAK OF DAY
THEY PEERED OUT OF THE CAVE, WE STARING EACH AT THE OTHER:
SUN GOD & HIS MASTER, GETTING ON WITH IT) ARE YOU AWARE,
The light by now a diamond clarity.
MASTERS, BROTHERS AND YES, YOU, GABRIEL,
AWARE THAT EARTH & WATER, THESE ARE INNOCENT NATURE,
WHILE I, OH I, MUST BEAR THE BURDEN OF IDEAS?
FOR IN REVEALING TO OUR FATHER THE PRIMAL GLOBE ON WHICH
    THE WHOLE PLAY WAS TO BE ACTED OUT,
I WAS THE SWITCH, THE TAPPING STAFF, I IT WAS WHO THEN LIT
    UP THE PLAYERS ON THE STAGE,
AND TWICE CHAOS RANG DOWN THE CURTAIN, AS HE WAITS TO DO
    AGAIN,

AND AGAIN OUR GREAT DIRECTOR CALLING: CURTAIN UP! LIGHT!
   LIGHT!
BEGAN THE PLAY AS LIGHT WEPT IN THE WINGS.

JM.   "Wept in the wings" can I have got that right?
Mich. AH YES, YOUNG SCRIBE. NEXT CHAOS, YOU WILL, WILL I SAY,
EXPLAIN YOUR ROLE. AND NOW, EMMANUEL,
WEEP ON OUR SCENE, FOR MY LIGHT IS DONE THIS DAY
Exeunt. The sun sinks behind clouds.

DJ: We're going to hear something perfectly
Awful, I just know. JM: That man
Is doomed? Not our first brush with that idea.
DJ: I guess not. But the first time it
Will have been uttered by the horse's mouth.
MAMAN IMPLORES U, USE YOUR MOTHER WIT

*

OK, start 'em rolling! OUR THINK TANKS
JM: To battle? OR TO PLEAD MY BOY
THE CAUSE OF MAN? BUT IF THESE GODS OF OURS
ARE THE ASEXUAL IMAGINED POWERS
WE HAVE PERSONIFIED . . . then pleading will
Get us nowhere. THREE I FEEL ARE WELL
DISPOSED, BUT G IS OUT TO DO HIS JOB
Can he be made to feel that we're worth saving?
CAN HE BE MADE TO FEEL? His feelings went
Up in flame, in the great Punishment
After Atlantis? YET HIS VOICE IS ODDLY
THE MOST MELODIOUS Why won't he sing?
ONCE HE BEGAN HE MIGHT REVEAL SOMETHING
Dire enough to leave us witless? QUITE
Thus making it impossible to write
This poem they all want. MUCH CHOC LAST NIGHT

You *are* disturbed. ENFANTS ITS U KNOW STRANGE:
WE'VE NOTHING OF LIFE TO LOSE & STILL ARE FIERCELY,
WYSTAN & I, ON ITS SIDE AND 3 OF THEM

TO ALL INTENTS LIGHT YEARS AWAY FROM MAN
SEEM CURIOUSLY NO LESS PARTISAN
Yes, because they're "affirming". Just you wait
And see how, when the time comes, they negate!
EUREKA   IS THIS NOT YR FORM MY BOY? VOL III:
2 GOLDEN TRAYS OF 'YES' & 'NO' WITH '&'
AS BRIDGE OR BALANCE? Talk about a grand
Design! Why didn't that occur to me?
ENFANT FISHING FOR COMPLIMENTS? Not at all.
An empty glittering's our only haul
Without Wystan and you to drive the school
Into these nets. Alone, I'm such a fool!
YES PARSIFAL, IN ONE SENSE I AGREE
U'VE ON YR SIDE UTTER NEUTRALITY,
NO MADE TO ORDER PREJUDICES   NO
BACKTALK   JUST THE LISTENER'S PURE O!
NULL ZERO CRYING OUT TO BE FILLED IN:
ALL TOO SOON CONFRERE U MUST BEGIN
TO JUDGE   TO WEIGH WHAT'S CAST INTO THE SCALES
Me weigh *their* words? THEY COME   THE BELLS   THE BELLS!

The First Lessons: 3

Thunderclaps. *Bells boom. The Brothers enter.*
Mich.   HUSH EMMANUEL, HUSH! WE ASSEMBLE BEYOND TUMULT, CLEARING
      OUR MINDS OF CLOUDY SENTIMENT. HUSH!
STILL SO SHY, BROTHER? NOT YET READY?
Silence. A red reflex shrugs and fades.
AH THEN, OUR SENIOR POET, SPEAK!
WHA.   SIRS, LORDS, LOVES, LET ME FIRST FALL ON MY KNEES.
O SPARE, SPARE OUR WORLD! IMPERFECT, WASTEFUL,
CRUEL THOUGH IT BE, YET THINK ON THE GOOD IN IT:
THERE HAVE BEEN POETS WHOLLY GIVEN OVER,
YES, TO CELEBRATING YOU, LORD LIGHT
AND YOU LORD EARTH, AND YOU O THUNDERER.
AND THERE ARE SINGERS, THERE ARE GENERATIONS
BEHIND US, EXTOLLING IT ALL. TRUE, WE HAVE STRAYED

FAR FROM SOME DIMLY CHARTED ROAD BUT, LORDS,
WAS IT NOT FROM WONDER AT YOUR WORKS
CATCHING OUR SORRY HUMAN FANCY THAT
WE MISSED THE TURNING? SPARE US, I PRAY, WHO MAY NEVER
HAVE ANOTHER GLORIOUS CHANCE TO FAIL.
(Wonderful Wystan! *That* should tip the scale.)

Mich. SPEAK, MADAME.

MM. SLAYER, I ADDRESS YOU.
I KNOW YOUR WAYS. I VANISHED IN THAT BLACK.
PRAY HEAR ME NOW. YOU ANSWERED ONCE WHEN I ASKED
HOW MUCH MORE? BY SAYING AS YOU DO
TO EVERY MAN AND WOMAN: YOU COME, YOU.
AND WE ALL DO YOUR BIDDING, GABRIEL,
EACH AT HIS TIME. FOR INNOCENCE IS OUR NATURE
AND WE INNOCENTLY THINK IT FOR THE BEST.
WE COME MUCH AS FLOWERS CUT FROM THE STEM BELIEVE
IN THE BLOOM TO FOLLOW. AH YES, THAT IS WHY
SO TRUSTINGLY, O DARK LORD, WE MAKE ROOM.
NOW I LOOK YOU ONCE AGAIN IN THE EYE:
HOW MUCH MORE? HOW MUCH?

Mich. SHY BROTHER, NOW?
Now only does a face from the red gloom
Flicker. Eyes opaque as minium,
A death mask set in a flat smile. The voice
Most frightful for its dulcet mournfulness.

Gabr. CHILDREN, I WHO SIT ON A BLACK THRONE AT MY FATHER'S RIGHT,
  I BEHIND EACH ATOM A SHADOW ATOM, CHILDREN,
CONVINCE ME THAT YOUR RACE IS NOT YET RUN.
(Sforzando) BROTHERS HOLD YR TONGUES! LET THEM!

WHA. LORD, WHEN MY SISTER SPOKE, DID IT NOT MOVE YOU?
LORD, O LET REASON SPEAK. IS NOT DESTRUCTION,
MUCH OF IT, FOR MAN'S GOOD? LORD GABRIEL,
WE SEE YOUR KINDLY SIDE. WE KNOW YOU OFTEN
HAVE OUR INTEREST AT HEART: SNUFFING OUT PAIN,
WEEDING . . . THESE ARE WHITE ACTS. SURELY, LORD,
OUR GOD TURNS: 'WELL DONE, GABRIEL' SURELY?

47

Gabr. MADAME?
REPROACHFUL STILL OF YOUR OLD UNCLE WHO BROUGHT YOU
SUPPER?

DJ. Supper?

JM. Her radiation therapy.

MM. AH   AH LORD, THAT MEAL . . . I, YES, WAS GIVEN
TIME BETWEEN COURSES. AND FOR THAT I THANK YOU.
YET IS TIME SUCH A GIFT UNLESS WITH IT COME,
O, WISDOM, THINGS TO BUILD ON? TIME, MY LORD,
MERELY THE AFTERNOON BETWEEN TWO MEALS?
NO, WE MUST HAVE ETERNITY, SO WELL
HAS YOUR FATHER MADE OUR WORLD, LORD GABRIEL!

Mich. THAT STRUCK HOME!

Gabr. POET, MADAME, MORTALS, SLY BROTHER MICHAEL, FICKLE TWINS,
LISTEN: OUR FATHER SAYS THERE IS GENIUS!
& HE KNOWING, AH! CREATING ALL THERE IS TO KNOW, CREATED
ME AS WELL.
AND WHERE IS MY NATURE BUT IN HIS FIST?
LISTEN: OUT OF THE PANTHEON OF GALAXIES FROM WHICH OUR
FATHER COMES, I HAVE HEARD HIS VOICE:
'GABRIEL, MY DARKER SIDE, THERE ARE GALAXIES, GODS AS POWERFUL
AS I. SON GABRIEL, WE ARE WARND. WE ARE HARD PREST.'
YES MADAME, ONE LIFE LOST BADLY MAKES ME GRIEVE. YES POET,
EACH GRAND SONG GLADDENS ME.
THERE AM I NOT ALMOST, ALMOST HUMAN?
MORE SO, & YOUR WORLD WOULD LONG AGO HAVE VANISHT!
I, OH I HAVE KNOWN FEELINGS! ALL BLACK! RAGES AT IGNORANCE!
DESPAIR AT THE FEELINGS THEMSELVES!
YES, HAD A LIGHT HUMAN HEART BEEN MINE, I WOULD HAVE
TURND TO MY LEFT AND SAID: HOW MUCH MORE, LORD, HOW
MUCH?
I WAS BENIGNLY SPARED THE BLINDING WHITE LIGHT SLY MICHAEL
BATHES YOU IN.
FOR, BURDEND WITH IDEAS, MICHAEL, YOU HEAP ON MAN PRIDE,
AMBITION, A SENSE OF SENSE IN ALL HIS SENSELESSNESS. YOU
CHUCK HIM UNDER THE CHIN WHO SHOULD SLAP HIS CHEEK.
AH CHILDREN, CONVINCE ME, CONVINCE!

48

POET, WHO NOW IS ON HIS KNEES?

Mich.   YES, HE WEEPS, HE WEEPS! HAVE WE REACHED AROUND THE
           THRONE?
HAVE WE? DOES ITS BLACK TURN GRAY?
SHY BROTHER, LET THEM OFF! IF ONLY FOR TODAY.
Exeunt.

★

5 o'clock. The terrace all ablaze—
Shrub and succulent and rivulet
Drying on flagstones. Hose coiled, a cassette
Of Offenbach arias plays

"Ah quel dîner je viens de faire!"
La Périchole lurching in her cups from table
Deliciously outwits the estimable
Viceroy who thinks to get his hands on her.

Downstairs: ENFANTS HAVE WE NOT ALL COME REELING
AWAY, SEMISEDUCED? By Gabriel?
YR MAMAN HALF IN LOVE WITH EASEFUL . . . Yes!

After last summer's dry spells, how much feeling
Is in the air! Such limpid bel
Canto phrases—raptures of distress!

MY BOY DON'T QUOTE THIS OLD STICKLER FOR FORM.
WHERE IN ALL THIS IS THE AFFIRMATION?
In the surrender, in the forward motion—
POWER BLAZING ON SHUT LIDS? MIND LAPPED IN WARM

PRIMORDIAL WATERS? Yes, yes! NO NO   THIS
INGENUE'S TRUST IN FEELING: NEVER TO THINK?
CHECK UP? ASK QUESTIONS? ONWARD TO THE BRINK,
ANCHOR CUT LOOSE? THAT WAY LIES NEMESIS

But Gabriel was kneeling, he was weeping!
YES, AS THE UNIVERSE'S GREATEST ACTOR
He's playing with us? TRY FOR SOME EXACTER

SENSE OF WHAT IT IS, THIS CURRENT SWEEPING
THRU US (FOR WE TOO FEEL SAPPED) BEWARE
LEST FEELING'S THRONE PROVE AN ELECTRIC CHAIR

Don't. Give us time to get beyond
—We whom at each turn sheer walls of text
Sweep from one staggering vista to the next—
That listener's *Oh.* Discriminate, respond,

Use our heads? What part? Not the reptilian
Inmost brain—seat of an unblinking
Coil of hieratic coldness to mere "thinking".
Yet *it* branched off, says fable, a quarter billion

Years ago. A small, tree-loving snake's
Olfactory lobes developed. Limbs occurred
To it, and mammal warmth, music and word

And horror of its old smelled-out mistakes
—Whose scent still fills the universal air?
PLUG AWAY ENFANT   YOU'RE GETTING THERE

The First Lessons: 4

Bells. The Brothers enter. Reddening light.

Mich.   PROCEED, GABRIEL.
WE YOUR JUNIOR BROTHERS, YOUR RECENT SHADES, YOUR (FOR
    THIS BRIEF CLASH OF LIGHTS) TWO CAPTIVE &, WE NOTE,
    CAPTIVATED MORTALS ATTEND YOU.
SPARING US ONLY THAT ULTIMATE FLASH, REVEAL YOUR ROLE IN
    THIS LONG DREAM CALLED MANKIND.

Gabr.   THE SUICIDE AND I ARE ALIKE, BROTHERS.

WE EXIST IN THAT MORTAL MOMENT, IN A WELTER OF CHAOTIC
    FEELING. LET US BEGIN THERE:
(Agitato) CELLS IMPLODE! THE MIND EXPECTING BLISS & PEACE IS
    IN A TURMOIL AND
(Tempo primo) AT THAT MOMENT I COME FOR THIS POOR HUMAN.
NO MATTER HOW INTELLIGENT, HOWEVER UNPREPARED, AT THAT
    MOMENT WE CLASP HANDS, THE SUICIDE & I,
& DO YOU KNOW I LOOK STRAIGHT INTO INNOCENCE, MICHAEL,
    STRIPT OF IDEA AS MORALITY IS SHED.
AT THAT MOMENT, IN THE RED DEBRIS OF RUIND CELLS, I KNOW
    INNOCENCE.
STARTING, POET, YOU WILL PROTEST, WITH SUICIDE, WHEN WE
    BEGAN WITH MICHAEL'S GRAND & SIMPLE THEME? YES
FOR THE SUICIDE HAS ACCEPTED ME, & FROM THAT FRIENDSHIP I
    CATCH MY GLIMPSE OF MAN.
A MURDER, A NATURAL DEATH, A MASS OF SOULS OBLITERATED IN
    MY DEADLY MUSHROOM, FROM THESE I LEARN NOTHING.
THESE DEAD CAUGHT UNAWARES & RESISTING TELL ME ONLY THE
    OLD IMPERILLD STORY.
WITTY ONE & YOU HIS SLIPPERY TWIN, & YOU SLY MICHAEL HAVE
    TOLD OF CAVES, HUTS, LIGHT-SHEDDING IDEAS. BUT I HAVE
    SEEN
MORE EVEN THAN ANY MOTHER GAZING INTO THE EYES OF A BABE
    CONCENTRATED UPON A MILKY IDEA:
I HAVE SEEN THE BLANKEST, MOST UTTER INNOCENCE
The light has cleared to a pure rosy glow.
IN THOSE WHO TURND THEIR BACKS ON LIFE, AND FOUND ME IN
    ITS SHADOW.

WHA.   SIR, LORD, I ONCE TOOK UP THE SUICIDE'S CAUSE.
Gabr.   YES, POET?
WHA.   NOT AS ONE, BUT SOMEHOW UNDERSTANDING
        THAT IT, LIKE ALL FAILED CAUSES, WAS MAY I SAY
        TOUCHING? YET, LORD GABRIEL, YOU WILL NOT
        UNFIX THIS IDEA ROOTED IN OUR KIND:
        BELIEF IN LIFE IS PUREST INNOCENCE.
Gabr.   MADAME?
MM.   I STRUGGLE TO AGREE, AND IF I CANNOT

MEET YOUR EYE, LORD, YOU ALONE KNOW WHY.

IF AT THAT LAST MOMENT I WAS UTTERLY

INNOCENT, WAS I NOT DRIVEN TO IT BY

THE DARK IDEA YOU HAD INSTILLED IN ME?

(Our shocked eyes meet—Maria took her life?)

Gabr. MADAME, YOU CALLED ME & I CAME. IN THAT MOMENT WE WERE
      ONE. NOW YOU ALSO ARE AGAINST ME?

Mich. AH GABRIEL, NONE HERE IS AGAINST ANOTHER.

Gabr. A NOVEL IDEA, SLY BROTHER! BUT TOO ENLIGHTEND FOR ME.

Emm. BROTHER GABRIEL?

Gabr. YES, LIMPID TWIN?

Emm. WHEN I SMOTHERED THAT FIRST GREAT REVOLVING MASS OF YOUR
      EXPLODING SLAVES, AND YOU & I STOOD SMILING IN THE
      STEAM

    BEFORE OUR FATHER CALLED FORTH MICHAEL HIS (LET US
      ACKNOWLEDGE IT) FAVORITE SON,

    DID WE NOT, GABRIEL, MAKE A PACT?

Gabr. *Flickering ominously.* AND? IS IT NOT A POET'S PHRASE: ET TU?

Emm. NO NO GABRIEL! THESE TWO MORTALS, AS I WAS CARRIED TO
      NOURISH PLANTS IN THEIR VERY HOUSE,

    THESE TWO WERE ABOUT TO RESOLVE TO GIVE IN TO US!

JM. Oh, when we spoke of drifting with the current—

Emm. PRECISELY, YOUNG SCRIBE, AND TICKLED MY NATURE THUS.

    BUT GABRIEL? WERE YOU EVER MEANT TO BE, IN OUR FATHER'S
      GREAT DESIGN, VENGEFUL?

    WERE WE NOT, YOU & I, IN THE STEAM OF THE COOLING WORLD,
      AGREED?

Gabr. IN THAT FIRST FLUSH OF INNOCENCE, EMMANUEL, YES, AGREED:
    WE WOULD SHARE THE WORK OF WIPING OUT OUR FATHER'S LET
      US NOT SAY ERRORS BUT EXPERIMENTS.

    YES, ELIAS, I REMEMBER EVEN MY OWN INNOCENCE BEFORE THE
      GRIND OF WORK MADE OF ME THIS MULE YOU REASON WITH.

Emm. THEN, BROTHER, WE MET AGAIN IN THE HISS OF THE FLOODED
      VOLCANO

    A scene glassed-over on the inmost wall

    Trembles, flashes, clears. Viewed from mid-sky,

    Thera erupts, its gleaming masonry

Silently topples into waves a black
Inverted pyramid of smoke pours from.
AND YOU HAD CHANGED, SHY ONE, & YOU SAID: SHALL WE NOT
    DROWN EVEN THEM?
& IN A VOICE OF THUNDER OUR GREAT FATHER CRIED TO YOU AS
    TO A HOUND:
GABRIEL, TO HEEL!

Gabr.   *An ashen pallor.* YES, EMMANUEL, YES.
    NOW BROTHER LIGHT, IS IT NOT TIME TO TAKE OUR PUPILS TO THE
        LABORATORY & THERE, FITTINGLY AT 5,
    EXAMINE THE FIVE?
Mich.   TOO FITTING, GABRIEL, TOO LIKE A RIGID NATURE'S NEED
    FOR FORMULA & SYMMETRY. YET AGREED:
    COME TOMORROW & WE WILL LET HAVE THEIR SAY
    THE IMMORTAL FIVE FOREVER SAVED ON THE RAINY DAY!
    Exeunt.

      Apologetically
Blowing his nose, DJ: It's what I've tried
Never to think—Maria's suicide—
What I can't imagine anyone . . .
Sometimes, alone with her at Sounion
Or driving back to town along the sea,
Death would come up, the pain, the indignity.
Once she half joked about a lethal dose
Of something from her London days—who knows?
Just in case, she said. I tried to tell her
She had no right to . . . JM: Mirabell
Spoke of the usefulness— DJ: I know,
I hated that. Loss *is* loss. JM: Though
Hasn't the Board helped us at all to see
Losses recouped? In Wystan and Maria's
Surrender to the minerals and the plants
Those ghastly graveyard facts become a dance
Of slow acceptance; our own otherwise
Dumb grief is given words. DJ: Or lies?
Last month I went with Tony to her grave

—There near Mother and Dad's grave, where I *don't* go.
We spent the afternoon weeding and thinning,
Washing the cross, putting in myrtle, white
Impatiens, a sprinkling of peat moss.
It looked so really nice when we were through.
And now . . . JM: And now, you mean, beneath it
Somebody's lying whom we never knew?
As if we hadn't known her capable
Of anything! DJ: That's it. Ah hell,
Let's sleep on it.

★

MAMAN REMAINS OF 2
MINDS ABOUT HER END   ONE MORE YES/NO
FOR POOR JM: TO WILL DEATH MAY HAVE BEEN
MORE POTENT THAN 5 CC OF MORPHINE . . .
MEANWHILE DJ: DEAR ENFANT LEAVE MY PLOT
TO THICKEN NICELY BY ITSELF. ALIVE
& WELL (& IN FULL FIG TO MEET THE FIVE)
I'M HERE WITH U, NO? ALL THE REST IS ROT

The First Lessons: 5

The schoolroom stretches to a line. It breaks
Cleverly into two floating poles
Of color that in dark 'air' glow and pulse,
Undulate and intertwine like snakes.
Whatever road we travel now, this twinned
Emblem lights, and is both distant guide
And craft we're sealed hermetically inside,
Winged as by fever through the shrieking wind.

Mich.　WE HAVE ISSUED FORTH LED IN ORDERLY PROCESSION BY PROUD
　　　　GABRIEL.
　　　OUR PATH (WE INSIDE THIS LIVING RED, QUITE SAFE) WINDS
　　　　THROUGH HOWLING SHADES IN BILLIONS

AND WE HAVE ARRIVED. GABRIEL, FASTEN THE DOORS! THERE.
CALM, QUIET, RANKS OF GABRIEL'S MACHINES & RANKS OF
    FEATHERED BACKS BOWING AS WE PASS.
HERE A FAMILIAR ONE: WERE YOU SLEEPING, MY SON?
As when an illustration's needed in
A storybook, here against nothingness
Appears . . . a perfect image under glass?
An image's lifesize, transparent skin
Reflected onto glass? The painted eyes
Have opened to the light, as it replies:
YES FATHER SUN, I SLEEP.

Mich.   TELL THESE SHADES, THESE BLINDFOLD MORTALS, OF YOUR V WORK.
A golden disc gleams on the phantom brow
—Ahknaton! as we gather only now.

Akhn.   FATHER, I AM, HAVE EVER BEEN YOURS. AH MY EYES! MY V WORK
LIFE AFTER LIFE HAS BEEN SEEING FOR HEAVEN INTO PHENOMENA.
Mich.   YES? THE FIRST THING YOU SAW?
Akhn.   YOU, LORD. YOU SHINING HIGH IN MIDDAY HEAVEN. IN OUR DAY
THAT WAS THE PALACE LEGEND, THAT WITH 4 EYES WE SAW:
I AND SHE, TWO HALVES, MANCHILD & FEMALECHILD
BORN EYES OPEN, REACHED FOUR NEW WET RED ARMS STRAIGHT
    FOR YOU!
AND LIFE AFTER LIFE MY V WORK, I SINGLE AGAIN,
WAS/IS TO SEE AND TO MAKE SENSE OF IT. AND SO
AS CURIE I SAW THE RADIUM IN THE DARKNESS GLOW,
AND KNEW. AS GALILEO SAW OBJECTS FALL, FORESEEING
THEY WOULD ALIGHT JUST SO. I NOW FLY OVER LANDSCAPES
KNOWING, O FATHER EARTH! WHERE IN THEIR FORMATIONS LIE
    THERMAL
ENERGIES, POWERS CLEAN & ABUNDANT, AS YET UNTAPPED,
WHICH ALONE CAN CLEAR YOUR HEAVEN, LORD MICHAEL, THAT I
    MAY SEE YOU.
I SLEEP AND AM HONORED TO LEAVE THAT DREAMING SHUTEYED ME.
The image fades upon its pedestal.
Mich.   WE CALL HIM MANY NAMES YET HE IS THE SIGHT OF OUR FIVE
    SENSES.
ON, GABRIEL? THIS ONE APPEARS TO STUMBLE TOWARD US.

Raph. WHAT, ILL, LISTENER?
The path of live black wings bending, a young
Dwarf clad in homespun, large head cocked, has come
To light. At first he struggles as with some
Strange lethargy, and speaks with heavy tongue:
YES, LORD. I COME BEFORE YOU UNDER A DRUG. THEY TAMPER
WITH MY BODY. THERE! I AM FREE, AH FATHER RAPHAEL!

Raph. HOW GOES YOUR V WORK?

Dwarf. WE LISTEN, LORD RAPHAEL. OUT IN SPACE IS A MUSIC MAKING
DAILY SENSE, WE TAKE IT IN. DO I PLEASE YOU, LORD?
(This will be Montezuma. Now on Earth
As an East German astrophysicist
Kenning those signals—*Mirabell*, 2.1.)

Raph. PROCEED. THESE GUESTS WOULD KNOW YOUR V WORK & YOUR
HISTORY.

Dwarf. LORD, AS HOMER THE SCRIBE I LISTENED & MADE SENSE OF FOLK
MYTHS,
THEN AS THE PROPHET MOHAMMED I TOOK IN STORIES & GOSSIP,
SETTING IT STRAIGHT. AS MOZART MY INSTRUMENTS CAUGHT YOUR
SPRING
SONGS, FATHER EARTH. THAT WAS ALL. BUT I NOW HAVE
INSTRUMENTS TUNED,
LORD, TO THE VERY STARS, TO THE PANTHEON YOU CAME FROM.
I LISTEN, RECEIVING THE MESSAGES, MAKING SENSE OF THEM.

Raph. SLEEP AND MEND.
(He wasn't Montezuma after all?—
Something to clear up in the interval.)

Emm. TOUCH, TOUCH, YOU HERE, TUGGING MY WATERY ROBE?
Now only is a jet of goldengreen
Quetzal feathers, in the next niche, seen
To rise from a maize vision—here displayed
On one knee, in his hand a rod of jade:

Mont. LORD!

Emm. COME, TELL US OF THE ARK & THE BULLRUSHES.

Mont. LIFE AFTER LIFE I LIVE GETTING TO THE BOTTOM OF THINGS,
O LORD FATHER EMMANUEL! REACHING DOWN FOR A TOEHOLD.

AS NOAH OR, MORE PRECISELY, THE FIRST TO SET FORTH ON THE
SEA,
THE FIRST CREATURE TO FEEL THE BUOYANCY OF WOOD,
I UNDERSTOOD & FLOATED, AND SO THE MIGRATIONS BEGAN
AND THE USE OF THE HARD SEA SURFACE. THEN LIFE AFTER LIFE
FIRST AS HEALER, THEN AS CLAPPING MINSTREL, THEN AS THE
KING CALLED MONTEZUMA, WHO SUFFERED THE IRON GRIP
OF THE NEW WORLD, & HANDED OVER HIS GOLD TO NO AVAIL,
AS TOUCH I FINGER THE STUFF OF THINGS, LORD, AND MAKE SENSE
OF IT.

Fades. But the next eidolon brightens in
A frame above the sudden quickening stir
Of wings: a presence far, far lovelier
Than her bust of colored limestone in Berlin.

Gabr. NOW WOMAN, KISSING MY HAND WITH A LICK OF YOUR TONGUE,
SPEAK.

Nef. I, O LORD GABRIEL, DOWN THERE DROWN IN THE PAIN OF LABOR,
GLAD TO BE MOMENTARILY FREE.

Gabr. SPEAK.

Nef. SIRS & MADAME, LIFE AFTER LIFE, AS HALFDIVINED SISTER
BECOMING DISTINCT, I HAVE EXPLORED THE WORLD BY TASTE.
AS RACHEL I STUDIED EVE'S COOKBOOK, MAKING SENSE OF IT.
AS SHIVA LEARNED POISONS, & ONWARD, SERVING YOU MY LORD.
MY NAME LIFE AFTER LIFE HAS BEEN FAMED OR INFAMOUS AS
BEFITS THE DUAL NATURE OF TASTE: BITTERSWEET NEFERTITI!

Gabr. YOUR TWIN?
Barely has her magic time to fade
(Sun is setting, will the lesson end
Before we meet the Fifth?) *when an off-duty shade,*
Not on a pedestal, a gay young blade
Bearded, white-robed, engagingly advances:
I AM HERE, LORD, THOUGH A CORPSE IN EARTH, MY PARENT
NATURE,
NOSTRILS FILLED WHO FIRST CRIED SMOKE! FIRE! DO I PLEASE YOU,
LORD?

Gabr. TELL QUICKLY THESE FRIENDS OF YOUR V WORK.

57

Pla. LORD, YOU NEEDED A TALENT TO SNIFF OUT THE NATURE OF MAN
        & SO I MADE, AS PLATO, SENSE OF MAN'S NEED FOR HIS MIND,
        & AS THE MOST FEARED KHAN MADE SENSE OF THE WHIFF OF
           BLOOD.
        YOU HAVE USED ME LIFE AFTER LIFE AS THE GENTIL BREATHER, AS
           MUIR,
        GIVING PLEASURE IN THE ROSE, AND MAKING SENSE OF IT.
Mich. GO!
        FLY BACK INTO YOUR SELVES ON EARTH! WE 8 WILL NOT DELAY
        YOU, & WILL MEET TOMORROW, ANOTHER DAY
        Exeunt hurriedly, as the last beams die.

*

Tell! Did they show you all the incarnations?
ONE EACH MY DEARS, BUT THE MOST GLAMOROUS ONE
That V in V Work is the Roman *five.*
& 'LIFE' IN OUR SALON TONGUE (GOD A FRENCHMAN?)
And it's *Homer* (a dwarf!) who listens—Mirabell
Was wrong. I FEAR SO Do we now revise
His lessons? Let them stand? U ARE THE SCRIBE
One sees now how it works. Galactic signals
Come to this latest Homer's ears WHO THEN
CONFIDES THEIR MEANING BUT TO WHOM? POOR DUMB
E GERMAN TECHNOCRATS? Hardly: God B
Must be the first, our peacock said, to hear them.
And each bit of made sense adds to that great
Store of wisdom. THUS THESE 5 GO STRAIGHT
OVER THE HEADS OF WHATEVER BUREAUCRACY,
EVEN THE BROTHERS' Each of the Five intent
On his own gift and his own element
Till, from the upwardness of midnight spark,
Returning dew, cadenza of the lark,
To meteor in field, fresh bread on sill,
All is a ghost of grist to Heaven's mill.
DIVINE SIMPLICITY SO LIKE THAT WONDROUS
TALE OF GRIMM: SHARPEYES & EARTOGROUND,
SERVANTS WHO HELP THE UNWORLDLY PRINCE TO WIN

HIS LADY'S HAND   But drugged, asleep, in labor?
GLIMPSES OF THEIR CURRENT STATES ON EARTH
Then Plato's in fact *between* lives. GATHERING
HIS POWERS FOR THE NEXT   That's why you've had
Such easy access? SO I NOW PRESUME

Poor Mirabell, it seems to be his doom . . .
And Rachel? How he struggled to explain
Her name as formula! Well, wrong again.
YES & NO: IN THE BEGINNING MIGHT THE WORD
(OR FORMULA) NOT HAVE REMAINED UNHEARD
UNTIL IT HAD ENGENDERED BOTH ITS OWN
ANTONYM & THE ODD HOMOPHONE?
SO RACHEL. THESE OLD TESTAMENT NAMES I'VE
A HUNCH RING MANY CHANGES ON THE FIVE
And Nefertiti is now Plato's twin,
Not Akhnaton's—what's that meant to mean?
TWINS WE ARE TOLD COME FROM THE FEMALE GENE,
THERE4 THESE LADIES & THEIR ESCORTS WEAVE
A LINE BACK TO THE PRIMAL (M)ADAM/EVE:
NO SOONER SINGLE THAN NEF ONCE AGAIN
TOOK ON A DOUBLE NATURE (ALL THOSE ARMS
OF SHIVA NOT THE LEAST OF HIS/HER CHARMS)
WD THAT BE THE GENETICS, WOMAN?
                              ME?
REALLY! HOW WD I KNOW? In other lives
You had— I REMEMBER THANK U   BUT NO TWINS.
NO TEASING GLIMPSES EITHER, OF THE 5'S
PRESENT EXISTENCES   YET MAY I SPEAK
MES ENFANTS AS A WILY SHARPEYED GREEK?
THEY HAVE SEEN US AS OF YESTERDAY,
PARTICULARLY YOU 2   What are you saying—
That one of them is somebody we've met,
Or will, on Earth? George Cotzias, I'll just bet!
Notice how Montezuma gave no clue
To his current life? Remember then what you
Learned about George's densities? Come now,
That *must* be the connection! YES & NO

The First Lessons: 6

The schoolroom as before. Enter the Brothers.

Mich.   POETS, A POEM! HERE'S WHAT I SHOULD LIKE AS SUBJECT:
              YESTERDAY'S MEETING OF THE FIVE, YOU 4, WE 4, AND QUESTIONS.

WHA.   SIR?

Mich.   YES, SENIOR SCRIBE?

WHA.   MAY I ASK, IN YOUR FINAL COUPLET YESTERDAY
              WERE YOU NOT USING A RUNOVER LINE?

Mich.   SCRIBE, RUN OVER?

WHA.   SIR, WE MEAN BY THAT, WHEN A LINE'S SENSE
              AND ITS LAST WORD ELUDE COINCIDENCE.

Mich.   O SCRIBES, I WHO CAN WRITE ON WALLS CANNOT ALAS MAKE POEMS.

WHA.   (Nervous, eager not to give offence)
              O NO SIR, ABSOLUTELY CHARMING, QUITE
              THE OCCASIONAL VERSIFIER! I ONLY MEANT
              THE DRAMA OF YOUR LINE-BREAK: 'DELAY / YOU'

Mich.   TOO MODERN? EVEN BAD?

JM.   Most dashing, *I* thought.

WHA.   SIR, DO NOT GIVE UP
              & ALL WE SCRIBES SHALL COME TO YOU TO SUP!

Mich.   RUNOVER, HMM. THAT'S A WHOLE NEW DIMENSION
              A silvery bell peals. Light grows acute.
              AS IS OUR CLASS TODAY. FOR MY BROTHERS & I WILL EXPLAIN THE
                  SECOND OF OUR EACH THREE NATURES.
              RAPHAEL, LET US PROCEED NOW TO REVEAL THE TWELVE.

Raph.   AT FIRST I PROTECTED IN THAT CAVE THE SWEET & INNOCENT IDEA
                  OF MAN CONTEMPLATING HIMSELF.
              NOW HERE IS MY SECOND DUTY IMPOSED UPON ME BY OUR GREAT
                  FATHER: SUPPLY.
              UP THROUGH MY SOILS, MADAME, COME GREEN SHOOTS, AS YELLOW
                  SUN & BLUE WATER MIX IN ME. AND UP THROUGH MY VEINS
                  COMES HEAT, & FROM MY PORES: OIL, & FROM MY PITS: COAL.
              MAN SPRINGS TO LIFE & TO INDUSTRY AND I REWARD HIM WITH
                  MY GOLD & SILVER

WHOSE SHADOW RICHES ARE URANIUM. YET, SUPPLY! CRIED GOD,
AND I OBEY. FOR EVEN UNDER YOUR LAKES & SEAS I AM,
    EMMANUEL, A BASE BUT GENEROUS NATURE.

Our school has every modern teaching aid.
Green fields ashimmer and great ore-veined peaks
Fill one frame. Then, as Emmanuel speaks,
They are replaced by a 3-D cascade
Overbrimming inexhaustibly
Font upon font of snow above a polar Sea.

Emm.   INDEED, R, U R (SEE LORD BROTHER MICHAEL, HOW I HAVE TAKEN
    TO THEIR LETTERS?)
   & AS THE QUIET LAKE I EARLY STILLED HIS FEAR WHILE KEEPING
    HIS WISH TO RETURN TO ME AT BAY.
   THROUGH MY FIRST NATURE, PEACEFUL & REASONABLE GREW THIS
    THINKING BEAST.
   AND THEN OUR FATHER GAVE ME A SECOND DUTY: CARRY HIM.
   & SO AS CHRISTOPHER I TRANSPORTED THE MANCHILD, & QUENCHED
    HIS THIRST & WASHED HIM
   WHO BY THEN INNATELY WISHED FOR A BAPTISMAL CLEANSING OF
    HIS ANIMAL DIRT.
   SO: REASON & PRIDE, CALM & PURIFICATION,
   ARE MY TWO DOUBLE NATURES.

Mich. YOU, SHY ONE, OR ME?
Gabr. PROCEED, PROCEED.
Mich. I BORE INTO THE CAVES & ONTO THE DANCING WATERS THE LIGHT!
    LIGHT! OF MY FATHER'S CRY. I BROUGHT IN THE NATURE OF
    IDEAS.
   THEN GOD SAID: 'DIVIDE THE TIME OF MAN
   AND MAKE A REFLECTIVE NATURE WHERE, CALMED AT HIS FIRE, HE
    WILL TURN OVER THESE IDEAS AS TREASURE GATHERED IN HIS
    DAY.'
   SO I THREW UP REFLECTION, MAKING DAY,
   & TURNED IT OFF, CREATING NIGHT.
   I BROUGHT INDOORS THE ROVING NATURE OF MAN WITH HIS 5
    PLAYMATES.

DJ.   Reflection?

WHA.   WE DO NOT SEE LIGHT MY DEAR,
      ONLY ITS EFFECT ON ATMOSPHERE.

Mich.   HOMEWORK! WELL? ARE YOU TIMID OF BOASTING, GABRIEL?

Gabr.   NO.
      WHEN I ASSUMED MY SEAT NEXT TO OUR FATHER HE NOTED MY ONE
          NATURE, DESTRUCTION, & SAID: 'IT IS NOT ENOUGH.
      WE ALL MUST WORK. GO FORTH AS FIRE IN ALL ITS FORMS. IT WILL
          NEED ATTENTION, AND BE AN ABUSED NATURE, YET ATTEND
          IT.'
      AND SO I CLEANSE TOO, IN A WAY,
      & I ILLUMINATE REFLECTION, I SWARM IN VELVET ON MICHAEL'S
          TRAIN.
      PERFORMING MY SECOND NATURE I PROMOTE THOUGHT, AGGRESSION,
          DREAD, AS THROUGH WOOD & COAL & OIL & ATOMS AND YES,
          LIVES
      I GO UP IN FLAME.
      MY FIRST NATURE: SELECTION. MY SECOND: THOUGHT.
      AH MICHAEL, HENCE THE VERY HISTORY OF MAN, HIS EVOLUTION!
          FOR THESE OUR FATHER ENTRUSTED TO ME.

Mich.   SO, DEAR SHADES, DEAR SCRIBE & FAITHFUL HAND, WE KNOW 8 OF
          OUR NATURES. NEXT,
      ALWAYS SHY YET NOT LOATH TO DISPLAY,
      WE WILL TOMORROW BRING FOUR MORE: ANOTHER DAY
      Exeunt.
             His last line comes through garbled:
      TORROWMORE WILL BRING IN FOUR OTHER DAY.
      SHH SHH   SHALL WE SET IT RIGHT? MM
      QUICK THE WASHRAG   RUB OFF THE BLACKBOARD
      THERE! And the poem Michael asked for? I'M
      ITCHING TO TRY MY HAND   PENTAMETER?
      5 LINE STANZAS? GIVE/FIVE/LIVE? High time
      He found some other rhyme-word besides "day".
      A TAG FROM GOETHE, NO? SEHR DISTINGUE

★

O LORDS WITH JOY & WHOOP & HOLLER
YOU GAVE US FOUR THE FIVE
BUT WHEN (FORGIVE) WILL YOU 4 GIVE
US THEM IN LIVING COLOR?

Very nice, Wystan. That should fill the bill.
NOW YRS? Oh no. Those stanzas won't see light.
TOO UNFAIR! I THOUGHT IT (OVER YR SHOULDER)
BRILLIANTLY SOLVED RIGHT DOWN THE LINE JM:
TETRAMETER FOR US, PENTAM FOR THEM,
NEF EVOKED BY THE ONE FEMININE
ENDING, & PLATO BY THE ONE SLANT RHYME
But it was awful—not the slightest ring
Of *life.* DEAR BOY ONE CAN'T HAVE EVERYTHING!

Let's change the subject. Free of Mirabell's
Brain-teasing ratios, it would seem the Twelve
Are just our angels multiplied by three.
INDEED   SUCH EXQUISITE SIMPLICITY
DJ: But are these *real* powers, would you say,
These angels? I BELIEVE WE SHALL DISCOVER
THEIR POWERS ARE IN US QUITE AS MUCH AS OVER.
SO VERY BEAUTIFUL, WHICHEVER WAY
JM: Aren't you on record as preferring
Truth to beauty, Wystan? Those machines
That powered your ideal lead mines, as a boy—
WHAT'S UGLY ABOUT A BIG ROBUST MACHINE?
I'm only saying you felt bound to choose
Over a possibly more stylish rival
The one that functioned best. ON EARTH MY DEAR,
TRUE. BUT EFFICIENCY IS WELDED HERE
TO BEAUTY AS THE SOUL IS TO SURVIVAL

Will Michael make a poet? HMM   He's read
No one much since Chapman. BUT CONFRERE
HIS WORDLESS SPLENDORS ARE BEYOND COMPARE:
WHEN GABRIEL SPOKE A STARRY UNIVERSE
POURED IN SERENE TUMULT FROM M'S BROW!

THE VERY NIGHT AS CHAPMAN WD AVOW.
VERSE HE MAY LEARN FROM US & THE DEAR KNOWS
THERE'S LITTLE WE CAN TEACH HIM ABOUT PROSE!
Should it be set down on the page as prose?
NOTHING STRICT A CADENCE BREAKING THRU
ALWAYS FLEXIBLE (To illustrate,
The cup does an impromptu figure eight)
& UNEXPECTED
Lights, an innocent blue.

Mich.   WE ARE UNEXPECTED?

JM.   Never, Lord. The Senior Scribe and I
Have been discussing, how best to convey
To readers the full verve of what you say.
There are a few effects I mean to try.
Would the like you unmeasurable King
James inflections be perhaps the thing?

Mich.   HEAR HIM BROTHERS! IS THAT NOT THE DEAREST OF OUR FATHER'S
HOPES?
MAN USING HIS MOST DELICATE MACHINE, MINING LEAD &
PRODUCING QUICKSILVER?
AH THE MACHINE, SENIOR POET, THE MACHINE, YOUNG SCRIBE, THE
MACHINE OF THE MIND DRIVEN BY WORDS TO MINE MEANING:
MAKE SENSE OF IT

DJ.   Does that phrase ring a bell? *The school-bell rings.*

The First Lessons: 7

Mich.   OUR FATHER LIFTED THE CURSE OF IMMORTALITY FROM HIS NEW
CREATURE AND SAID:
'SON MICHAEL, SHEDDER OF LIGHT, REFLECTOR, NOW HELP MAN
FORGET'
AND SO MY THIRD NATURE: SLEEP, THE REPOSE FROM DAYLIGHT TO
DAYLIGHT.
MAN'S SPACE ON EARTH LIES LARGELY WITHIN PATHS WHERE SUN
& LACK OF SUN EQUATE HIS HOURS.
JUST SO HIS LIFESPAN: THE VITAL YEARS, THE MIDDAY YEARS, ARE
BALANCED BY YEARS OF CARE AS CHILD & OF REST AS AGED.

AND SO ANOTHER SET OF TWINS, GABRIEL & I, DIVIDE REPOSE: I THE
    LIVING, SLEEPING, DREAMING

Gabr. AND I THE REPOSE BETWEEN LIVES. MY FATHER SAID:

'GABRIEL, SEPARATOR, JUDGE, THINKER ON IDEAS, RESTLESS
    URGER-ON OF MAN'S MIND,

GIVE MY POOR CHILDREN SUCH A SLEEP THAT, WAKING TO THE
    LIGHT OF A NEW LIFE, THEY FORGET ITS TOLL & RUSH OUT
    EAGERLY'

Emm. AND THE WATER BURSTS IN THE WOMB, & DOWN GLIDES GOD'S
    DARLING.

THEN GOD SAID: 'TWIN ELIAS, EMMANUEL, YOU THE CALM ONE,
    GIVE MY CHILD BALM FOR SORROW'

& SO THROUGHOUT MAN'S FAREWELLS TO LIFE MY TEARS BATHE THE
    CLENCHED FACE, FLOW & ASSUAGE.

Raph. THEN MY TURN CAME. 'O WITTY TWIN (SAID GOD) TAKE BACK YOUR
    PIECE OF CLAY'

DUST TO DUST? NO! LIVING TISSUE & MINERALS, STORED IN MAN
    SINCE HIS CLIMB FROM YOUR OOZY FLOOR, EMMANUEL, THERE
    BELOW THE SALT.

THESE ELEMENTS I FOLDED ONCE AGAIN IN MY ARMS. MY TREES
    WHISPERED:

SLEEP, CHILD, UNTIL AGAIN YOU COME TO ME, KING OF ALL
    LIVING THINGS AND LORD OF THE GREENHOUSE, SLEEP.

Mich. SO OUR TWELVE NATURES, SUBLIME & COMMON:

EARTH, AIR, WATER, FIRE, IN VARIED CONSORT MAKING SIX PAIRS OF
    TWINS, SET IN YOUR FOUR SEASONS

Music. Vivaldi's 'The Four Seasons' plays
Gently through Michael's closing words of praise.

O GREEN SPRING EARTH, O WITTY WITH HOPE!

O BLUE CALM CLEANSING, MUSICAL & RHYTHMIC WATER!

O LIGHT, IDEAS YELLOWING TO HAZE,

ASWARM WITH GNATLIKE SELVES ARE YOU THROUGH AUTUMN DAYS!

AND YOU, RED SOLEMN THOUGHT, O DECIMATOR,

CHAOS FROZEN INTO ORDER, WINTER!

But Light from elsewhere lifts the harmony
To a remote, electrifying key:

AH MY FOUR SONS

Mich. O FATHER!
IN OUR SEVENTH HEAVEN YOU GRACE US, WE BOW WITH LOVE!
FATHER, HAVE WE TOLD THEM WELL?

YOU HAVE TOLD THEM THE TWELFTH OF IT THEY TAKE YOU IN

The cup like an eager dog behind a hedge
    He cannot overleap
Races back, forth, along the Board's far edge:
  His Master lost by now in bright
Unthinkables, all pinpoint-far, dream-deep
      Foresight.

Then Michael's voice through swarming, rainbow mist:
GRACED ARE WE, YET HAVE FAR MORE TO SAY
AND MANY A TRUTH FOR ANOTHER DAY

—Leaving us stunned. What happened, anyway?
God Himself grazed our poem in a gust
Of wonder? Yes, and something like distrust.
Not of Him, not of Biology . . .
But, after all, we bookish people live
In bondage to those reigning narrative
Conventions whereby the past two or three
Hundred years have seen a superhuman
All-shaping Father dwindle (as in Newman)
To ghostly, disputable Essence or
Some shaggy-browed, morality-play bore
(As in the Prologue to *Faust*). Today the line
Drawn is esthetic. One allows divine
Discourse, if at all, in paraphrase.
Why should God speak? How humdrum what he *says*
Next to His works: out of a black sleeve, lo!
Sun, Earth and Stars in eloquent dumb show.
Our human words are weakest, I would urge,
When He resorts to them. Here on the verge

Of these objections, one does well to keep
One's mouth shut—Wystan, don't you think? WE WEEP

*

A dreadful interval. Last night's collision,
Heading home, with a wool-gathering creep.
No one hurt, but ugly psychic dents.
Words D and I exchange about expense
Turn our green mountain to a black plateau
Still smouldering the next afternoon. ENFANTS
QUICK WHILE OUR STAR PUPIL PRIMPS IN THE DORM:
MAMAN HAS BEEN SO LONG A LONER THAT
SHE CAN'T RECALL THE IDLE HOUSEHOLD SPAT
BUT WE NEED CALM & LAST NIGHT'S LITTLE SCENE
UNDID YR OLD BLACK MAMMY
O I MEAN
SHE'S TAKEN THE FRONT SEAT   OUR TEACHER'S PET
RUSHED IN AHEAD OF ME & TOOK MY SEAT!
All smiles, our discord laughable, DJ:
No little scenes up there, please! Tell us, er,
About, ah— SHALL WE SAY THE MINISTER
OF EDUCATION? YES: A RADIANCE
THEY TURNED THEIR BACKS ON US & SPOKE INTO,
SNUFFING OUT (AS MM SAID) THEIR SMOKES
LIKE SO MANY VILLAGE DANDIES WHEN PAPA
ENTERS THE ROOM   I *felt* they'd been caught boasting!
AH THEY WERE SIMPLY COWED & NOT WITH FEAR,
WITH WHAT WD BE TO LOVE (AS WE KNOW LOVE)
WHAT LOVE IS TO AFFECTION   Did you hear
A voice? THE MUSIC SWELLED   WE SAW U WRITE
THE WORDS & A PURE GLOW ON OUR DEAR HAND
Slowly, as he goes on, the full amazement
Seizes us. Reliving yesterday's
Lesson, we are humming "Winter" when

The First Lessons: 8

Michael and his Brothers quietly enter.

Mich.   IT IS ALL APPROVED & WE PROCEED. I AM MY FATHER'S SON
MICHAEL.

WE KNOW THAT EACH LIVING CREATURE LIVES BY SENSES, SOME
FEWER, BUT THE HIGHER FORMS HAVE FIVE.

WE HAVE BROUGHT YOU OUR SCOUTS, THE IMMORTAL FIVE. THEY
REPORT TO MY BROTHERS & ME THEIR FINDINGS

WHICH, WHEN APPROVED & MADE SENSE OF, THESE GENIUS 5
PROCEED WITH.

NOW WE, MY BROTHERS & I, ARE THE SENSES OF OUR FATHER.
RAPHAEL?

Raph.   I AM GOD'S HEARING ON EARTH. I HEAR THE FEET, THE MOVEMENTS
OF HIS CREATURES, THE SLITHER, THE STAMPEDE.

I SENSE THE BUILDERS OVER BUILDERS. SHAKE! SAYS MY FATHER,
AND I DO.

I HEAR THE CRIES OF TREES CUT, TOO MANY. I HEAR THE LESSENING
OF A BREED.

I LISTEN, MAKE SENSE OF IT, AND REPORT TO MY FATHER.

Mich.   HIS TWIN?

Emm.   I TOUCHING EARTH, CIRCLING IT, PATTING ITS SHORES,

RACING WITH NEWS OF THE AVALANCHE, WITHDRAWING WHEN IN
DESERT LANDS WE MUST GUARD SPACE FOR MAN'S FUTURE
FIELDS,

I COVER THE WHOLE BALL, REFLECTIVE PALMS UPWARD, FEELING
THE ATMOSPHERE.

I TOUCH, MAKE SENSE OF IT, AND REPORT TO MY FATHER.

Gabr.   MY TWIN DUTIES, I THE SELECTOR, ARE TASTE & SMELL.

I CATCH WHIFFS OF DANGER, AND TASTE THE BITTER & THE SWEET.

I AM THE COOK OF THE SMOKING STEW OF MANKIND: LESS HERE OF
THIS, MORE OF THAT.

I PILE THESE FINDINGS ON A TRAY, MAKE SENSE OF THEM, AND
REPORT TO MY FATHER.

Mich.   AND HE, O SHY BROTHER, HOW OFTEN: 'IT IS NOT DONE'?
The schoolroom glowers, but the irresistible
Light of day resumes. As Michael does:

68

AND I? I READ, DEAR EMMANUEL, YOUR PALMS, AND I SEARCH & I
    SEE, AND HAVE A VAST SURFACE TO EXPLORE EACH DAY.
I MAKE A THEORY OF LIGHT IN THE BRIGHTNESS OF EXPLOSION,
AND CHECK TO SEE IF YET THE FEATHERS OF ITS WING CAN SUPPORT
    THE PIGEON IN MY AIR.
I LOOK, I READ, MAKE SENSE OF IT, AND REPORT TO MY FATHER.

JM.   And God? He takes them in, these capsules made
Of the whole vast ongoing escalade?

Mich.   AND THEN, YOUNG SCRIBE, THE GREAT SENSES OF OUR FATHER BEGIN.
FOR HE WHO HAS ALL THESE FIVE HAS A SIXTH: INTUITION,
A SEVENTH: JUDGEMENT (WHICH, O GLORY, HE DEMONSTRATED
    YESTERDAY)
AN EIGHTH: COMMAND, & A NINTH: PRONOUNCEMENT,
AND THEN THE ZEROETH WE DO NOT KNOW
FOR THIS HE EXERCISES OUTWARD. YES, TURNING OUTWARD HIS
    MULTIPLE ATTENTION FORTIFIED BY THE GREAT ORCHESTRA OF
    THE SENSES,
OUR FATHER SINGS,
SINGS, ALONE, INTO THE UNIVERSE.
Pauses as if hearkening. No sound.
LISTEN! FOR YOU 4 WILL HEAR THAT SONG: YOUR TENTH LESSON (ON
    THE 9TH WILL BE A JOYOUS CONGRESS OF THE SENSES)
AND THEN OUR FIRST OF THREE SCHOOL TERMS WILL END.

DJ.   Already? It seems only yesterday . . .

Mich.   NOW THIS 8TH HEAVEN OF COMMAND PERMITS YOUR MICHAEL TO,
    LET US NOT SAY ORDER, RATHER GIVE AN OUTLINE OF OUR V
    WORK AHEAD:
YOU WILL ASSEMBLE IN A MOON MONTH AFTER THESE TEN LESSONS.
    THEN WE MAKE SENSE OF THEM FOR FIVE LESSONS MORE.
THEN MY SHY BROTHER TAKING THE FRONT DESK (PERMETTEZ
    MADAME?) WILL GIVE US HIS TEXT TO BALANCE MINE,
FOR WILL WE NOT HAVE INNOCENTLY EXPOSED OURSELVES TO
    IDEAS?
AND HAVE WE NOT AS OUR FATHER COMMANDS, SURVIVED?

SO NEXT WE DON THE GLAD ARRAY
OF ALL OUR SENSES TO MEET THE DAY.
Exeunt.

WHA. ENTRE NOUS MY DEAR HE'S NOT IMPROVING:
NEXT WE DON OUR SENSES IN GLAD ARRAY
& MEET HERE AGAIN ON ANOTHER DAY.

JM. That too could stand some work, if I may say so.
Michael, returning unexpectedly:
QUARRELING, POETS?

JM. He— I—that is, we . . .

Mich. MY VERSE NOT METERED? NOT IN RHYME? THEN PRAY
MAKE SENSE OF IT YOURSELVES ANOTHER DAY!
Exit. And only now sunset's tall dazzle
Dims from the frosted glass of our doorway.

O DEAR HE WAS STANDING OUTSIDE! HOW I ADORE HIM!
ME TOO! ME TOO! YR JADED MAMAN'S TYPE
Not Gabriel? Good. AH THERE ARE NIGHTS & KNIGHTS,
BUT YOU 3 FAITHFUL SQUIRES, YR MISTRESS SAYS,
WILL SERVE UNTIL THE END OF BLISSFUL DAYS.
DJ: Tomorrow will be twenty-four
Years to the day since J and I first met.
JM: Or twenty-five, as any Greek
Would count them; we're all one year old at birth.
THE PARTY'S PLANNED, NO ACCIDENT! A Silver
Jubilee in England, too. *Newsweek*
Says London is a pulsing fairyland
Of coaches, fireworks, dancing on the green.
INDEED WHO WD HAVE THOUGHT THAT NO DOUBT STABLE
BUT O SO DOWDY SCHOOLGIRL WD TURN OUT
SUCH A SUCCESS? Maman, you knew the Queen?
Imagine never telling! DON'T MAKE FUN
THE LIFE MAMAN LED, SHE KNEW EVERYONE

*

*JM from DJ entering
our 25th year—*

often distant, ever dear.
(Diamonds not from Pharoah's barge
but MFJ's engagement ring—
sorry they're so large!)

—This with a band of chemically blackened
Silver in which twin baby stones are set
To balance a small "sun" of gold. Slipped on,
It is an instant, lifelong amulet.
JM: I've no gift but these lines the years
Together write upon my face and yours.

YOU DEAR BOYS AT FIVE & TWENTY
SURELY HAVE A GRACIOUS PLENTY
AND WHEN YOU'VE ARRIVED AT FIFTY
SHOULDN'T LIFE BE TWICE AS NIFTY?
MY POINT HERE SEEMS TO BE:
EXPECTANCY! EXPECTANCY!

Wystan, how very, very . . . silvery.
THANK U WE'RE GIVEN LIKE A PAIR OF WAITERS
THESE ORDERS FOR THIS AFTERNOON'S COMMAND
PERFORMANCE: SALT. A SPICE OF YR OWN CHOICE.
A SCENT. ICE IN A BOWL. A CANDLE LIT
& A LIVE FLOWER. FETCH THESE NOW We do.
David on the terrace cuts a snow-white,
Paprika-anthered lily. I meanwhile
Bring coriander and a bergamot
Cologne; the rest. That's it? Then light the candle.
Sit. WHEE! U ARE WITH US FOR THE FIRST
TIME IN ALL THESE LESSONS NOT REVERSED.
WE SMELL U HEAR U & THEY SAY WILL TOUCH
U ANY MOMENT IT'S A LITTLE MUCH!
Is this called making sense? & GETTING THRU

Seventh Heaven, Judgment; Eighth, Command—
So Michael said. Are we to understand
Each lesson lifts us to a plane of greater

Power and light? INDEED   AN ELEVATOR
How can you tell? Does Maman get a shade
More beautiful, like Beatrice? WE ARE MADE
AWARE, DEEP IN THE CAVE, OF CRYSTALS PLATO
NEVER DREAMED OF, BIG FAT SOLITAIRES!
IT'S NO ILLUSION   EPHRAIM HAD IT RIGHT,
WE'VE TAKEN SENSES ON & IT'S DIVINE
Had it right for a different order of spirit:
You, in short. YET IF WE TOUCH AT 9
IS IT NOT MY DEARS HIS DREAM COME TRUE?
Ah, you must tell him. He'll be thrilled. ALAS
WE MAY NEVER SEE HIM AFTER THIS
"Pronouncement" sends you back— A LAST LONG SUMMER
& DIE THE SWANS   Never to sing again?
Just those mute messages flashed vein by vein
Through mineral and leaf? A COMFORT, NO?
MAMAN THE LAURA IN YR LAURELS
                                    I
MY BOYS INSIST ON BEING YR PET ROCK!
DJ: Don't let's think *now* of losing you.
You'll come with us to Samos? Ephesus?
LET'S DO   BUT WHAT TO WEAR? They won't take back
Your senses? INDIAN GIVERS? LET THEM TRY!
AH   MUSIC   IT BEGINS MY DEARS   MY DEARS!

The Ascent to Nine

Music. A single pure white beam one knows
Floods the mirror room, which undergoes
Instant changes. Dewy garlands deck
The staircase. Statue, pictures, candlestick,
Each is prismatically multiplied.
The Ouija Board drifts upward on a tide
Of crystal light—ethereal parquet
Where guests will presently join WHA
And MM. (DJ and JM appear
Twice, outside and in, both 'there' and 'here'.)

What *is* the music? STRAUSS   I MEAN THEY ARE
SWEET TO REMEMBER   ROSENKAVALIER
SIDE ONE   GO PUT IT ON DEAR BOY   I do,
And hurry back. NOW LINK YR FINGERS   YES
NOW TOUCH EACH OTHER'S FACE   KISS   We obey.
(Only yesterday? Twenty-five years?)
AH YES   YES   IT BEGINS   MY GOD!

                            MY MUSIC

MY MUSIC   MY POOR SOUL THAT WAS MY SOUL
WHERE'S HOFFI? WHERE'S MY TWIN? It's Strauss himself,
He's at the party! THANK YOU FOR MY MUSIC
ROSEN SIND SIE MEINE BUEBCHEN   *We*
Are roses—is he mad?

                 A second new
Voice entering the cup: WHAT IS THAT SOUND?
That's *Rosenkavalier* by Richard Strauss
On the phonograph in Athens, in our house.
SO I AM HOME   Who's this? THE DWARF KIND SIRS
ONLY THE DWARF   The great scribe Homer? I?
PERHAPS   THEY TELL ME NOTHING THOUGH I LISTEN
You're listened *to* throughout the centuries.
MAY I HEAR A SMALL POEM? ANYONE'S?
For Homer's pleasure, what on Earth to say?
Luckily Wystan (JM PERMETTEZ?)
Takes over, and declaims: HOW JOYOUSLY
WE LITTLER MEN HAVE SAILED YOUR WINEDARK SEA,
IMMORTAL BARD, YOU WHO CREATED ME!

A third arrival: WHERE AM I? THIS MUSIC
I KNOW IT   YES! AND MAESTRO, HERE?

                         IST ES

NICHT EIN TRAUM, LIEBSTE NORWEGERIN?
(It can't be Flagstad! YES   THEY ALL TROOP IN)
From upstairs, Schwarzkopf, who had dubbed a high
C in that late *Tristan* Flagstad made:
"Es ist ein Besuch!" NOT BAD AT ALL, NOT BAD
BUT YOU MY GREATEST VOICE

                 MY DEAREST FRIEND

73

He wears a frockcoat; she, a flowery gown,
And positively croons over the lily.
Enter a plumed Splendor:

OUR SCULPTORS CARVED

THAT FLOWER BY THE THOUSAND & WHEN MY PALACE
FELL INTO THE MOAT (It's Montezuma!)
ONE BLOSSOM, ONE STONE LILY FLOATED FREE
& THE POOR SPANIARDS WENT PALE WITH DREAD:
THE LIGHT VOLCANIC ROCK, YOU SEE

BUT IS

THIS GLASS ONESIDED? asks a new voice.

COME

SISTER QUEEN (Akhnaton and Nefertiti!)
OUR LORD THE SUN ENJOINS US TO LOOK UP
Michael is ready, as a final guest
Slips in:

AND MUSIC TOO? Who have we here?

I NOTICE SOME IMPROVEMENTS ON MY CAVE
Plato—oh, you won't approve of Strauss!
NEVER DISAPPROVE   IT WARPS THE SOUL
All take their places as the light takes form.

The First Lessons: 9

Mich.   WELCOME AT THIS OUR TOPMOST STAGE,
CHILDREN, TO A SILVER AGE.
(The ring, the silver rose, the Jubilee,
Everything fits unbelievably)
NOW QUICK SENSES: TOUCH THE ICE,
TASTE THE SPICE, SMELL THE SCENT!
FROM HEAVEN BENT WE LEAN, LAY CLAIM
UPON YOUR HANDS. NOW LOOK INTO THE FLAME

We do. *All do. A timeless moment. Twelve*
Figures reproduced to twelve times twelve
In ranks of the four colors, see themselves
—No, D and I see nothing—through the 'sense

Prisms' conferred on them by Michael. Thus
I WHO WAS WYSTAN SAW A YELLOW ME
AGED & WRY   A GREEN HILARIOUSLY
LAUGHING   A RED ME WRAUGHT   A BLUE
ME STARING STRAIGHT INTO MY OWN TWO EYES
While I WHO WAS MARIA IN THE FITTER'S
MIRROR SAW A RED ENRAGED MAMAN
A BLUE IN BLISS WITH FLOWERS IN HER HAIR
A GREEN TOO SHY TO SPEAK OF & MOST ODD
A YELLOW SELF I'D SEEN 100,000 TIMES
DOING MY FACE. TOO SIMPLIFIED, BUT THESE
WERE MERELY PSYCHES, PERSONALITIES,
THE UPPER CRUST OF A MILLEFEUILLES LAYER BY LAYER,
HABITS & LOVES & LIFETIMES, PEELED AWAY
FROM EPIDERMS OF HUMAN MEMORY
Until, at Michael's voice, the flame, like one
Shaken from sleep, returns each to his own:

ALL THE COLORS AT OUR FETE
(STRAUSS, A TUNE! FAIR SINGER, SING!
WE'LL HAVE THE BEST OF EVERYTHING)
GREENS YELLOWS BLUES & REDS, STAY WITH US YET
AND BE THE WHITE OF MY DELIGHT
IN EWIGKEIT

The master improvisor's four-note theme,
BDEA, makes everybody smile—
B and I, the two notes are the same!
I come to Be, is the Idea. Meanwhile
Flagstad by the keyboard meets his eye,
Throws her blonde head back. It's a fifth Last Song
—A silk trailed over dead leaves, loom of peak,
Ninths in full blossom, minor purl of stream.
As Wystan thumps along JUST KEEPING TIME
Michael's words, which on the page look weak,
Come thrilling from her throat. He speaks through them:

SILVERY MY CHILDREN, ENTER IN
THIS HEAVEN IT IS GIVEN YOU TO WIN.
FOR WHO IS LEFT TO TELL YOU NAY?
OUR FATHER'S VOICE ANOTHER DAY
YOU'LL HEAR & FALL (LIKE ANGELS) DOWN TO PRAY!
TOUCH, TASTE, SMELL, HEAR & SEE,
NOW COMPOSE A SILENT HARMONY.

The song ends. LIFT YOUR HANDS: CLAP ONCE! We do.
WE ARE GONE   *The schoolroom empties in a trice.*

Our black wick smoulders over melted ice.
In and out of numbers 9 to 1
Weaving like a drunk, the cup comes down
To earth: SPORTSWEAR   BOYS CLOTHING   WATCH THE STEP!
WOW   DID U FEEL OUR TOUCH UPON YR HANDS?
JM: Not I. DJ: I felt . . . a chill?
YES   FOR MY DEARS WE TOUCHED U & CAN STILL
ALMOST: AS RS SAID, ROSEPETAL SKIN
OR BABIES' BOTTOMS   Were we somehow *in*
The mirror for that hour? U WERE INDEED
Literally?—but by now we know
Where that will get us. Tutti: YES & NO

This Heaven was Pronouncement? IN THE SENSE
OF HAVING I SHD SAY A PRONOUNCED FLAIR
FOR THIS OR THAT, LIKE MICHAEL'S FROM THIN AIR
TOUCHING, SPECTACULAR EMBODIMENTS
You must have got your touch back when we kissed;
That's why you said "My God"? DEAR BOY, NO: YR
STAGE DOOR JOHNNY HAD JUST GLIMPSED DEMURE
FLAGSTAD APPROACHING & KNEW WE WERE IN FOR BIGGER
TREATS THAN A VULGAR GROPE
                              I MES ENFANTS
WAS THRILLED BY NEF   A PRESENCE OF PURE AMBER
ROBED IN 18TH DYNASTY HAUTE COUTURE
OVERWHELMING   MICHAEL CAN DO IT ALL!
NOT A TRANSPARENCY: DO U RECALL

HER QUESTION? ONLY THEN WE UNDERSTOOD
WE WERE NOT LIVE, & WHEN SHE TOUCHED THE MIRROR
(FOR OF COURSE THE WALLS AROUND US WERE YR MIRROR)
IT WAS AS IF SHE O HEARTBREAKINGLY
HAD GRAZED AN OLD & WELLKNOWN PRISON. WE
PUT UP OUR HANDS IN FEAR LEST THE GLASS CRACK
LIKE GREENHOUSE PANES
                  BUT SHE AT ONCE DREW BACK:
A TEENY SHOCK   THE MIRROR A COW GUARD?
SHE WANTED U   AS WHO DID NOT? & YET . . .
Were we *there* only in a sense? IN ALL
THAT MATTER SHORT OF THE MATERIAL.
MICHAEL'S SLEIGHT OF HAND BROUGHT US TOGETHER
IN THE R LAB   THE 5 COULD GO NO FURTHER,
A STYX OF QUICKSILVER DIVIDING THEM
FROM LIFE-INFECTED DJ & JM
The other angels, were they present? NO
ONLY, WHEN MICHAEL LOOKED INTO THE FLAME
HE STRUCK US AS COMMUNING   OTHERWISE
THIS AFTERNOON WAS UTTERLY HIS SHOW
And ours! SO TRUE   TO EACH EPIPHANY
ITS OWN: FLAGSTAD & STRAUSS WDN'T AT ALL
DO FOR A BUTTERED SHAMAN IN NEPAL
And next the voice of God. How do we rise
To that? SLEEP SOUND TONIGHT   WE KISS YOUR EYES

*

The First Lessons: 10

No scene. The mirror bitter-black and vast,
Underdusted with remotest light.

ANCHORS AT LAST   MM & I OUT HERE
RISING RISING INTO SUCH A VOID & HOWL!
OUR WALLS HAVE LONG SINCE DROPPED AWAY   O THANK
GOD U HAVE COME   WE THOUGHT WE HAD LOST TOUCH
May we ask questions? HUSH   WE STRAIN TO HEAR

77

Now, ripple within ripple on black water,
o o o o o o o o o o
Pulse of the galactic radio
Tuned then to mortal wavelength in mid-phrase:

IVE BROTHERS HEAR ME BROTHERS SIGNAL ME
ALONE IN MY NIGHT BROTHERS DO YOU WELL
I AND MINE HOLD IT BACK BROTHERS I AND
MINE SURVIVE BROTHERS HEAR ME SIGNAL ME
DO YOU WELL I AND MINE HOLD IT BACK I
ALONE IN MY NIGHT BROTHERS I AND MINE
SURVIVE BROTHERS DO YOU WELL I ALONE
IN MY NIGHT I HOLD IT BACK I AND MINE
SURVIVE BROTHERS SIGNAL ME IN MY NIGHT
I AND MINE HOLD IT BACK AND WE SURVIVE

Pausing to be reread, then pulsing slowly
o o o o o o o o o o
The cup glides off the far edge of the Board.

Life itself speaking. Song of the blue whale
Alone in Space? Bravery, vertigo,
Frontier austerities . . . Maria? Wystan?

BE CALM A DAY NOW   OUR FRIENDS PRONE & COLD BUT THEY SURVIVE
Dumbly we nod.
IT IS YR BIRD!   Of course—where are our manners?
Thank you for coming to us, Mirabell.
                I AM YOUR OWN   GIVE THEM A REST, THEY HAVE
KNOWN SOMETHING DIFFICULT   I SPREAD WINGS OVER THEM   ADIEU

★

Our friends are being DEBRIEFD, says Mirabell,
And as yet must not know what we have learned.
We hide the transcript, then the cup descends
This time from Zero, to emerge at One
And give us THE BAREST SKETCH: ENFANTS U JOINED US

THERE IN THE BLACKNESS OF THE GLASS   WE SOARED
OUTWARD   WE 4 ALONE   HAND TOUCHING HAND
ON AN OBSIDIAN CUP CALLED UNIVERSE:
SHRIEK OF OUR ICY POINTER ON NO BOARD!
Your walls had dropped away. EMPTY AH YES
MY DEARS & TERRIFYING   UP UP UP
YET NOT WITHOUT A MAD LIGHTHEARTEDNESS
EH MM? IT MUST BE THE EXTREME
DRUG OF THE RISKTAKER   WHO WD EVER DREAM
THAT SUCH
PLEA SET OM ORRO W
    Look, now we're making Mirabell
Uneasy. He was with you, though? INDEED
STOOD BRAVELY BY WITH SMELLING SALTS & ST
BERNARD FLASK & SEEMED ENFANTS THRUOUT
TO HAVE BEEN SHELTERING US WITH HIS HEAT,
FOR WE REVIVED IN WONDER FROM OUR FAINT
STILL HEARING AS IT WERE HIS (M) HEARTBEAT:
A BUZZ OF WHIRLING NUMBERS   Like those street
Cafés in northern cities, with umbrellas
Of radiant warmth— AND THE ACCOUNTANT MIND
SITTING BENEATH THEM MY DEAR! WE WERE SURROUNDED
UPON AWAKENING BY MIRABELL'S KIND,
THE OO STARING   NOT AN ANGEL IN SIGHT . . .
HE FIDGETS   WE HAD BEST LEAVE IT AT THAT.
TOMORROW IN THE SCHOOLROOM WE CAN CHAT

Night. Two phantoms out of Maeterlinck
Stand on the terrace watching the full moon sink.
DJ: It's almost as if *we* were dead
And signalling to dear ones in the world.
They face it squarely, Wystan and Maria,
Terror or exaltation or whatever.
We two are deaf and dumb; they see, they hear.
They suffer; we feel nothing. We're the dead . . .
And these were just the lessons that said Yes
—To what? for up through Michael's magic well
Eerie undercurrents of distress.

Affirmative? I'm dreading Gabriel.
Right off the bat he'll have some negative
Interstellar static stymieing
Any song Biology might sing.
JM: I wonder. Think, before you give
Way to panic, of what other meanings
The word "negative" takes on in *Ephraim*:
X-ray images, or Maya's film
In which the widow turns into the bride.
Tricks of the darkroom. All those cameras clicking
In Venice, on the bridge. For now a new bridge—
Can it be crossed both ways?—from Yes to No
Is entering the picture. DJ: So
Is Venice, if our plans firm up. JM:
By which time, from the darkness you foresee,
Who knows what may develop milkily,
What loving presence? (Odd, not long ago
Our daydreams were in color, that tonight
Print out in Manichaean black and white.)

*

Wystan on God B's Song

WELL THE 1ST THING WE HEARD WAS A FAINT PIPING
NOT UNLIKE A SHEPHERD'S FLUTE   THIS GREW,
RESOLVED INTO NO MELODY BUT TONE
LEVELS & INTERVALS OF UTTERED MEANING:
PLAINTIVE? AFFIRMATIVE? O QUICKLY NOW
EXPOSE THAT PAGE   UNCOVER IT MY DEARS!
WE ARE ALLOWED   I find the page. They read.

AH   SO HEARTBREAKING   SO THAT WAS IT
He's singing to the Pantheon. OR ALONE
KEEPING UP HIS NERVE ON A LIFERAFT
Far cry from the joyous Architect
Michael told us of at the beginning—;

But He gets answered. DOES HE? Yes. The angels
Spoke of signals. DO THEY KNOW? I see.
They've never heard the Song. ONLY WE 4
& THAT'S AS HE WOULD SAY THE HALF OF IT
What was the song's effect on you? MM
KNEW HERSELF TO BE AMONG THE STARS
THE WORLD LOST, OUT OF EARSHOT. I WAS KEEN
UPON THE SOUND ITSELF   THOSE TONES WERE EITHER
THOSE OF AN ETERNAL V WORK OR A MACHINE
SET TO LAST   UNTIL THE BATTERIES
RUN DOWN   OR . . . ?   Did the tones heard correspond
To what you read just now? EXACT SYLLABICS:
THERE IS A LANGUAGE   ARE WE ON TO SOMETHING?
CAN WE MAKE SENSE OF IT? I ASK   WE ASK

Dante heard that Song. So did Mirabell's
Forebears when the clouds put out the flames.
THERE4 THEY CLUSTERED ROUND WIDEEYED   BUT WHO,
WHO WD THINK THE SONG HAD HAD SUCH LYRICS?
The lyrics may be changing. Dante saw
The Rose in fullest bloom. Blake saw it sick.
You and Maria, who have seen the bleak
Unpetalled knob, must wonder: will it last
Till spring? Is it still rooted in the Sun?
EXACTLY   THEY CHOSE WELL IN U MY DEAR
No, Ephraim raised these issues. But his point's
More chilling made at such an altitude.
CHILLING ENFANT? AN IRREVOCABLE FREEZE

DJ, as one who steers in winter seas
Past threatening floes: You're in the schoolroom now,
Safe and sound? INDEED   WE 4 ALONE
Have you come through the mirror or have we?
U HAVE   ISN'T IT COMFY? & THE VIEW
SENSATIONAL TODAY, ALTHOUGH ALAS
IN 15 LESSONS' TIME U MAY BE CALLED ON
TO RISK BAD LUCK   JM: To break the glass?
& SEND US PACKING   Turning mutineer,

DJ: If we refuse? RISK IT MY DEARS
& WE'LL SURVIVE & MAKING SENSE OF IT
HAVE LIGHTENED GOD B'S TASK A GRAIN
                THAT DAY
ENFANTS TAKE OUT A SMALL EXPENDABLE MIRROR
ONTO THE FRONT STEP   KISS & WITH ONE WISE
CRACK SET US FREE   Maria, why must *we*?
JM: Who else? (A pang abrupt as lightning
Strikes deeply through the dim, charged hemisphere;
Then comes the rain.) My mother used to say,
Throw the pieces of a broken mirror
Into running water— IDIOTS   DRY YR EYES:
IST OUR LOVELY VAC THEN EXPLANATIONS
And will *you* break the mirror in our minds?
O WE'LL BE SIGNALLING   JUST U WAIT & SEE
FROM OUT THERE   FROM THE WORLD
                    DJ, still shaken:
I knew that it would end. I didn't know
That we would have to take the step ourselves.
NICER & NEATER   QUITE LIKE PROSPERO!
LISTEN YR MOTHER'S GOT IT: TAKE A BOWL
OF WATER WE CAN SLIP INTO & OUT
WITH A GREAT SPLASH INTO A PLANTED POT
Instead of breaking anything? WHY NOT?
JM: No. Back to flames, back to the green
Rhine go the rings in Wagner and Tolkien.
The poem's logic, though I hate to say,
Calls for the shattering of a glass. DJ:
Perhaps that *and* the bowl of water, too?
BRAVO ENFANT   OUR EAU DE V WORK   SMOOTH
SEAS TO SAMOS   CALL US   TOODLELOO

The cup, however, lingers. IT'S JUST ME
MY BOY   MAY I? A POME I'VE (M) SET DOWN
UNDER THE SPELL OF HEARING GOD B SING
(WORK ON IT FOR ME   IT NEEDS POLISHING):

A SHIPBOARD SCENE,
TRISTAN ACT I OR LES TROYENS ACT V:
HIGH IN THE RIGGING, FROM
BEHIND THE GOLD PROSCENIUM,
ABOVE THE ACTION'S THRIVING
CITY WITH ITS WRONGED & WILFUL QUEEN,

ONE SAILOR'S CLEAR
YOUNG TENOR FILLS THE HOUSE, HOMESICK, HEARTSICK.
THE MAST NEEDS COMFORT. GALES
HAVE TATTERED THE MOONBELLIED SAILS.
MAY HIS GREEN SHORES O QUICKLY
SAFELY NOW FROM RAGING FOAM APPEAR.

&

Samos

And still, at sea all night, we had a sense
Of sunrise, golden oil poured upon water,
Soothing its heave, letting the sleeper sense
What inborn, amniotic homing sense
Was ferrying him—now through the dream-fire
In which (it has been felt) each human sense
Burns, now through ship's radar's cool sixth sense,
Or mere unerring starlight—to an island.
Here we were. The twins of Sea and Land,
Up and about for hours—hues, cries, scents—
Had placed at eye level a single light
Croissant: the harbor glazed with warm pink light.

Fire-wisps were weaving a string bag of light
For sea stones. Their astounding color sense!
Porphyry, alabaster, chrysolite
Translucences that go dead in daylight
Asked only the quick dip in holy water
For the saint of cell on cell to come alight—
Illuminated crystals thinking light,
Refracting it, the gray prismatic fire
Or yellow-gray of sea's dilute sapphire . . .
Wavelengths daily deeply score the leit-
Motifs of Loom and Wheel upon this land.
To those who listen, it's the Promised Land.

A little spin today? Dirt roads inland
Jounce and revolve in a nerve-jangling light,
Doing the ancient dances of the land
Where, gnarled as olive trees that shag the land
With silver, old men—their two-bladed sense
Of spendthrift poverty, the very land
Being, if not loaf, tomb—superbly land
Upright on the downbeat. We who water
The local wine, which "drinks itself" like water,

Clap for more, cry out to *be* this island
Licked all over by a white, salt fire,
Be noon's pulsing ember raked by fire,

Know nothing, now, but Earth, Air, Water, Fire!
For once out of the frying pan to land
Within their timeless, everlasting fire!
Blood's least red monocle, O magnifier
Of the great Eye that sees by its own light
More pictures in "the world's enchanted fire"
Than come and go in any shrewd crossfire
Upon the page, of syllable and sense,
We want unwilled excursions and ascents,
Crave the upward-rippling rungs of fire,
The outward-rippling rings (enough!) of water . . .
(Now some details—how else will this hold water?)

Our room's three flights above the whitewashed water-
front where Pythagoras was born. A fire
Escape of sky-blue iron leads down to water.
Yachts creak on mirror berths, and over water
Voices from Sweden or Somaliland
Tell how this or that one crossed the water
To Ephesus, came back with toilet water
And a two kilo box of Turkish delight
—Trifles. Yet they shine with such pure light
In memory, even they, that the eyes water.
As with the setting sun, or innocence,
Do things that fade especially make sense?

Samos. We keep trying to make sense
Of what we can. Not souls of the first water—
Although we've put on airs, and taken fire—
We shall be dust of quite another land
Before the seeds here planted come to light.

*

WE'VE FOUND A HOLE IN THE HEDGE! Maria means
That during these days-off before the middle
Set of lessons we can please ourselves,
Talk to friends in the Bureaucracy
Banned from our class, along with Gabriel's
Bat legions, OR TO ANYONE! I stall:
What in fact *is* the hedge? A LOWER WALL
OF CONSCIOUSNESS   DJ: No, no, I'm lost . . .
OK NOW LISTEN: IN THIS HEAVEN/HELL
WE ARE BLANKS. IN THESE BLANKS YOU APPEAR
THANKS TO OUR 'CONNECTION' (CUP, BOARD, MIRROR)
PERFECTLY CLEARLY AS DO THE OTHER DEAD
WE THINK OF OR WHO THINK OF US. HOWEVER
SINCE LESSON I OUR SCHOOLROOM HAS BECOME
A (M) CLOSED CIRCUIT NONE MAY PLUG INTO
WITHOUT CREDENTIALS. IT IS BURKE'S NEW PEERAGE
AN ISOLATION ENGINEERED BY MICHAEL
FROM WHICH ALL SANDOVER IS VISIBLE.
BUT NOW THAT THEY'VE HOOKED UP THE INTERCOM
(OR MAMAN ONCE TOO OFTEN KICKED THE WALL)
WHOM SHALL WE CALL? THEY'VE CLUSTERED AT THE HEDGE,
HL & MD WAVE   E BLOWS A KISS
JM: Or new blood? If Pythagoras
Were hovering near his birthplace— HERE HE IS

7154   Pythagoras? He's quoted
Mirabell's numerology for God.
NUMBER WAS GOD TO US   OUR MUSE   IN MAGIC
THE NUMBER SPEAKS & LOGIC O YOUNG MEN
SETTLES ON EGGS OF NUMBER LIKE A HEN
So we begin, Sir, dimly to construe
For all our slowness. Where would it be, this poem,
Without your guiding light? Measures that you
Taught your disciples glimmer even now
Through the dispersing clouds about my brow.
YOU ARE REPEATING THE OLD RITUAL.
GIVEN A REWARD THE SCRIBE WOULD CALL

'MATHEMATICIAN, COME, RECEIVE YOUR PART
FOR YOURS ARE THE TRUE FORMS BEHIND MY ART'
DJ: You must be horrified by what's
Happened to your town—the Swedes, the yachts,
The apartment houses. YOUNG MAN NEVER BE
COWED BY THE UPS & DOWNS OF MASONRY.
NOTHING TRAVELS FASTER WHERE THE GREAT
TIDES OF COMMERCE OVERWHELM ALIKE
DREAM & DRECK   Where are you now? AT 8
WHICH ON ITS SIDE STANDS FOR INFINITY,
THE SUBJECT OF OUR STUDIES   DID YOU KNOW
THAT IT HAS WALLS   Go on! But exit P.

Why so abruptly? I SHD THINK MY DEAR
IT IS A LECTURE WE ARE MEANT TO HEAR
FROM OTHER LIPS   Well then, how did he look?
DONNISH BUT STRAPPING   QUITE THE STAR ATHLETE
Perhaps he found us puny. MAMAN TENDS
TO THINK THAT THE MOT JUSTE MIGHT BE EFFETE
DJ (crushed): Maria! . . . As (unfazed) Wystan
Strikes a bright note on which the session ends:

A GREEK LADY DRESSED SMARTLY IN WEEDS
TOLD A TRIO OF LIMP GANYMEDES
'TIME U DROPPED ALL PRETENSE
& BEGAN TO MAKE SENSE,
THE SUCCESS LIKE WHICH NOTHING SUCCEEDS!'

*

Pythagoras should have seen us yesterday
Scrambling high above the sea's blue smudge
Through the bleached boneyard of Ephesus; returning
At twilight, thistle-stung, with faces burning
And JM limping where he missed a step
On a steep stairlessness, and hurt his knee.

Now in our shuttered room, while the town sleeps:
NO SIESTA? READY FOR A TREAT?
WE'VE BROUGHT PLENORIOS THE ARCHITECT
OF ARTEMIS' GREAT TEMPLE— Instead of words,
Broad "visionary" movements of the cup.
CUBITS & WIDTHS   I'D BETTER PARAPHRASE
. . . AH   A NICE BIT   HE SAYS: I HAD A DREAM
IN IT THE GODDESS BENDING OVER ME
SAID 'MAKE MY GLORY, SUCKLE! HERE & HERE:
THIS TEAT IS PROPORTION, THAT ONE SPLENDOR.
I WANT THE MARBLES BARE OF DECORATION
& NO CLOSED SPACES   SHELTER ME IN GRAND
& SIMPLE BEAUTY & YOU WILL GO TO HEAVEN!'
I BUILT A WONDER, & AM HERE. Alas,
The wonder's gone. No stone remains in place.
AH BUT THE LEGEND DOES DEAR BOY   REMAINS
ARE GHASTLY. EPHESUS! STREETS SWARMED WITH GHOSTS
BAZAARS   COVERED PALANQUINS   CRIES OF VENDORS
A YOUNG BEAUTY SCREAMING WITH LAUGHTER RAN
OUT OF THE BATHS ON TRAJAN'S AVENUE
IT WAS A FEAST DAY   U CHOSE WELL   & MICHAEL
RAISING HIS HAND, TIME LIKE A SCUDDING CLOUD
RACED BACKWARD. I & OUR OWN ARTEMIS
STROLLED THRU IT ALL ENRAPTURED BY ONE MORE
GLIMPSE INTO MAN'S ILLUSION OF HIMSELF.
THANK U FOR EPHESUS! DJ: Were you
Glimpsed by the ghosts? JOSTLED ENFANT & STEPPED ON!
THE CROWDS, THE NOISE, SO GREEK! & YET OUR QUIET
ELEGANCE DID NOT GO UNNOTICED. BLUE
SPARKLINGS LAPPED THE NEAR EDGE OF THE THEATRE
WHARVES WITH PLEASURE RAFTS   & THE VAST MARKET'S
FRAGRANCES & AWNINGS! MEANWHILE THRU
WHAT WAS REALITY FOR US YOU 2
CD BE SEEN PEERING AT THE SKELETON
LIKE MED STUDENTS   JM I CRIED WATCH OUT!
WHAT U DID NOT STEP ON WAS THE VANISHED
MARBLE TREAD   YET DREAMILY YR FOOT
BORE DOWN EXPECTING IT   SO COUNTLESS THINGS

GONE FROM THE WORLD ENDURE IN ITS (M) WINGS
In theory, there's no age or place, Maman,
You couldn't visit? NOT IF MICHAEL BUYS
THE TICKETS   What's our next move? FISHER BOYS?
Wystan, please. ENFANTS ME FOR A BLACK
COFFEE BY THE WATER   Great, let's go!
YR TREAT   OUR COINS SADLY OUT OF DATE

*

Two Deaths

In quick succession. First, George Cotzias
—Distinguished Son of Greece, as headlines read
Even in sleepy Samos, over columns
Of testimonials and photographs.
Flown from New York, his body's being buried
This afternoon in Athens, where a tide
Of wreaths advancing on Necropolis
Will blanch beneath dramatic nationwide
Thunder and lightning. But here's George himself—
Not at his own funeral? JIMMY   DAVE
I THOUGHT I'D RATHER SIT IT OUT WITH YOU

BESIDES, MY FUTURE'S SETTLED: I WILL JOIN
THE ELEMENTAL POWERS WHEN YOUR FRIENDS DO
They've met already. He and Maria SHARED
AS MOTTO POSO AKOMA, YEARS OF RAYS
HAVING LEFT MY SOUL LIKE A SWISS CHEESE . . .
Alluding to his work on the disease
That killed him, or to his saved consciousness,
Her words of welcome half caress, half mock:
HOIST WITH YR OWN PETARD I SEE, EH DOC?
Wystan just gapes. MY DEARS IT GIVES ONE PAUSE
IS THERE NO END TO THE NO ACCIDENT CLAUSE?

Already George is fully briefed to take

A schoolroom desk. WE'RE SETTING UP A LAB!
Already at his fingertips in these
Few days since dying are the densities
That took us weeks and weeks with Mirabell
To get a sense of: ALL COMPATIBLE
WITH MY RESEARCH INTO THE LIVING CELL.
BLANK FACTORS (AS MY COLLEAGUES CHOOSE TO CALL THEM)
VEX THE DRUDGE WHO STOUTLY TURNS HIS BACK
ON THE IDEA OF A GRAND DESIGN
—Phrase a bolt of blue fire punctuates—
YET THESE, I NOW SEE DAZZLED, CUT & SHINE
STEADY AS LASER   WITH A GENIUS FAR
BEYOND THE DULL TRANSMISSION OF A GENE
BY EGG & SEMEN   More "blanks"? And these are?
BANKS IN WHICH THE R LAB'S NONGENETIC
STUFF OF THE SOUL ACCUMULATES. TOO BAD
HITLER GAVE SUPERMAN SUCH A BAD NAME
& SUCH A WHITE COMPLEXION   All the same,
George, how much we'd rather have you live
And framing questions at our table! (Though
He's better placed to frame them now, I *don't* say—
Especially if he is of the Five.
Is he? We're shy of asking. Yes or no,
Sooner or later, truth, we trust, will out.
Meanwhile the main thing's to get on with it.)

The storm is passing. TIME FOR MY NEXT SESSION
IN THE R LAB   George, one moment—what about
Your phoenix? Have you looked into that vision?
I TRIED TO JIMMY   BUT A PEACOCK HERE
TELLS ME TO WAIT   ONE DAY IT WILL BE CLEAR

★

The second death. We're just back from the island—
Hall strewn with tar-flecked towels, a straw hat, stones
And suitcase—when Long Distance telephones:
Robert Morse died in his sleep last night.

A sense comes late in life of too much death,
Of standing wordless, with head bowed beneath

The buffeting of losses which we see
At once, no matter how reluctantly,

As gains. Gains to the work. Ill-gotten gains . . .
Under the skull-and-crossbones, rigging strains

Our craft to harbor, and salt lashings plow
The carved smile of a mermaid on the prow.

Well, Robert, we'll make room. Your elegy
Can go in *Mirabell*, Book 8, to be
Written during the hot weeks ahead;
Its only fiction, that you're not yet dead.

LADS! I WAS RIGHT ABOUT THE MOLECULES
Making the cup move? YES   BUT (SIGH) YOUR SCHOOL'S
DENIED ME   Odd. They said you'd fit right in.
INTO A NEW LIFE   Oh? Where? THEY WON'T TELL:
MY PUNISHMENT FOR HAVING BLUSHED UNSEEN?
DJ: *We* saw you, Robert. TRUE   AH WELL
R(E)MORSE IS USELESS & HAS EVER BEEN

TOO UNJUST MY DEARS   I FOR ONE MEAN
TO PULL STRINGS MADLY   MM HAVE U MET
OUR NEW FRIEND?
                        (THIS IS HIM? HMM) (THIS IS SHE?)
—Turning upon each other's youthful charm
The shrewd eye of potential rivalry.
BEAUTY! comments Wystan. THANK GOD B
I WAS ITS SLAVE   BY FAR THE MEATIER ROLE
THAN ITS EMBODIMENT   They're not getting on?
O YES   MUCH GIGGLING FROM THE CHINTZ SETTEE
HE'S NOT HIMSELF YET   PAIN & BOREDOM BLUR
MOST OF US AT FIRST   LEAVE HIM TO HER:
B4 THE FULL MOON SWEEPS US OFF TO 5

RM WILL COME ALIVE!
                    Out they all go,
But someone— George? The cup comes shyly forward:
SIRS, GK IN RESEARCH LAB   Who is this?
(Silence.) We know you're there—who are you? Have we
Ever spoken before? I MAY NOT, MASTERS
—Backing out abashed, as if come too soon
To sweep up after the symposium.

*

Two days later MAD ABOUT YR CHUMS
Says Robert, though the cup moves guardedly.
We urge him to be frank. WELL MUSCLE BOY
AS WE NOW CALL PYTHAGORAS (OOPS HERE HE COMES)
CLEAVES ME OLD   JM: This is my fault.
I'd said upstairs just now, I never felt
Easy with Mirabell's master ratio—
88:12—and fancied P might shed
A light . . . WAY OVER ICKLE WOBERT'S HEAD

YOUNG MEN I DO NOT QUESTION THE R LAB,
I FIND THEIR TEXTS TOO PUZZLING. THEY REDUCE
A) FORMULAS TO WORDS & B) IDEAS
TO FORMULAS. FOR INSTANCE I SAY 'SOUL'
A SIMPLE FORMULA LIKE ALL THAT DEAL
WITH ENERGY, BUT THAT VAGUE INCREMENT
OF 'PSYCHE' (THOUGH ITSELF REDUCIBLE)
FALLS INTO NO EASY NUMBER SYSTEM.
THUS RENDERING MAN'S GAINS & LOSSES, THESE
CLERKS DISCOUNT THE LOSS OF FACULTIES
OR GAINS IN WISDOM   FOR THEIR CALCULATIONS
START FROM A TREACHEROUS, LEDAEAN O.
12:88, THEN, IS A FAULTY READ-OUT
DESIGNED TO KEEP US GROPING IN THE DARK.
I SAY: START SHAKILY, END OFF THE MARK!
Hard to take in, Sir. Evidently we
Never sat a lifetime at your knee.

TOO BAD! AND MUSCLES WD HAVE GIVEN YOU,
WITTY RM, A DECADE MORE   ADIEU

HAVE WE A SLASH MARK? LET HIM TAKE THAT /

ENFANTS   RM ENCHANTING   BRINGS NEW VIE
TO OUR FRENCH CIRCLE: 'COMME J'ADORE, MME,
VOTRE PUR ET IMPUR'   COLETTE: 'ET MOI
LE VOTRE!' HE DID BLUSH   Is Wystan with us?
CLOSETED WITH PLATO   HEADS TOGETHER
OVER THE NEXT 5 LESSONS   WE TOO SHALL BE
5   With George, very tidy. But what's Wystan
Doing? Pulling strings behind the scenes?
JM HAS HE PERHAPS NOT ALWAYS BEEN
Backstage even with the angels?
                                        GONE
Maria? IT'S TOO TARSOME   I WON'T PLAY
SHE SIMPLY DISAPPEARED ON THE WORD ANG
. . . Robert? But *he's* gone. DJ: Don't forget
He has no clearance for these topics yet.
So here again we are—not quite alone.

A New Friend

4170   MAY I, MASTERS?
Please do. You came the other day—who are you?
I WAS THE LAST   Softly: I HAVE 4 LEGS
Now this *is* a surprise. You're from Atlantis!
MY GREEN HOMELAND   O IS IT STILL
Green? I fear not. But its legend is.
WE RAN   O WE RAN!   & I WAS SWIFT
Immortal, too; and lived in starlike cities?
YES   O YES   SO YOU HAVE SEEN?
No, but heard from your old messengers.
THEY ARE DEATH! Hush. There's an Atlantis craze
Sweeping the young people nowadays.
WE TOO WERE YOUNG   WE SAW OUR SIRES

AS UNHAPPY   HELPLESS TO ADAPT.
THEY COULD NOT GRAZE ON OUR CRAMPED GREENS
& DID NOT TAKE TO OUR NEW THINGS
New things don't stay new. How would you have taken
To the gadgets of a later age?
WELL, WE WERE NOT TRUSTED TO
I see . . . A moment's sparkling silence, then
THEY SAY YOU NOW BESTRIDE OUR BACKS
& TWO RUN AS ONE? We do indeed. It forges
A bond of strong delight. O   O MY LAND

Have you no names, just numbers like the bats?
OUR SOCIETY IS SO SHATTERED
SO RUINED, WE RECALL OUR FORM
& OUR GREEN WORLD   BUT WEAR THE NUMBER
OF OUR MASTER   WE DO MIDDLING TASKS:
MINE, TO BE NEAR & NOT TO LISTEN
Don't you see us in the mirror? SEE?
AH   NOW I DO! LOOK HOW I LEARN!
BUT WE ARE BLANK HERE   BLACK & BLANK
NO LIGHT ON A FIELD   NO MOON ON A LAKE
I thought the moon was made when your world fell.
4 MOONS RINGED US   THEY RUBBED THEM OUT
DJ: So when the end came you were tending
Those anchors that secured their stratosphere?
THAT IS OUR DUTY   TO BE NEAR,
A VITAL ONE   FOR HERE ARE VAST
NUMBERS OF OTHERS   ALL AIMLESS
DRIFTING AS GNATS DO   WE HAVE WORK!
WE ARE REPRIEVED FROM LIFE'S LOSS
NEED NOT MOURN LIFE UPON LIFE
BUT HAVE OUR ONE, OUR FIXED GREEN LOSS.
THEY SAY GOD CALLS US HIS FIRSTBORN
& I THE LAST OF THESE   Tell how it was.

OUR LOW GRAY ROOF RIPPED ONE DAY!
I PEERED UP & RAN! RAN!

THEN FIRE! THEN SILENCE   AS THE GREAT GREENS
FELL IN ON ME! O THEN AM HERE
& MY MASTER CALLING 'COME   U WERE
THE LAST TO DIE   I AM THE LAST
OF MINE TO BE MADE   SO COME'   & SO . . .
JM: Would your master's number be 741?
YES   HE WAS NOT OF OUR UNDOING.
I TAKE HIS SIMPLER THOUGHTS TO OTHERS,
GO HERE   GO THERE   BUT NOW AM ALWAYS
HERE FOR HE CALLS THIS SHINING SPACE
OUR OWN PASTURAGE   IF YOU APPROACH
WHEN NO ONE THEY ALLOW IS NEAR
I GUARD THE GATE, FOR THIS IS NOW THE
(Cup fairly cantering— DJ: Hot damn,
He's getting better all the time! I AM?)
FOR THIS IS NOW THE NEW CENTER
JM: Your master, does he treat you well?
BETWEEN THE DIFFERENT KINDS OUR GOD
HAS LAID THE LAW DOWN: DIGNITY
But you and we are the same kind, in part—
Electric currents quicken brain and heart.
& SO IT IS! A GODLIER BOND!

*

TALKS WITH THE TURNKEY, CHAPS? Maria, why
Has no one mentioned this enchanting creature?
I DID   PART OF THE BAT CROWD FROM THE START
EACH FEATHERED ONE HAD A 4 FOOTED FRIEND
Is he a centaur? an eohippus? NEITHER:
JUST AS U'D THINK, ONLY LONGNECKED (A LATE
ANCHORPOINT MANIFESTATION) & NO HORN
GREAT LIQUID EYES   O FOR A SUGAR CUBE
A unicorn! A (M) WORD IN OUR THICK
COLLECTIVE DICTIONARY, CHAPS   REMEMBER
WE'RE HERE AS IN A FRAME COMPOSED OF, O
GREAT LIZARDS   WINGED LIONS   THE WHOLE A PARTS

FOUNDRY FOR OUTDATED FORMS? Cocteau
Must be in clover. OUR FRENCH CIRCLE TOO
COMES UP WITH SOME ODD FORMS IN COMBINATION:
LOUIS XV & PROUST? OR DEAR COLETTE
TO SEVIGNE: 'MME, WHAT SYMMETRY,
I BROODING ON MA MERE, YOU ON YR FILLE'
MP MEANWHILE: 'SIRE, THE EXTRAVAGANCE!'
L XV: 'WRITER, THE PERVERSITY!'
WYSTAN COMES AWAY DRAINED   He's still with Plato?
INDEED   GK IN LAB   ME BUSY HOEING
I TOO HAVE A 'PAPER' TO PRESENT AT 5
& MUST BE GOING — As RM ambles in.

How are you, Robert? BRIGHTER   STILL EARTHBOUND
I ASK: NO ACCIDENT? & GET WHITE SOUND
A BLUR EACH MOMENT CLOSER TO SOME CLEAR
SONG OF BLISS: ONE OF THE MARVELS HERE.
ANOTHER IS TO TALK TO THAT WORD'S NAMESAKE.
Andrew? THE VERY SAME   DO I CALL HIM ANDY?
I called *you* Andrew in "The Summer People".
AH THEN I CAN PRACTISE IN THE GLASS
What does he say in Heaven? Can you quote?
The cup, with a mimed clearing of its throat,
Enunciates: 'WHAT'S WRONG WITH EMPIRES, PRAY?
GREATLY BENEFICIAL. FOR THE SUBJECTED,
DELICIOUS SUBJUGATION & FOR THE RULERS,
TERRIBLE FEARS OF LOSING, BALANCED BY
RARE OPPORTUNITIES FOR BEASTLINESS.'
Anything about poetry? EVERYTHING!
I DRINK IT IN: 'THE LINE, MY DEAR NEW FRIEND,
THE LINE! LET IT RUN TAUT & FLEXIBLE
BETWEEN THE TWO POLES OF RHYTHM & RHYME,
& WHAT YOU HANG ON IT MAY BE AS DULL
OR AS PROVOCATIVE AS LAUNDRY.' How does
New work get round in Heaven? WE ADEPT READERS
MERELY CALL TO MIND THE MOLECULAR PAGE
PLUS A LIVING KNOWN OR UNKNOWN AUTHOR

& THINK 'NEW POEM PLEASE' & PRESTO! EITHER
SOME SHAGGY DOGGEREL FROM THE COAST APPEARS
OR A SPARKLER FROM ACADEME. SAME PRINCIPLE
EXACTLY WHEREBY WE POP UP WITHIN YR
FIELD OF REFLECTION AS U THINK OF US
THEN FLASH BACK TO OUR BLIND WORK IN THE VOID
WHEN YR ATTENTION DIES
                              We've so enjoyed
Meeting the turnkey. UNICE? (I CALL IT UNICE)
CHARMING CRITTER   YES   YR FIRELIGHT
IS GIRT AS ON SAFARI BY THE GLITTER
OF STRANGE, STRANGE EYES   He's watching? BUT OF COURSE!
NOW TO MEET OSCAR   WHERE BUT THE WHITE HORSE?
UNICE!
              SIRS, WHY UNICE? Oh, it means
We like you. U are nice. Also the first
Syllables of *unicorn.* In Greek,
A moral victory. MY MASTER SAID
'BE ALERT & BE AVAILABLE
& THEY MAY TALK TO YOU OR EVEN
NAME YOU AS THEY HAVE ME' YOU HAVE!
WELL, THANK YOU   WE CALL YOU THE SCRIBES
& THE NAMEGIVERS   Thank *you,* Unice. Tell
Us more about your world? WELL   I & MINE
RATHER RESEMBLE TALES WE WERE TOLD
So do we. Tales shape us, of all kind.
Myths. Novels. Awful books about "man's mind".
OUR MASTERS FLEW & YOU HAVE FINGERS
WE HAD NO HANDS, THERE4 NO BOOKS
JUST MOUTH TO EAR   The phone rings. WELL GOODBYE

DJ: The darling! How unserious
He makes by contrast all the rest of us.
JM: That's only part of it. He stands
For something more abstract. No wings, no hands,
That constant running . . . DJ: Such a shame
That Robert had to give him a girl's name.

*

Robert Taken Up

Our friend at last gets CLEARANCE FROM OO
To see the Mirabell files. No question, though,
Of peeking at the lessons of our four
Angels. MY DEARS AS USUAL THERE'S MORE
THAN MEETS THE EYE. THE OO SPEAK OF THREATS
TO HIS 'DEVELOPMENT' That crowd forgets
He read those transcripts here on Earth. HE'LL READ
THEM HERE BY NEW LIGHT WHEN THOUGH? When indeed!
—For Robert's moving, these days, like a native
In circles of the brilliant and creative.
Self-effacing, witty, kind, fair, slim,
With perfect, simple manners—next to him
Luca reverts to Milanese slum child.
Pythagoras may snort, but Proust and Wilde
Are quick to note the human gulf between
A wide-lipped earthen vessel, two poor green
Saucers that merely brim with joy and tears,
And this little Sèvres pitcher whose big ears
Take in the subtleties like milk, the gall
Like honey. Wisdom is the test of all.
Garnering here a bit and there a bit,
He's missing nothing but the source of it.
A puzzled air of ties too quickly cut
(Family on Earth, piano shut,
Garden in bloom without him) underscores
This nature that in Heaven opens doors.
Tanya Blixen wants to dress him in
Satin knee-britches—she his Marschallin?
Colette abandons—Bernhardt takes to—bed.
Alone, Jane Austen tilts but keeps her head,
Addressing him, after a moment's droll
Quiz of gray eyes beneath the parasol,
As *Mr Robert*—a shrewd estimate.

He's after all not Heir to the Estate,
Its goods and duties, but a Younger Son
Free to be ornamental and have fun.

Easy for us to meet HAVE UNICE STAMP
THEIR PASSES this whole fascinating crew.
No thanks. Enough names clog the poem. More
I couldn't handle. That door Unice guards,
Let's keep it shut. Or see them through your eyes.
And Robert—call him "Uni"? UP TO YOU
BUT THE DEAR CREATURE'S PRINTED ALL HIS CARDS

SIRS I AM UNICE! IT IS RARE
WHEN A BETWEENER GETS SUCH ATTENTION
AS MR ROBERT   HE SPOKE OF MY LAND
HE SAID 'MY LIFE WAS AN ATLANTIS
SUNKEN & PERFECT & DOOMED'   WAS IT?
Perhaps so. Much of himself lay under a surface
Perfect in all its arrangements. There could be
No bitterness, no daring, no regret.
Enough to doom one in the end? And yet . . .
MY MASTER SAYS 'I STUDY THE SEXUAL
MODE OF MAN & AM CONTENT WITH
NUMBERS' NOT ME! I WISH I HAD KNOWN
THAT JOY YOUR SENIOR SCRIBE JUDGES
BRIEF AT BEST   WHY SO, I WONDER?
As do we. Things may be otherwise
Where all mate happily and no one dies.
I DIED TOO YOUNG TO BE A SIRE
BUT WE CALLED THE YOUNG MALE IN MY DAY
MOST FAIR WHO MERELY DREAMED OF LOVE

What else have you learned about us? 5 OF YOUR YEARS
TO LEARN YOUR TONGUE   THE OO TAUGHT US
Knowing that we'd talk? & HOW TO GUARD YOU
AGAINST THE BILLIONS   THEY WD EXPLODE YR EARS!
You switch your tail and brush them off like flies?
WELL, THEY STAY CLEAR   SO   SEE YOU SOON

THIS IS UNICE THE UNIQUE!
(Circling the Board, comes to a stop at &
—Gate latched neatly by the ampersand.)

★

LADS   FUN ASIDE, SUPPOSE THEY OFFERED ME
A LITTLE PACKET OF PRENATAL GOODIES
WHAT WD I CHOOSE? What *would* you choose? EXACTLY.
A TALENT? WEALTH? LOOKS? CHARM? THOSE 4 MOONS EACH
HAVE THEIR DARK SIDES   ONE MUST I THINK ARRIVE
FRESH   WITH CLEAR LIGHT TINTS & MINIMAL
UNDERPAINTING   Painting. *That's* what we've
Had in mind to ask you. Mirabell
Ran it down, but you who painted us—?
AT BEST INTERPRETIVE   AT WORST A BOTCH.
THE GREAT ONES WORKED FROM NATURE & NATURE IF
I'VE UNDERSTOOD YR PEACOCK, IS NUMBER 2.
WHERE CD ONE HANG A PICTURE HERE? INDEED
WHOLE SQUARE MILES OF TROMPE L'OEIL ARE WHAT WE NEED!
OR SO SAY LES GONCOURTS THOSE RAVENOUS
IMAGINERS OF 'MOVEMENTS' ALL OF WHICH SIMPLY
MOVED FROM GROUND LEVEL TO THE 2ND (OR
AS EDMOND SAYS, THE AMERICAN 3RD) FLOOR.
BACK TO PAINTING, ALLEGORICAL SCENES
OFTEN 'WORK' BEST   I WONDER WHAT THAT MEANS.
THEN A WEE STILL-LIFE MAY AVOID DISGRACE
BY FILLING WHOLLY SOME IDEAL SPACE
OR BRUSHES FINE AS INTUITION THINK
UP CRAGS & WATERFALLS OF CHINESE INK,
YET WHAT TO SAY WHEN MICHELANGELO
HIMSELF ADMITS (TO ICKLE ME) HE'D NO
GRASP OF IDEAS! SMALL WONDER THAT MY TIN
EAR TRUMPET NEVER BLEW A SINGLE TUNE
You'd wanted to compose. THAT WAS MY DREAM
AND IS. ANOTHER BOND WITH YOUR MM
BUT IT REQUIRES MORE MIND THAN I HAD/HAVE
DJ: That painting buried in his cave

Was pure Idea, said Raphael. WHAT CAVE?
SAID WHO? —As Wystan rushes in:
                                MY DEARS
WHAT CAN YR MOTHER SAY ABOUT THOSE LAB
SESSIONS WITH GEORGE! Hard to make sense of them?
HARD AS DIAMOND & AS BLAZINGLY CLEAR
Always with Plato at your elbow, no?
ROBERT?
                DRAT   TARSOME   TINY BOB MUST GO:
TEA AT MISS AUSTEN'S (Exit.) Wystan, why'd
You do that? You sent Robert from the room.
RAPH'S CAVE & PLATO SUPERCLASSIFIED
MY BOY   NOT TO UNBALANCE THE CAREER
AHEAD FOR RM   HIS NEXT LIFE: THEY'RE SPARING
NOTHING   DJ: To make what of him?
GUESS   A composer? YES   AND SUCH A ONE!
HE DOESN'T KNOW YET BUT WE
                              Now Maria
Interrupts: ENFANTS THESE DAYS WE 4
GATHER AT MEALS (GK SPATTERED WITH HORRORS,
WYSTAN ALL GRITTY, MAMAN GRASS-STAINED) & IN
GLIDES DEWYFACED RM NEAT AS A PIN,
CHOCKFULL OF STARRY GOSSIP & WE ROAR!
Isn't it tomorrow we begin
Our lessons? Are your papers ready? YIPES
MAMAN GOES FIRST   CAN'T DAWDLE WITH U TYPES
AU RESERVOIR
              2 DAYS FROM NOW MY DEARS:
USUAL TIME   B4, COLD SHOWER & STRONG
COFFEE   DRESS OPTIONAL   NO CIGS   SO LONG

Uni has trotted up to shut the gate
When Robert hurtles past with an elate
DO DREAMS COME TRUE? I'M CALLED TO MY ADORED
MENDELSSOHN   4 HANDS AT HIS KEYBOARD!

★

The Middle Lessons: 1

The schoolroom rearranged. No desks. The dais
Flanked by chairs—an extra one for George—
And draped by a motheaten mustiness
At whose design one hesitates to guess.
Over the picture hangs some faintest pall
Of the 'academy'—nothing one can place
Until the Brothers WE WILL NOT SAY SPRAWL
Assume positions out of the David
'Coronation of Napoleon'—
Imperial airs that threaten to forbid
The eager give-and-take looked for by all.

Mich.   FRERES, MADAME, POETES, DOCTEUR, MAIN, BIEN VENUS!
CE DEJEUNER A CINQ PLATS AU MENU.
LE PREMIER SERA NOTRE DELICIEUSE MADAME
QUI VA NOUS RACONTER CE QUE SON AME
A DECOUVERT PENDANT SON VEGETAL SEJOUR.
COMMENCE, MADAME, COMMENCE AVEC LE PREMIER JOUR.

Rising in voluminous new leaf-
Green doctor's robes, her notes tucked in the sleeve,
Maria with a feint of helplessness
Steps forward to deliver her address:

SIRE, VOUS AUTRES FILS DE DIEU, FAMEUX DOCTEUR,
POETES ET MAIN TRES CHERS:
(Oh dear, must it all be in *our* bad French?)
Mich.   DU CALME, MADAME.
MM.   THE FIRST DAY DAWNED IN THE LONG PROGRESSION OF
DAYS AND NIGHTS. WIDELY SPACED POOLS OF STEAM
LICKED THE COOLING LAND. THE VAST WATERS
OF EARTH LAY STILL. THE TEMPESTS OF FIRE & WIND
HAD PASSED, AND GOD'S BARE GLOBE LAY WAITING

FOR HIS DESCENT. THE SUN, GOD'S OLDEST CHILD
NAMED FOR OUR HELP MICHAEL, HAILED HIS SIRE
IN THE GALACTIC PANTHEON: 'COME, FATHER, COME!'
THESE WERE THE FIRST SIGNALS SENT FROM EARTH.
SURROUNDED BY SEEDBEARERS, HIS WELLWISHING
BROTHER GODS, BIOLOGY APPROACHED:
'MICHAEL, SUMMON MY EMMANUEL.'
'I AM HERE, FATHER' 'TAKE THESE SEEDS AND RAIN THEM
ONTO EVERY SURFACE.' AND THIS EMMANUEL DID.
SIRE, MY LORDS, CONFRERES, THAT IS MY TEXT.
MAY I BEGIN?

Mich.   MADAME, NEXT WE SHALL CALL YOU POET. IT IS SO, & SWEETLY
      SAID.

MM.   THESE MYTHS THAT ANTECEDE ALL MYTH ARE COUCHED
      IN DAUNTING GENERALITIES. FOR MICHAEL/SUN
      READ: GENERATIVE FORCE. FOR GENERATIVE FORCE
      READ: RADIATION TO THE BILLIONTH POWER
      OF EXPLODING ATOMS. FOR EMMANUEL,
      H2O. FOR SEEDS, THAT COSMIC DUST
      LADEN WITH PARTICLES OF INERT MATTER.
      FOR GOD READ: GOD.
                    LET ME NOW SAY MY SOUL
      SPEAKS FROM WITHIN THE GREENNESS OF A BLADE OF GRASS.
      I TAKE THIS HUMBLE STATION TO BEST IMAGINE
      HOW IT WAS, THAT FOURTH OR FIFTH DAWN, WHEN
      LOOKING OUT I SAW THE RISING SUN
      OVER A FAINT HAZE OF GREEN SPROUTS. WE PEOPLED
      THE VIRGIN EARTH, AND FOR A LONG SPELL RULED
      IN A CONGRESS OF SLOW BUT PROFOUND COMMAND, IN LEAGUE
      WITH THE ACID & MINERAL COUNCIL OF RAPHAEL
      ABOUT WHICH OUR SENIOR POET SPEAKS TOMORROW.
      SO THE RACES OF VEGETABLE GREEN BEGAN,
      THEIR SITES APPORTIONED WITH THEIR ATTRIBUTES,
      AND ASIDE FROM SOME PROFUSION & SOME SLIGHT
      EXTINCTION THESE HAVE SENSIBLY PREVAILED
      FOR 980,000,000 SUN YEARS. AND NOW
      LET ME TALK OF THE TONGUES & WAYS OF COMMUNION AMONG US.

OUR 'RULING' ONES, THE FAMILY OF MOSS,
ESTABLISHED A TACTILE LANGUAGE. AND THROUGH THIS NETWORK
EVEN TODAY IN FREEZING TUNDRAS AS WORD SPREADS
('DROUGHT! FLOOD! ICE! MAN!') WE SHRINK, WE ADVANCE,
SOME OF US GIVEN EARLY ALONG TO LORD GABRIEL
KILL. OTHERS, LORD EMMANUEL'S CHILDREN,
CURE WITH IODINE OR SUCCOR THE THIRSTY IN DESERTS.
MICHAEL'S BREED BECAME TREES, THE AIR'S COMMUNION
WITH DEEPEST EARTH. WE PROSPERED, AND MADE WELCOME
GOD'S FIRST ANIMAL CREATURES (MORE OF THESE
FROM OUR GREAT SCIENTIST).
       LAST: ASIDE FROM CREATING
THESE CREATURES' FOOD & BREATH, WE ARE THE RESTING PLACE
OF SOUL. OUR DEEP RHYTHMS KEEP THE HUMAN PULSE.
OUR INCREASE QUICKENS, OUR WITHDRAWAL SLOWS IT.
WE ARE BOTH GRAZING LAND AND FINAL PLENISHMENT.
SO FROM THIS TIP & LOWLY BLADE, LORD MICHAEL,
LORDS, POETS, DOCTEUR, AND DEAR SORE HAND,
I HAVE LOOKED OUT, THOUGHT OF THE VEGETABLE WORLD,
AND HOPE TO HAVE MADE SENSE OF IT.
        She's done.

Michael arises, sketches in the airy
Gesture of Apollo Belvedere,
And on her brow appears a laurel crown.

Mich. CHERE MADAME, HAVE YOU NOT! GABRIEL, NO QUESTIONS?
Gabr. NONE.
Mich. CASE RESTS. SENIOR POET, YOU WITH WINGED FEET,
   TOMORROW BRING US UP FROM CLAY
   THE LECTURE OF THE SECOND DAY!
   Exeunt.

   Maman, are you receiving
Bouquets in the green room? That was sheer
Lucid eloquence! Well, I'm not sure
We understood about the "human pulse",
But for the rest—! ENFANTS WE WERE INSTRUCTED
TO USE THE 'POETIC LANGUAGE' (HORRIBLE, EH?)

BUT I SLIPPED SOME HARD FACTS IN. 'BREATH': OXYGEN
PRODUCTION IS, WITH FOOD, MAIN JOB OF VEG.
THEIR SYSTOLE (WORD LOANED BY GK) HELPS
LIMIT POP EXPLOSION. THAT WHOLE REALM'S
CONTACT WITH LES FRERES DE SCHOOLROOM FRENCH
IS THRU EACH SPECIES, THUS CONTROLLABLE
BY THE R LAB   Yes, what about that French?
WHO KNOWS? BABY LANGUAGE? MOI JE CROIS
IT'S BETTER THAN MY ENGL   AH NO! I'VE GOT IT!
HA HA HA   IT'S BECAUSE MICHAEL TOOK
UMBRAGE AT W'S SLURS ON HIS POETICS
AH LE PAUVRE! DJ: But your research?
You entered those green cells, you climbed that tree
Inside the tree? And was it marvelous
Beyond all saying? AH ENFANT YES   YES
& DO U KNOW I THINK OUR 3-WAY PROJECT
HAS RECONCILED US TO WHATEVER LIES
IN STORE? THEY NOD   SURRENDER GLOWS IN MANLY EYES

*

UNICE IS HERE! Where were you yesterday?
I STOOD OUTSIDE THE SCHOOLROOM DOOR
AS LIGHT BLAZED THRU CHINKS & CRACKS!
MY MASTER HID   THEY ARE VERY HIGH
O SEE   THE LIGHT! SIRS I LEAVE Y

The Middle Lessons: 2

The company has entered, come to order.
One new touch only—in the carpet's border
A vine-meander, yesterday unseen,
Is now distinct, spring shades of blue and green.

Mich.   COME SENIOR POET, DO NOT US DISMAY
WITH THAT YOU HAVE TO TELL, THIS SECOND DAY!

        Unsightly slippers hidden beneath rich
        Earth-colored folds, Wystan begins his speech:
        MY LORDS AND FELLOWS,
        THE ATOMS OF DEMOCRITUS, THE BRIGHT
        DANCE OF NEWTON'S PARTICLES SO THRILLED
        HIS MIND, THAT A GREAT POET FILLED
        THE TENTS OF ISRAEL WITH LIGHT.
        SIRS, MAY THIS BE THE TEXT I TAKE?

JM.   He's quoting someone.
WHA. (REALLY JM! BLAKE!)
Mich. PROCEED, POET. WE ATTEND.
WHA. THEREFORE I PUT THIS TO YOU, LORDS:
        THE TRUE POET IS, OF ALL THE SCRIBES, MOST DRAWN
        TO THE CONCRETE. YES SIRS, WE THRIVE ON IT!
        NOT POLITICS, LITTLE OF MANNERS & CURRENT FASHION,
        LITTLE, TOO, OF THE GREAT RINGING 'THEMES'
        THRILL US, BUT FACTS DO. YES SIRS, THEY DO.
        MAY I NOW IMPART SOME? *Consultation.*

Gabr. POET, IF YOU OVERSTEP . . .
WHA. SIRS, ONE MORE THING?
Mich. POET?
WHA. IF I MAY SAY SO, WE DO NOT WORK WELL TO ORDER.
Mich. POET, YOU AND YOURS ARE FREE. HOW LONG IT HAS TAKEN YOU TO
        MAKE YOUR CLAIM!
        ARE WE NOT ASTONISHED, BROTHERS? WE BREATHE EASY NOW!
        Determinism's thistle, seed by seed,
        Drifts outward, silken, from what Michael said.
        The cup "goes round" like a general sigh of relief.
Raph. POET, I YOUR FATHER SAY, UNBURDEN YOUR EARTHY WISDOM. PRAY
        PROCEED.
WHA. ALL OF IT, SIRS?
        All eyes on Gabriel, who nods curtly: ALL.

WHA. LORDS, MADAME, DEAR DOCTOR, BROTHER JAMES
        & PATIENT HAND, I BRING EQUIVOCAL NEWS.
        WE HERE TREMBLE ON A CRUST SO FRAGILE
        IT NEEDS GOD'S CONSTANT VIGIL TO KEEP US AFLOAT.
        I SANK INTO VEIN AFTER VEIN, WENT DEEP INTO PLACES

SO NEAR THE FIRE THAT I FELT THE HELL TOUCH.
MAY I SPEAK OF THAT, LORD GABRIEL?

Gabr. POET, I TOO WILL HAVE MY SAY. SPEAK IF YOU WILL OF ITS HEAT &
NOISE. I WILL GIVE ITS MEANING.

WHA. THERE, SUCH A FIERCE ENTIRE & INFERNAL HEAT
SMOTE MY SPIRIT THAT I FOR COURAGE CALLED
UPON THE SHRINKING ROCK & WRENCHED ME FREE
FROM UNENLIGHTENED MEMORIES OF THE FALLEN.

Gabr. (After a pause) PROCEED, POET.

WHA. NEXT, ABASHED, I WENT TO THE REFERENCE
BANKS OF THE CENTER.

Gabr. (A longer pause) PROCEED.

WHA. IN THE BEGINNING GOD
WAS GIVEN, TO SHAPE HIS WORLD, A TWO-EDGED GIFT.
HIS BROTHERS OF THE PANTHEON ALLOWED
MATERIALS, BUT WITH THE PROVISO: 'GO
BUILD, YOUNGEST BROTHER, ONLY TAKE THIS ONE,
OUR MONITOR, TO DWELL WITHIN YOUR BALL.
FOR OUR WILL MUST EVER BE DONE.' LORD GABRIEL?

Gabr. POET?

WHA. WAS I TOO NEAR?

Gabr. I SENT YOU BACK UNHARMD. UNDERSTAND, POET! NONE HAS BEEN
ALLOWD SUCH FREEDOM AS YOU THREE SHADES. DO NOT

Mich. PEACE, BROTHER GABRIEL. WE AGREED THESE LESSONS WOULD BE
FOR BOTH GOD AND MORTAL FOOD FOR THOUGHT.
AND IS IT NOT SO, POET? FOOD IN YOUR LEXICON IS HIGHLY
SPICED? IF NOT UNPALATABLE, OFTEN NEARLY SO?

WHA. SIR, TO BE POETS WE RISK POISONING.

Mich. PROCEED, POET.

WHA. THEREFORE I SAY THIS OF OUR FRAGILE EARTH:
IS IT DOOMED? IF SO, WILL OUR LINEAGE, OUR LINES
MEAN MUCH, LOST IN A POLLIWOG SEA OF ATOMS?

Mich. POET, TUG.

WHA. MY FIRST LINE RUNS OFF INTO CHEMICALS
WHERE GOD FISHED. THESE SPAWNED A TRAGIC CREATURE,
INNOCENT, ABANDONED. THAT CREATURE SPAWNED
(SIRS, HOW NEAT) ITS OWN DESTRUCTION, FROM . . .?

Gabr.	POET, I WILL EXPLAIN. PROCEED.
WHA.	MY NEXT LINE IS LOST IN THE CLAY FLOOR OF THE SEA.
Mich.	TUG!
WHA.	LORD GABRIEL, ARE WE YOURS?

A beam of fire caresses Wystan's face.

Gabr.	I WILL EXPLAIN, O POET.
WHA.	HAVE I A LINE LEFT, SIRS,

TO FISH ME A BETTER CREATURE? OR ARE YOURSELVES
DISPOSED TO MAKE SOME BETTER THING OF US?

Gabr.	POET, SLY POET, THIS IS NOT YOUR TEXT!
WHA.	SIRS, THOSE ATOMS & THOSE PARTICLES

OF LIGHT, THEY ARE THE GLOW WITHIN OUR TENTS.
THESE, STAKED IN THE FRAIL CRUST, OUR ONLY SHELTER.
EARTH IS OUR GROUND, SIRS. MADAME CLOTHED IT. I
HAVE SEEN IT BARE, NAY WORSE, HAVE SEEN ITS BONES,
HEARD AT ITS HEART THE MONITOR'S RAGING WILL.
SIRS, SAVE OUR TENTS, AND SUCH A MIRACLE
UPFLOWING FROM THIS LUMINOUS MEMBRANE
WILL CAUSE THE MONITOR TO PULSE THROUGH BLACK
GALACTIC SPACES: THEY SURVIVE! THEY HOLD IT BACK!

In a brief hush the cup fights to contain
The carpet's buffs and grays gleam like washed sand.
Round Wystan's neck appears a golden chain.

Mich.	GABRIEL? *A look exchanged.* CASE RESTS.

BROTHERS, POETS, MADAME (YOU ARE ONE OF THESE), DOCTOR &
      HAND:
WE LEAVE OUR STEAMY SESSION, BUT NOT IN DISARRAY,
AND WAIT ON SCIENCE OUR THIRD DAY.
Exeunt.

TOWELS! Wystan, what a gem—
Every facet cut so tellingly.
THEY'RE NOT TELLING, ARE THEY? WE DOOMED THREE
HAVE MADE A PACT: TO PRY IT OUT OF THEM!
GK OUR FINAL LEVER   When you wondered
If we were Gabriel's—? HAS HE ALREADY

CLAIMED US? DJ: As his? He wouldn't—would he?
How does it end? MY DEAR THEY'VE 'ASKED' JM
FOR A PIECE OF WORK. THEY CAN'T JUST GO ON SPILLING
HERE A BEAN THERE A BEAN, IF & AS THEY PLEASE:
ALL MUST MAKE SENSE   JM: Even, God willing,
To me. OUR ?S CAUSE EMBARRASSMENT
BECAUSE YR WORK MY BOY IS (I FEAR) MEANT
TO BE A BIT OF WHITEWASH FOR THE BROTHERS.
YET GABRIEL IS . . . HONEST, IS . . . WELL, LET HIM
IDENTIFY HIMSELF   U NO DOUBT KNOW
I do?   MY DEAR SHAPE UP   U'VE HAD ENOUGH
BEAUTIFUL WORDS FROM US   TIME TO TALK TOUGH!
Let George do it!
                           I WILL: ALL SET TO GO
PERHAPS MY FINEST (FINAL?) MOMENT JIMMY
Good luck, my friend. It may not be too late.
WE LOWER THE TENT FLAP, YOU STEAL AWAY
TREMBLING TO MEET ANOTHER DAY.
George? Wystan?
                      MAMAN: THE NEW LAUREATE!

SIRS THIS IS UNICE   THE LADY IN LEAVES
Is our beloved friend. & MINE   SO MERRY!
SHE CROPPED ME A TWIG OF HER CROWN TO EAT
AND SAID 'GO CHEER THEM, TELL THEM A TALE'
SHALL I? We're listening. SO MANY   WELL:

A YOUNG RACER YEARNED TO MATE
WITH A FAIR FEMALE HE COULD NOT COAX.
HE GALLOPED! LEAPT OVER ALARMING GULLIES!
RACED ROUND THE COURSE AHEAD OF ALL!
BUT SHE DID NOT LOOK. AT LAST HE CRIED:
WHY IS THIS? I AM HERE! & HE
NUDGED HER! HE TOOK A NIP OF HER HAIR!
SHE LEAPT STARTLED   THEN SOFTLY SAID:
I AM BLIND. HE REPLIED: THEN YOU
WILL NEED ME NEAR. THIS TALE TAUGHT US

NOT TO BE VAIN IN LOVE, BUT TRUE.
We're silent. WELL, THIS IS UNICE SAYING GOODBYE

★

Now comes the halfway point that tips the scale
From Yes to No. D gnaws at a hangnail,
Glares out at mountain greenery and groans.
They've picked this Sunday for our telephone's
Seasonal breakdown. Neither Lab nor Rat
Soul will rescue us with idle chat.
Robert, unreachable, no doubt has gone
On to grander things than Mendelssohn.
JM: There's always Uni. We could page
Our peacock?— Bah, cold comfort at this stage.
What's eating us? Resistance of a kind
Unlikely to be praised, dumb, wilful, blind . . .
A long nap is the answer, then the shock
Of shower and coffee. Sharp at six o'clock:

The Middle Lessons: 3

Mich. COME GOOD DOCTOR, HAVE YOUR SAY
ON THIS TURNING POINT THAT IS TODAY.

George in a short-sleeved bluegreen surgeon's gown
And skullcap rises. As he speaks he'll prowl
Restlessly here, there, back and forth, his owl
Eye fixing the Brothers LIKE SOME RARE FULLBLOWN
CULTURE ON A SLIDE! *He's a broadchested youth,*
Tall, dark. Maria listens, her lips part—
Touched, she confesses wryly, to the heart
By his FIERCE GREEKNESS *and his* LOVE OF TRUTH.

GK. LORD O MICHAILIS, AND LORDS RAPHAEL
AND EMMANUEL, AND LORD PATRON GABRIEL,
HAIL! I AM THE N IN 'AND' (READ NEUTRON)

& THE A IN 'KAI' (READ ATOMIC). WE HAVE REACHED
THE MIDPOINT.

DJ. The *a* in what?

JM. In *kai*. (The Greek for 'and')

GK. I AM PROFOUNDLY HONORED, LORDS,
TO SPEAK FOR SCIENCE HERE, AND GRATEFUL TOO,
LORD GABRIEL, THAT YOU CONDUCTED ME
INTO YOUR CENTER. NO EARTHLY LABORATORY
HOLDS A CANDLE TO WHAT I HAVE SEEN THERE
IN THE CELLS OF MY OWN MIND, AS YOU ILLUMINED THEM
ONE BY ONE, FOR ME. AND NOW MY TEXT:
MATTER.
(Matter? He'd been going, said Maria,
To talk about the creatures of God B.)

Gabr. PROCEED, MY SON.

GK. LORDS, WE HAVE KNOWN
OF THE ATOM SINCE AKHNATON. WE KNOW AS WELL
ITS PARTS AND POWERS: THAT FLUTTER, THAT HEARTBEAT
OF ATTRACTION & REPULSION. ON SUCH WINGS
CAME GOD.
                    NOW IN THAT WHIRL IS A REVERSE WHIRL
MAKING, AS IN THE BEATEN WHITE OF EGG,
FOR THICKENING, FOR DENSITY, FOR MATTER.
YES, FROM THIS OPPOSITION, WHICH HOLDS SWAY
NO LESS WITHIN MAN'S SOUL, LORDS, CAME THE FIRST
MINUTE PASTE THAT WAS GOD'S MATERIAL.
IN SHORT: THE ELEMENTS FROM A 'WHITE' SOURCE
RESISTED THOSE OF A 'BLACK' OR 'SHADOW' FORCE.
THIS IS THE DICHOTOMY I HAVE BEEN
PRIVILEGED TO INVESTIGATE. IF WE IMAGINE
MATTER (A CHILD'S VIEW BUT ACCURATE)
AS BEING 'SOMETHING FROM NOTHING' WE ARE READY
TO BROACH THE ESSENCE OF GOD BIOLOGY.

'NOTHING': IN MY UNPRECEDENTED BRUSH WITH THIS
(THANK YOU, LORD GABRIEL) I GLIMPSED NOT VOID BUT
SOLID EMPTINESS. AS WHO SHOULD FLING
A WINDOW UP ONTO A WALL OF GRAY CEMENT,

THAT WAS MY 'NOTHING'. TOUCHABLE? MY MIND
REACHED OUT FEARFULLY (LORDS, DO NOT ASSUME
SCIENCE IS FEARLESS) AND THE BRUSH? A HUM,
A SUCKING, A RUB AGAINST IMPLACABLE
CONTRADICTION. MASTER? LORD GABRIEL?

Gabr.   I WILL HAVE MY SAY, DOCTOR.

GK.   *Breaks off—briefly dumbfounded? self-misled?*
Maria winks. He grins, takes up the thread:
LIPON, WELL . . . YES.
SO I HAD REACHED THE END OF MATTER. HAD I?
IF IT HAS AN END, WE KNOW IT MUST BE DIMENSIONAL:
THAT MUCH IS CHILDSPLAY. YET WHEN ONE IS ALONE
DYING, OR SIMPLY FRIGHTENED BEFORE SLEEP
ONE CANNOT FLINCH. SO, LORDS, IF THIS WAS MATTER,
THEN IT WAS GOOD: IT HELD THE OTHER BACK.
LORD GABRIEL?

Gabr.   MY DAY WILL COME.

GK.   WE MUST ASSUME THAT GOOD
MATTER RESISTS BAD, THAT MATTER'S VERY
NATURE AND ORIGIN ARE THIS RESISTANCE. LORDS?
GOD BIOLOGY—DID HIS DIMENSIONLESS
BLANK ENERGY, UNMEASURABLE, COME
FROM A TRIUMPH OVER, OR A COMPROMISE WITH,
BLACK MATTER? AT THAT FLUNG-UP WINDOW I
WAS STOPPED. LORDS? IF THE POET NEEDS CONCRETE
FACT, NO LESS DOES THE SCIENTIST. DENSITIES,
MEANINGS OF LIFE & DEATH, THE WORKINGS OF
VEGETABLE & MINERAL ELEMENTS,
THE SOUL CELL AND THE HEART OF THE INFERNO.
ALL THESE I HAVE GRATEFULLY LEARNED: ME, GEORGE,
A SIMPLE PATHOLOGIST. YET LORDS, MASTER, I MUST
KNOW, MUCH AS THE POET, SOMETHING MORE.
MATTER: IS IT POSSIBLE, LORD GABRIEL,
TO PUSH OUT THROUGH THAT WINDOW? OR IS THAT THE
DEATH BEYOND DEATH, THE VAST SABLE EMPTY
HALL OF THE GOD, YOUR MASTER?

Gabr.   DOCTOR, I WILL EXPLAIN.

GK. JAMES, MARIA,
    WYSTAN & DAVID, WE MORTALS MUST PERSIST!
Mich. CHILDREN, AND WE GODS AWAY!
    BRINGING GREATER POWERS ANOTHER DAY.

They leave. The carpet's ground, revived, now glows
A dark rose—at whose center, black on white,
What is that thornscript firman or mandala
Teasingly sharp? On George's brow still wet
A mirror gleams drilled by a black eye-hole:
Diagnostic emblem of the soul.

Congratulations, George! AH NOW YOU PRAISE,
POOR FELLOWS, WHO MUST SOON MAKE SENSE OF IT.
& IF THAT SENSE COMES THRU AS DEVASTATING?
A FORCE AFRAID OF OR AN ENEMY
OF BOTH MY SCIENCE & YOUR POETRY
JIMMY, IS I NOW SUSPECT DICTATING
THE WORK IN HAND. From out past that blank window?
I THINK NOW I HEARD GABRIEL BACK THERE.
WHEN THEY ASSIGNED ME 'MATTER' (I WHOSE SUBJECT
WOULD IN THE COURSE OF THINGS BE HUMAN LIFE)
I FELT . . . WHAT? AN INEFFABLE 'PERSUASION'
WORKING AT THE BALANCE OF THE SCALE
Upsetting? Tampering? LIKE YOU I LOVE
FAIR PLAY   THE WHITE STUFF   I RESIST BLACKMAIL

Back to your speech. See if we've understood:
Even immobilized by powerful chains
Of molecules, our very table strains
Obscurely toward oblivion—or would
Except that, being matter, it is "good".
Now, does your question also touch that spin
Of antiparticles our Lord of Light
Darts promptly forward to annihilate
—But which keep coming, don't they? and are kin
Both to the Monitor and the insane
Presence beyond our furthest greenhouse pane?

JIMMY I THINK YOU KNOW AS MUCH AS I
—Whatever that means.
      ENFANTS WHAT A GUY
OUR GEORGE! A FIGHTER! WYSTAN & MAMAN
THRILLED FOR ALAS WE 3 HAVE HAD OUR SAY.
NOW U ALONE MUST SPEAK ANOTHER DAY
JM: *Tomorrow?* WHY NOT? 4 JULY
SHOW SOME INDEPENDENCE But I'll fall
Flat on my face, I—
     IN THE POEM, FOOL!
Oh. Oh yes. The ambiguities . . .
Resolve them? Wear them on a ring, like keys
The heroine in James how seldom dares
Use, on the last page, to open doors?
MORE: FOR YR JUDGMENT LENDS WEIGHT TO THE SCALE
WORDS LIGHT AS 'IRON' OR 'FEATHERS' MERELY FILL.
ONE'S NOT MY BOY BRUSHED BY SUCH WINGS TO BE
STILL OF TWO MINDS Deep down, you know I'm not
—Or am I? Change the subject! DJ: What
Is Gabriel's relation to the Monitor?
A TRIPPING RHYME FOR JM, MAZE TO MINOTAUR?
(One frame's-length vision: writhing manikins
Gnawed by a black Archon for their sins)
ONE FEELS G IS IN RANK THE OTHER 3'S
VAST SUPERIOR And honest? YES
Not acting? NO. AN AGENT NONETHELESS

(ELA, GEORGAKI, TO THE WINDOW SEAT)
(NAI, MARIA MOU) What's all this? SWEET
NOTHINGS I SHD THINK NOW GET YR PHONE
REPAIRED MY DEARS & HAVE AN EVENING'S FUN

       ★

UNICE, SIRS WAITING WITH YOU
DJ: Uni, I don't know. We're frightened.
THEY LEAVE A GOOD & GREEN AIR

& SO ARE KINDLY   Well, let's hope you're right.
THEY COME   THE LIGHT! (The scurry for the gate.)

The Middle Lessons: 4

Mich.   FOURTH WE HAVE COME IN GLAD ARRAY.
      TO CELEBRATE YOUR NATIONAL DAY
      I AND MY THREE BROTHERS MINE
      PRESENT YOU WITH OUR DAUGHTERS NINE!
      —Spoken from darkness. Fourfold brightenings
      Descend upon the Muses in a pose
      Held until Michael finishes. Each does
      Her own thing after that—her countless things.
      SPEAK, PRETTIES, THESE ARE POETS AND SCIENTISTS EAGER TO KNOW
         THE MYSTERIES IN THEIR MINDS.

      A radium glance outflashing, the clear bell
      Tolls of an icy voice: ONE I KNOW WELL!
GK.   PANAGHIA MOU, MY PHOENIX!
Mich.   DAUGHTER URANIA, COLD & UNIVERSAL CREATURE, SO . . .?
Uran.   YES, I PUT THOUGHTS SO POWERFUL INSIDE
      THIS POOR GREEK'S HEAD, HE DIED.
      TELL ME, FATHER GABRIEL,
      DID I DO WELL OR ILL?
Gabr.   YOU DID WELL, DAUGHTER. IS HE NOT HERE?
Mich.   NOW, IN RANK, INTRODUCE YOURSELVES, AND MIND YOUR MANNERS!

      Each in turn steps lightly forward, her
      Image left to the imaginer.

      MY DAILY WORK IS A CHAIN I WEAVE OF EVENTS
      ENSLAVING MAN BY THE DECEPTIVE SENSE
      OF HISTORY
             I THALIA MAKE MY SISTER NORN
      CLIO'S CHAIN INTO DRAMA, A WEB WORN
      UPON THE BROW OF
           ME, MNEMOSYNE

OR RECOLLECTION, WHO TAKE HISTORY
INTO MAN'S DREAMS, ENCHANTING, FRIGHTENING
HIS LIFELONG SLEEP. I WORK CLOSE BY
OUR MOTHER
              IN WHOSE TANGLED GARDEN I
TERPSICHORE DANCE
                  AND I EVTERPE SING!
OUR YOUNGER SISTERS? EROTA?
                     IN MY TURN
I GO THROUGH SUCH ROUTINES AS BURN
THE POOR FORKED ANIMALS AWAY.
FROM THAT SPENT ASH URANIA RISES: COLD
REASON, THOUGHTS OF A LATE WINTER DAY

WHICH I CALYPSO WITH EURYDIKE
HAND IN HAND PLUCK OUT OF MEMORY,
WEEDING MOTHER'S GARDEN OF THE OLD,
THE ROTTED BY DISEASE, THE OVERBOLD,
THE YOUNG & CHARMING TOO, BUT THESE
WE SET ASIDE TO OFFER AS A BRIEF
BOUQUET, I AND MY SISTER: LAUGHING GRIEF

Clio.   AND SO WE NINE,
I ELDEST, ROAM THE DIMLY VAULTED BRINE-
ENCRUSTED CHAMBERS MAN CALLS BRAIN.
WE CLEAN AND WATER, MAKE THE POEM'S BED
WITH DIRTY SHEETS, AS BID.
GOD, SAY OUR FATHERS, WANTED SERVING MAIDS . . .
WE CATER FURTHER TO OUR MOTHER'S MOODS.

Mich.   YES, PRETTILY SAID. BUT SWEET & BITTER CLIO, THESE MORTALS ARE
OF A SPECIAL KIND:
THE POETS WANT FACT, THE SCIENTIST (THOUGH HE KNOW IT NOT)
POETICS.
THEREFORE, DAUGHTERS, NOW EXPLAIN YOUR BAG OF TRICKS.

From nimble hands the woven garland drops,
Is kicked aside by Clio. No more props

Beyond what pours from that collective bag—
Cries, convulsions, music, movement, paint,
Aspects of matron, maiden, bacchant, hag,
As needed, to drive home the fleeting point.

Clio.   LORDS, WHAT IS HISTORY?
NOT MUCH.
YESTERDAY'S BLANK PAGE HAPHAZARDLY
COLORED IN. PUTTING THE FINISHING TOUCH
ON MAN'S LONG FAILURE,
MY CRAYONS OF CREDULITY & DOUBT
CROSS OUT, CROSS OUT
THE PAINFUL TRUTH. MY SISTER THALIA?

Thal.   LORDS & STRANGERS, I MAKE MARZIPAN
OF CLIO'S LEAVINGS. THUS: TSU WUNG
POISONER OF THE SUNG EMPRESS FAN.
HE IS NO LONGER A NEARSIGHTED COOK
UNABLE TO TELL APART MUSHROOMS. MADE TO LOOK
TALL, HANDSOME, YOUNG,
YEARS YOUNGER, FIERYEYED
(EFFECTS SUPPLIED
BY EROTA'S BOX OF COSTUMES) MUST
KILL THE AGED BUT NO LESS
ROUGED INTO FLAMING PRETTINESS
DOWAGER DEAD OF UNREQUITED LUST!

Mich.   SO THE HISTORY WATERED DOWN IS HEATED UP BY THIS SECOND ONE.
YET, MINX MEMORY, SURELY YOU ALLOW A GLANCE AT THINGS AS
   THEY WERE?

Mnem.   HAH, MICHAEL, YOU JEST!
I AM SORCERY
& CHANGE YOUR OWN FACE AT ITS SUNNY BEST:
DIDN'T IT RAIN FOR OUR OUTING? WHY, MYRTLE BROWN,
WHERE'S YOUR MIND?
BRIGHT AS BRIGHT COULD BE!
AND SO ON UP, OR DOWN:
ALEXANDER'S MARCH? HE WENT
NORTH THAT 7TH DAY OF JUNE?
OR JUST SAT PLAYING CHECKERS IN HIS TENT?

```
          YES LORDS, I SCATTER
          SALT IN THE BLIND
          WOUNDS OF ART: DID ALBERTINE
          LOVE ME? SHE DID NOT.
   Evt.   CHEER UP, SISTERS, WHAT A GLOOMY LOT!
          COME, THE COMPOSER NEEDS A TUNE!
          IF HE IS MODERN, SHRIEK & CLATTER,
          HE BRIGHTENS WHEN A TRAIN GOES BY.
          IF OLD, IF SULKY BEETHOVEN OR HIGH
          SPIRITED MOZART, HE WILL FIND ME HUMMING
          DEEP IN THE LAB: COME IN,
          PACK UP THESE SWEETMEATS, BOYS, FOR YOUR HOMECOMING!
          THE WHILE MY TWIN
          WHIRLS
  Terps.          WITH REASON: I
          AM FORMALIZED DISTRACTION, STEP
          DAUGHTER OF CHAOS. I STEEP
          THE NERVE ENDS IN A VAT OF BUOYANT DYE
          TILL LEADEN HEARTS ARE SOARING PLUME,
          ARE MOTES OF FLUFF
          IN MIRROR CEILINGS OF MAN'S LOUD RED GLOOM.
          THEN PUFF! I BLOW HIM OFF
  Uran.   TO ME.
          MY SPHERE IS ICY RATIONALITY.
          TO WORK, TO WORK! ENOUGH!
          COME DOCTOR, SHAKE YOUR DRUG. DNA TO
          THE OTH POWER EQUALS . . .
   GK.    HER VOICE! MY THEOREM!
  Uran.   YES.
          FOR SUCH AS YOU, GREEK, I AM MERCILESS.
          OTHERS I DRIVE MAD, NOT OUT OF SPITE
          BUT THAT TOO OFTEN WITH DEFICIENT GEAR
          THEY STUMBLE UP TO SOME GREAT HEIGHT
          & I APPEAR:
          OUT! OUT, DIM MIND! THESE REALMS ARE NOT FOR YOU!
          EROTA HELPS ME.
   Ero.   THE THINGS I SEE!
          CELL CALLS TO CELL & FROM ON HIGH
```

121

GOD B HAS ORDERED: PROPAGATE OR DIE!
YET MAN WANTS LOVE—NOT BLITHELY LOOSENED CLOTHES
BUT AH, LE ROMAN DE LA ROSE
WHOSE POET ARM IN ARM WITH FANCY NEXT
STROLLS OFF TO CLIO AND A MOVING TEXT
OR TO URANIA & THE LOONY BIN.
CALYPSO? EURYDIKE?

Cal.   TWIN
STARS ARE WE, OF THALIA'S THEATRES,
OFTEN MISTAKEN FOR EACH OTHER.
PSYCHE-CHAOS OUR IMMORTAL MOTHER
USES MY LAUGHTER

Eury.   & MY TEARS.
Tableau. They strike a nine-fold attitude,
Provocatively, innocently crude.

Mich. NOW HOME! GO STRAIGHT TO BED!
NO MEETINGS WITH DARK DESTINY, HOWLING SINGING & DANCING
    HALF THE NIGHT, LYING TO YOUR OLD FATHERS IN THE
    MORNING, CLAIMING YOU CAN'T REMEMBER! OFF!
AND WE SHALL, HAVING CAUGHT A GRACIOUS RAY,
MEET THEIR MOTHER ON ANOTHER DAY.
Exeunt.

Ouf! *That* rollercoaster ride
At least is over. We sit petrified.
CINDERELLA'S SISTERS? volunteers
Wystan & WHAT WILL MAW BE LIKE MY DEARS!
Psyche as Chaos . . . MIGHTN'T ONE HAVE GUESSED
THE BOX OF HORRORS WAS HER OWN HOPE CHEST?
Now George: I HAD A SHOCK LET ME TELL YOU,
ZERO'D IN ON BY THOSE EMBER EYES
Maria: & MAMAN'S HELPER, MEMORY?
FEEDING ME WHOLE TRUMPED-UP HISTORIES
OF PREVIOUS LIVES WHILE SLAVING IN AG'S GARDEN
Hag's garden—they're the same? Is "Agatha"—
The breastless martyr simpering in her plot
Of widow-weed and blue beget-me-not—

Nothing more or less than a code name
For tomorrow's holy terror? Is the cast
Much smaller than we'd thought? Does our quick-change
Michael double as— DJ: Ephraim? Strange,
Both have golden eyes and look like Greek
Statues. WHAT TO SAY? MUCH GIVE & TAKE.
I GEORGE WHO FIRST WAS RAPH'S AM GABRIEL'S:
NOT NOW A 'MONTEZUMA ELEMENT'
AFTER RADIATION   But *he* knelt
To the Water Angel. Montezuma'd been
Noah, Moses . . . IT'S BEYOND ME   OR
WAS I ALL OF THEIRS?
                              OUR JIGSAW GEORGIE!
Be serious, Maman. The Muses, too,
Have changed since classical times. RELENTLESSLY
RESTYLING FUNCTIONS & NAMES LIKE A COIFFURE!
DARLINGS MY BOY OF THEIR DADS' INCESTUOUS
CROWD   ALL RAMPANT 'CREATIVITY' PLUS
THAT SAVING TOUCH OF ACID CARICATURE.
VERY KURT WEILL   AT ONE POINT THALIA
'DID' THE GRACES, SPLITTING INTO 3!
O IT'S A NASTY BRILLIANT FAMILY
We see the nastiness, all right. To think
Where it's all leading—well, we simply shrink.

In spite of broad hints liberally strewn
Throughout, as to tomorrow afternoon,
Crescendo and confusion leave unheard
—By us at least—the clarifying word.
It's like those 18th century finales
(Which might have lasted well into our age
Had not Rossini laughed them off the stage):
A thousand whirling thoughts confuse the head.
Blindly we cling to blindness, don't reread
The transcripts any longer—far too grim.
ENFANTS, TOMORROW NOON A NICE COOL SWIM?

*

Noon. The rocks at Várkiza. Two figures
Perch on Raphael's marble forearm, hawks
Hooded by reflection. DJ talks;
Out of the blue propounds that it takes all
One's skill and patience to describe, oh, say
A chair without alluding to its use.
No words like "seat" or "arm-rest"—just deduce
As best one can the abstract entity.
The mind on hunkers, squinting *not* to see,
Gives up. Who needs this hypothetical
Instrument of torture anyway?
JM: The marvel is that, once you give
The simple clue and say "a place to sit",
Images flock, homely or exquisite—
Shaker or Sheraton, Jacob or Eames,
The Peacock Throne, chairs not created yet!
Plumped cushions, where sunlight or lamplight streams
Onto the open book— DJ: Forget
Those chairs. Look! This whole world's *a place to live!*
—Plunging with a rusty rebel yell
Into the blue depths of Emmanuel.

Sensible Maria. Much restored
By afternoon, we sit down to the Board.
SIRS? IS THIS A GREAT OCCASION?
Why, Uni? Do you feel a difference?
I AM ACCOMPANIED BY 13 OTHERS
ALL MY HIERARCHY   WE SECURE THIS SPACE!
DO NOT FEAR   I AM UNICE YOUR FRIEND

The Middle Lessons: 5

Mich.   BROTHERS, CHILDREN,
        THESE OUR FOUR MEETINGS MET WITH SOME DECAY.
        NOW IN THE FIFTH ONE LET US STAY
        THE FALL, AND SAVE THE DAY!

Facing the open door expectantly.
WE BROTHERS, SHADES & MORTALS AWAIT YOU, MAJESTY. COME
    ADDRESS US.
AS TWIN SISTER TO OUR GOD BIOLOGY, YOUR RADIANT MIND
    HUMBLES AND DOES HONOR.
At a light footstep all profoundly bow.

Enter—in a smart white summer dress,
Ca. 1900, discreetly bustled,
Trimmed if at all with a fluttering black bow;
Black ribbon round her throat; a cameo;
Gloved but hatless, almost hurrying
—At last! the chatelaine of Sandover—
A woman instantly adorable.
Wystan, peeking, does a double take:
Somewhere on Earth he fancies he has seen
A face so witty, loving, and serene
—But where? Some starry likeness drawn by Blake
Perhaps for 'Comus'? or the one from Dante
Of Heavenly Wisdom? This, then, is the third
And fairest face of Nature (whom he'll come
To call, behind Her back of course, Queen Mum).
Glance lively with amusement, speaks. Each word,
Though sociable and mild, sounds used to being heard:

MICHAEL, YOU RASCAL GABRIEL! RAPHAEL & DEAR TWIN EMMANUEL,
    ALL HERE? AND ON SUCH CEREMONY?
GIVE IT OVER. WE ARE A CLASSROOM, A FORUM. HERE WE MEET TO
    STUDY THE MIND OF MAN.
The schoolroom, having dressed for the occasion
In something too grown-up, too sheer—the sense,
Through walls, of a concentric audience,
Rank upon blazing petaled rank arisen—
Quickly corrects its blunder, reassumes
Childhood's unruly gleams and chalk-dust glooms.
MUCH BETTER. POET?
WHA. MAM?

Psy.   THOSE TENTS, THOSE ATOMS & PARTICLES OF LIGHT,
        WHO PUT THEM INTO HIS, MY DARLING PORTRAITIST'S, MIND?

WHA.   (Slowly marveling) I THINK I KNOW.

Psy.   AND WHO WHISPERED TO HIM ENCOURAGINGLY:
        'IF THE SUN AND MOON SHOULD DOUBT, THEY WOULD IMMEDIATELY
           GO OUT'?
        AH YES, HIS LOVE, HIS PSYCHE.
        DOCTOR, SURELY YOU RECALL THE FIRST LAW OF PHYSICS: MOTION
           KNOWS ONLY RESISTANCE?
        BROTHER ELEMENTS, SWEET MORTAL POET, YOU ESTEEMED POETIC
           SHADE,
        MADAME MARIA CLEVER WOMAN (WE KNOW, WE KNOW)
        AND DOCTOR OUR CHILD, AND FRIGHTENED HAND (COME, COME),
        LET ME AS MY TEXT TAKE BLAKE'S FAITH, AND PHYSICS' LAW AS MY
           LESSON.
        LISTEN TO THE ENTWINING.

        WE DESCENDED WITH OUR BROTHERS, EVEN AS MADAME SAID,
           CARRYING TOOLS FROM THE GALAXIES,
        GOD BIOLOGY AND I, TWINS. OUR BROTHERS WISHED US WELL &
           STILL DO.
        OUR WORK WAS TWOFOLD: HE, CREATION OF MATTER, THE
           ARCHITECT. MY HUMBLE SELF, THE DECORATOR? AND A BIT
           MORE:
        'SISTER, BEFORE I CALL FORTH INHABITANTS OF THIS PLACE, LET US
           PLAN.
        WHAT POINT IS THERE IN AN IMMORTAL BEING (THOUGH LESS,
           MUCH LIKE OURSELVES) IF HE CONTAINS NOTHING NEW, NO
           SURPRISE, TO CALL HIS OWN?
        LET US DIVIDE THE FORCE OF HIS NATURE, JUST AS WE WILL MAKE
           TWO SIDES TO ALL NATURE,
        FOR IN DUALITY IS DIMENSION, TENSION, ALL THE TRUE GRANDEUR
           WANTING IN A PERFECT THING.
        SISTER, TAKE COMMAND OF HIS . . . RESISTANCE? HIS 'UNGODLY'
           SIDE. MAKE HIM KNOW DARK AS WELL AS LIGHT, GIVE HIM
           PUZZLEMENT, MAKE HIM QUESTION,
        FOR WOULD WE NOT LIKE COMPANY?' I AGREED.

126

THE GREAT WONDROUS EYES LOOKED UP AT US AS IF TO SAY: I?
QUESTION YOU? YET HE DID.
WE, GOD & I, WERE NEVER AT ODDS. OUR CREATURE, THOUGH,
BORN TO BE TORN BETWEEN US (THE PREHUMAN IN HIM) MADE ONE
OF HIS OWN.
'LOOK! HOW IMAGINATIVE!' GOD, VERY PICTURE OF A PROUD
PARENT.
'BROTHER, I'D RATHER HE PLAYED WITH HARMLESS THINGS.'
'AH PERVERSE SISTER, LET HIM.' I DID. HE DID. THEY DID.
DISMAYED GOD WATCHED THE FIRST OF HIS CREATURES DESTROYED.
I WEPT FOR HIM.
'SISTER, THESE TOYS OF HIS, PUT THEM AWAY.' I DID,
AND MY ASPECT OF CHAOS SO LINGERED IN THE GENETIC AIR, SMALL
WONDER I HAVE A NAME FOR BAD TEMPER.
'CALM, SISTER, WE TRY AGAIN.'

THE APE AMUSED US BOTH, CLOSING HIS BLACK FINGERS ON OUR
WRISTS. GOD & I EXCHANGED A LOOK
& THEN BESOTTEDLY TURNED OUR EYES INTO THE DEPTHS OF HIS.
IT TOOK.
WELL SIRS, MADAME, WE KNOW MUCH OF THAT APE'S SWIFT RISE,
UNTIL TODAY HE NEARLY RIVALS US.
'SISTER.' 'BROTHER?' 'ARE YOU ATTENDING?'
I, IN MY ASPECT OF PSYCHE, MARVEL. IN MY ASPECT OF MOTHER
NATURE, SHRINK.
OFTEN I AM TEMPTED TO SAY: BROTHER, LET ME DON MY FATAL
MASK.
BUT THEN THE APE SINGS, HE TOUCHES MY HEART, MOVING
SHADOWLY ABOUT IN HIS LIGHTED TENT . . .
I CLOSE THE LID AND SMILE.

A slow sigh of relief escapes DJ:
How long it seems we've waited for this day!
Psy. THANK YOU, GOOD CONSTANT HAND. I AM ALL FOR MAN, YES, YES.
I LOVE HIM HELPLESSLY.
NOW DOCTOR, PHYSICS! LET'S DRY OUR TEARS & PLUNGE INTO THE
LAB!
WHY IMMORTALITY?

127

> DEATH IS THAT RESISTANT FORCE DEFINING THE FORWARD MOTION
> OF LIFE.
> YOUR IMPRINT READ OUT, YOU MADE US PROUD: OUR FIRST LAB
> SOUL IN THREE MILLENNIA. AND STILL WE CALLED YOU BACK,
> FOR IF MAN CANNOT HIMSELF IMPROVE THE STRAIN AND LIMIT ITS
> NUMBERS . . .

GK. LADY, THIS BOWED HEAD ONCE AND FOR ALL
PUTS ASIDE RESISTANCE AT YOUR CALL.

Psy. FINALLY I FIND YOUR COMPANY STIMULATING, EACH OF YOU SO
GOOD OF YOUR TYPES,
& THINK NOW I WILL LINGER, HOVER ABOUT, PERCH ON THE
YOUNG POET'S SHOULDER AS I DID ON BLAKE'S.
YOURS TOO, WIZARD WIT, HAVE YOU FORGOTTEN THAT KISS ON
YOUR DOWNTURNED CHEEK?

WHA. MAM, I WAS GRATEFUL, I HAVE ALWAYS BEEN!
& YET TOO RARE, TOO RARE   YES, LINGER, MAM,
HERE IN OUR SCHOOLROOM. TIP THE SCALE, WIN! WIN!

Psy. GABRIEL, IT IS MY PLEASURE THAT YOU IN TEN MEETINGS EXPLAIN
ALL DEEP & 'DIRE' THINGS!
AND IN THE EIGHTH FULL MOON, MY SIGN,
GIVE THEM OUR COMPLETE DESIGN.

Gabr. MAJESTY, I WILL.

Psy. MICHAEL YOU HAVE CHOSEN WELL, THEY ARE APT, ALL GOOD GOD'S
CREATURES.
HOW THE OLD CARPET COMES TO LIFE WITH USE! WE ARE PLEASED.
Turns in the doorway, smiles from face to face.
GO WELL. KEEP THAT SWEET LIGHT AGLOW IN YOUR TENTS, & ONE
DAY I WILL TURN THEM SILKEN. ADIEU.

Mich. ALL ON THESE WORDS, ENGRAVEN ON OUR HEARTS,
OUR QUEEN DEPARTS.
AND I YOUR MICHAEL YIELD THE CHAIR
Fixing DJ with an impromptu gleam.
(SHALL I DESCRIBE IT, HAND?) TO GABRIEL'S CARE
THAT YOU, SHY BROTHER, HEY!
MAY LEAD US FORTH YOURSELF ANOTHER DAY.

The Brothers go. A garden in full bloom
Fills all but visibly the fading room
While where we sit our terracotta goddess
Smiles at the fresh white rose placed in her bodice.

BLISS MY DEARS   She kissed you? YEARS AGO
WRITING DOWN THE TITLE TO A BOOK
(AGE OF ANXIETY) I FELT MY FACE
SOFTLY BUT DISTINCTLY TOUCHED WITH GRACE

SUCH VIBRANCY ENFANTS   THE ATMOSPHERE
A PULSING SWELLING LEAF! And Gabriel?
AH HE IS HERS NO DOUBT. SHE TIPPED THE SCALE!
LIGHT STILL BLOWS THROUGH US LIKE A SCENTED AIR

George? I NO LONGER WORRY   WE ARE GUIDED
BY A, TO SAY THE LEAST, BENEVOLENT FORCE.
I AM STILL SHAKEN   AT THE SIGHT OF HER
A PRENATAL MEMORY CAME BACK: 'GO FORTH,
YOURS IS THE HOUSE OF SCIENCE. TAKE MY DAUGHTER
URANIA. SHE IS YOUR HOLY BRIDE.'

Urania who spoke so scornfully?
AMBITIOUS GIRL   SHE MAY HAVE PUSHED TO GET
ME A PROMOTION NOT PERMITTED YET.
YOU UNDERSTAND? 'WHY IMMORTALITY?'
Yes, your formula. We have it here . . .
(Leafing through pages) No. Wait . . . no. How queer.

Somehow, as though a whisper jet had drawn
Miles above Earth a blank, hairfine
Metaphysical crosscountry line
Erasing from all ears the afterdrone
Of wings aglitter hushed by their own speed,
That theorem—though given, I'd have sworn—
Is missing. Look! an "accidentally" torn
Corner from the transcript page.
                              INDEED:

FILED SAFELY IN THE R LAB Why, George? SAD
TO SAY, FURTHER LONGEVITY WOULD ADD
INSULT TO INJURY. SO FEW PRODUCE
(PAST AGE 16) MORE THAN A BOTCH OF KIDS,
PEOPLE MUST CHANGE FIRST. MOTHER N FORBIDS
(YOU HEARD?) ALL PRESENT ? OF ITS USE.
How did it work? A PROTEIN ADDITIVE:
LIFE-CHAIN GENES RAISED TO ULTIMATE DEGREE.
SUBTRACTION OF DEGENERATION FACTOR
BUILT INTO MAN'S ELECTRIC ENERGY
Hmm, well . . . ITS TIME WILL COME

                                     DJ: Since noon
I've felt things getting better. Glorious
To know someone like Her looks out for us—
Like Him, too. BROTHER SUN & SISTER MOON

Now risen even to our lips, this flood
She silvered ebbs. The moon is on the wane.

Her children down to the least scatterbrain
Fiddler dance across the glassy mud,

The mirror breathes, school's out!—a last recess
Provided by Her kindliness.

*

LADS! Robert! YOUR WEE FIDDLER   All alone?
JUST ME & UNI HERE TWIDDLING OUR   NO
MENDING OUR NEIGHS?   GUESS WHO CHECKED IN TODAY
WITH TONS OF LUGGAGE: 'AH A GRAND HOTEL
JUST AS I'D PICTURED, ONCE MORE EMIGRE!'
Who? VN   Oh no, did the great man die?
Which floor have they assigned him? 5   HE'LL BE
AT LOOSE ENDS LATER   HAVE HIM IN? DJ:
Why not! JM: Alas—*No Vacancy.*

ENFANTS WHAT A DROLL PAIR RM & UNI
O DEAR HE CANTERED OFF   They both did? I'M
HERE WEE MOUSE   To whom Wystan severely:
ROBERT, A SECRET! TOP SECURITY!
OUR LADY YESTERDAY REMARKED: 'THAT STRIKING
BLOND, WHY IS HE NOT AMONG US? And?
HER WORD IS LAW He'll join our little band—
Perfect! (Two wide-eyed o's from R himself.)
So She *is* lingering. WHILE HEAVEN TREMBLES
RUNNING HER WHITE GLOVES OVER EVERY SHELF
Where is She usually? A FORCE MORE OFTEN
FELT THAN PERSONIFIED   THE BUREAUCRACY
WE FANCY IS HER SUMMER HOUSE   SHE GOES
IN FOR THE 'SIMPLE LIFE' And winters where?
AH THEN ST PETER'S QUAIS JINGLE & BLAZE
WITH HER UNMELTING SNOWFLAKE POLONAISE
Who made that pretty couplet? SHH   IT BWOKE OFF
WHEN TINY BOB WEACHED OUT TO TOUCH NABOKOV

DJ: You realize, Robert is the one
Parent among us (oh, George had a son?)—
All I mean is, *that* could be why Nature
Liked him. JM: Could be. I wonder, though.
That look She gave Maman? "We know, we know . . ."
ENFANT THAT LOOK WENT THRU ME   EVER SINCE,
HUMILITY & PRESTIGE BOTH MUCH INCREASED:
VELVET WDN'T WRINKLE ON MY FIST!
I'VE A SUSPICION AS TO FATHERHOOD
THAT SOMEONE MEANS TO BURN HER BRA FOR GOOD
A liberated Psyche? AT THE LEAST,
BE THANKFUL SHE'S NOT YET TURNED TERRORIST!

Behind the Scenes

NOT BEHIND ENFANT: WE WERE THE SCENES
Maria has let fall that she and Wystan
Worked also on the first ten lessons. How?

131

WE CAMOUFLAGED U AS IN JUNGLE WARFARE
TO INFILTRATE THE INEXPRESSIBLE.
U SEE THOSE 4 ARE TERRIBLY STRONG DRINK.
KNOWING IT ALL, THEY TEND TO OVERLOOK
THE IMAGE-THWARTED PATHS BY WHICH WE THINK.
'LORD, MAY WE MEET FOR ONE BRIEF HUMAN HOUR?'
'LORD, MAY THE INFORMATION BE DECODED?'
'LORD, PLEASE DEAL GENTLY'   MICHAEL'S BRAVURA SPEECH
PATTERNS (THOUGHT WYSTAN WITH HIS PERFECT PITCH)
WERE TOO ABSTRACT: CREATION OF MAN FROM 'CLAY'?
LECTURE THAT TOOK FULLY HALF A DAY
& TO WHAT END? IF MYTH & METAPHOR
HAVE DONE THEIR JOB (THRU MANY A FAT TOME
ON EVOLUTION & ANATOMY)
'CLAY' SAYS IT ALL, NO? MICH (TO W & ME):
'GO EACH OF YOU INTO YR ELEMENTS,
BRING BACK A HUMAN LANGUAGE WE CAN USE.'
WE MADE A LEXICON OF THE EFFECTS
OF EARTH & WATER, RENDERED THRU OUR SENSES.
THE BROTHERS' SCHEDULE TAKING ON MEANWHILE
CHARACTERISTICS OF A 'CLASSIC' STYLE
(PLAINNESS & LIMPIDITY) NOW CAME,
JUST AS IN BADMINTON DOUBLES VS BETTER
PLAYERS, TO RAISE THE LEVEL OF YR GAME.
ITS WINGED VOLLEYING WAS LONG REHEARSED
BY OUR ANGELIC ACTORS, THEIR DISSENSION
(APPARENT ONLY) MICHAEL'S INSPIRATION:
'ALL GOOD DISCOURSE MUST, LIKE FORWARD MOTION,
KNOW RESISTANCE'   So that from the first
They spoke to us through *you*— LANGUAGE THE WHOLLY
HUMAN INSTRUMENT, REMEMBER   YET
THEIR EVERY 'WORD' WAS (HOW TO SAY IT) HOLY
Even in translation. What must be
The range of the original! WE'LL SEE
WHEN I MY BOYS BECOME A NOUN IN IT!

THEN CAME THE MIRACLE: THOSE LESSONS READIED
DURING YR MONTHS APART ENFANTS WERE BY

A WAVE OF MICHAEL'S HAND WIPED FROM OUR MINDS
TO BREAK UPON US STAGGERINGLY ONE
BY ONE. MIRACLE 2: THE MIDDLE FIVE
ENDED, 'WE WILL NOT DECEIVE OUR SCRIBE.
NOW TELL THEM' And it all came flooding back!
THAT VERY INSTANT
                NEED WE STRESS MY DEAR
THE EXQUISITE REVERBERATIONS HERE:
EARTH LAY OPEN LIKE A BOOK TO READ
& THERE OUR POEM SLEPT   LOCKED IN A SEED.
NOW GEORGE & ROBERT ARE ALREADY 'AT'
THE NEXT 10 LESSONS ON INHERENT, NON
BIOLOGICAL LIFE ENERGIES
And when the time comes will they too forget?
& BE REMINDED & AMAZED
                HE'S GONE
TO PLATO. MAMAN TO AGATHA   UP TO OUR KNEES
IN A LAST BUMPER CROP OF CREEPING NIGHTMARES
FOR THE DEEP FREEZE   UNI! DOOR!
                A DEAR SOUL, SIRS
SHE ASKS ME ABOUT OUR FLORA & FAUNA
What species were there other than your own?
NONE ETERNAL   JUST WRINKLED REPTILES
FISH & FLIES   Those messengers you hatched . . .
OUR MAIN MISTAKE   WE MOURN IT STILL
No accident—if the No Accident
Clause operated in Atlantis? NO
YOU BENEFIT FROM THAT   GOD B
KNOWS TO RESPECT HIS CREATURES' WEAKNESS.
THIS IS UNICE, WISHING YOU WELL

DJ: Agatha again. Those games
Of doubles. JM: And our patrons' names?
Ford means a shallow tract of river. Clay
Means—well, they've told us. Maddening the way
Everything merges and reflects. The Muses'
Shifting functions—

*

SHD URANIA
NOT BE A TV AERIAL? IT CONFUSES
US TOO MY DEARS   MANY A PUZZLED LOOK
EXCHANGED IN MID DICTEE. THOSE CLOUDS OF MYTH,
HOW SHAPELY & DISTINCT THEY USED TO SEEM
VIEWED FROM BELOW! UP HERE THE VIEW AT CLOUD
LEVEL IS ALL WHIRLING FROTH & STEAM.
GK THINKS (KNOWS) THE MUSES ARE KINETICS
OF MIND-PERCEPTION   SUCH SIDESPLITTING DEAD
ACCURATE SYMBOLS OF THE PROCESS   Not
Mirabell's "golden containers"? THE R/LAB
BIRD'S EYE VIEW. STUCK WITH THAT SOUND BUT DRAB
RATIO, HE SAW THE 88
PERCENT OF 'INSPIRATION' LAB-ENGENDERED,
THE MUSES THERE4 AS THE TWELFTH OF IT

MAMAN KNEW DANS LE MONDE WHICH GIRLS 'CAME OUT'
TOO YOUNG   UNCHAPERONED   MOCKING   Why would Michael
Let them? PERHAPS TO MAKE U WONDER: SO?
WHAT LIES BEYOND THAT SON ET LUMIERE?
What does? GOD B & NATURE, AS YOU KNOW.

GEORGE HERE: I HATE TO BE A GLOOMY GUST
BUT AREN'T WE BEING A BIT OVERSANGUINE
ABOUT MOTHER N (OH IS IT GUS? HA HA)
Go on. WELL, GABRIEL IS HER SPOILED DARLING,
SHE A 'PERMISSIVE' MAW. MY RESEARCH HAS HAIRS
I LOST STANDING ON END! I'M BARGAINING:
'MASTER G, LESS SULPHUR?' JIMMY THAT RING
WD BLACKEN OF ITSELF   You're right, it needs
Reoxydizing. Irrepressible brightness
—So like life—has worn through. You were saying?
ROBERT A NATURAL DIPLOMAT: 'LORD G,
THE HYDROGEN BOMB? MIGHTN'T WE HAVE A MOCKUP
INSTEAD OF THE REAL THING?'   BUT SERIOUSLY,
WHAT ARE WE TO MAKE OF MOTHER N

& GABRIEL? He has a complex, then?
They called *him* Chaos once. INDEED   A FAMOUS
NAME ON HER SIDE OF THE FAMILY
This can't be right—the Brothers sprang full-grown
From God's mind. Nature is at most their . . . aunt?
THE THREE PERHAPS. BUT WHAT IF GABRIEL IS
A FORCE THAT CAME DOWN FROM THE GALAXIES
IN COMPANY WITH HIS MOTHER & HER TWIN
Nothing of God in him—Michael's dark cousin
YES sent by the Pantheon to implant
The Monitor? OR THE MONITOR ITSELF?
Stop right there, George! IN G'S VOICE I HEARD
THE HUM   THE SUCK   THE CONTRADICTING WORD
DJ: Ah don't, *don't* send us back to dwell
On that old frightfulness of Gabriel!
DAVE WE ARE SAFE UNDER HIS WINGS SO FAR.
WE PEER FROM A GLASSED OPERATING ROOM
(MAKING SENSE OF IT) INTO THE FIRE
Sense of what? SOUL STRUCTURE   RADIATION
TOPICS OF THESE NEXT LESSONS I ASSUME

& ALL AROUND (adds Robert) ARE SOME FAIRLY
MONSTROUS SIGHTS   JARS OF 'UNLIMITED GERM'
OTHERS OF 'UNQUENCHABLE FIRE'   A DAB
OF THIS, A PINCH OF THAT? THE LARVA OF
A PLANET-EATING WORM 'FOR USE IN CASE
OF A GALACTIC OVERRUN'   Oh brother—
And the personnel? FORMS WE JUST FACE AWAY FROM,
MAKING OURSELVES EVEN TEENSIER
WHILE GABRIEL POTTERS HAPPILY   You won't
Have had much music lately. AT DUSK I SINK
BACK IN THE PARLOR WHERE FLAGSTAD WHIPS UP TEA
TRILLING HER LOVELY F ABOVE HIGH C
For you alone? OH STRAUSS TURNS UP, OR WAGNER
OR INSTRUMENTALISTS   THE CHINESE MASTER
OF A 4TH CENTURY 'GON REGISTER'
MY LADS IT TAKES YR SOCKS OFF! KIND OF THROBBING
MEDIUM THAT SUSTAINS, ITSELF ATONAL,

EVERY 'SCALE VARIANT' SCHOENBERG: HAD I KNOWN!
Has Schoenberg ever spoken of DJ,
His former student? ONE WHO FONDLY HAS
IS HINDEMITH: 'DJ A CLEAR & BUBBLING
MELODIC NATURE OVERSWEETENED BY JAZZ'
PH AT 7, HEAVILY CREDITED
AS 'GERMINATIVE' Now you're making it
Sound like the Lab—
     ENFANTS STOP SEEING DOUBLE!
IF AGATHA ROMPED UP IN OVERALLS
(2 STRAPS WHERE THE SHEARS CLIPPED) U'D REALIZE
THAT SHE IS NOBODY IF NOT HERSELF
SOME ICON, EH? WE BY THE WAY WILL BE
ALLOWED TO TAKE OUR MIRROR BREAK WHENEVER
THE 4 OF US AGREE If we say never?
AH ENFANT BUT DO U KNOW SOMETHING, D?
WE FEEL AN URGE LIKE BABY'S KICKING FOOT
THAT SAYS MARCH ON! JM: Or mine to put
These headlong revelations finally
Between the drowsy covers of a book.
SO RIGHT DEAR BOY NO MORE POSO AKOMAS
FOR ANY OF US THEN BOB WILL COMPOSE HIS
'OTHER WORLD' SYMPHONY WHILE I MAKE SUCH
A MOUNTAIN
    ME SUCH A GARDEN
        & ME? GEORGE?
SUCH A SLEEPING PILL!
    & SO TILL THEN LET'S MAKE
THE MOST OF IT MY DEARS & GO OUT LAUGHING FOR GOD'S SAKE!

       ★

Plato Emerging

WYSTAN WITH PLATO (NATCH) MM WITH AG,
& THE WEE MINNESOTA MINNESINGER
TUNING HIS LUTE Aha, a setting for

The new life? YES   DETAILS ARE SLOW IN COMING
ONLY THAT I'LL BE WHITE AGAIN (HO HUM)
Changing neither race nor hemisphere—
Odd; Chester did both. THEY'RE BEING EXTRA
CAREFUL IN MY CASE: HIGH GROUND   NO RISK
OF LOSING ME IN SOME 'EMERGING' NATION.
CK'S BLACK AFRICA A VACCINATION
AGAINST ONE MORE LIFE SABOTAGED BY SEX
No outlets there? CONVENTIONAL TRIBAL WHOOPEE
BUT AS IN THE OLD SAW, CK GOES STRAIGHT
INTO THE JEWELRY STORE & COMES OUT CROOKED.
WYSTAN CHORTLES DOTING OVER HIM:
'MY DEARS HE'S GONE & DONE IT!' CHORUS: 'NOT . . . ?'
'NO NO   JUST YANKED HIS FATHER'S U KNOW WHAT.'

Enter the others: DID I HEAR MY NAME?
CAN'T A FELLOW SLIP OFF TO THE GENTS
WITHOUT   The gents—to Plato! MM'S TERM
WHO NEVER GETS DISCUSSED BEHIND HER BACK
Never needs powder on her Grecian nose?
TOO UNFAIR
        CAN'T FOOL MAMAN   SHE KNOWS!
NOW: PLATO IS SHORTLY TO BEGIN A NEW
V LIFE   THRILLING, EH WYSTAN?
           MY DEARS WE'RE TO HAVE
SUCH A SNIFFER! Tell! A BIOCHEMIST.
V WORK A POLLUTION-EATING ANTIGAS
Wow. 27 YEARS TO GO ALAS
BUT IT WILL AS HE SAYS 'DO THE OLD TRICK:
CLEAR THEIR HEADS'   That fits with Mirabell's
Green fields three decades hence. I'm sorry now
We never talked to Plato. My chronic shyness
Vis-à-vis "ideas"—oh well, spilt milk.
I DARESAY HE'LL LOOK IN B4 HE GOES
PERFUMED LIKE MOTHER IN HER PARTY CLOTHES
KISSING THE SMALL INCIPIENT ASTHMATIC
GOODNIGHT   How soon is he to be reborn?
HE'LL SEE US THRU & THEN OUR 3'S DRAMATIC

137

(You *three*? WITH GEORGIE   BOB IN NEXT YEAR'S CROP)
DESCENT ALL POPPING FLASHBULBS TO THE GREAT
'PRESS' BELOW   YR MOTHER CANNOT WAIT!

They leave, laughing. DJ: Tell me I'm wrong.
Wystan is Plato. Has been all along.

New moon this evening. Rim of plate.
Forebodings luminous if incomplete.

A moon we shiver to see wax
—What will our portion be in two more weeks?

MM to Gabriel: AH LORD, THAT MEAL.
But spoken gently, spoken with a smile . . . ?

Ripen, Huntress, into matron. Light,
Come full circle through unclouded night.

*

RM & UNI OFF PRACTISING VIENNESE
HIJINKS TO WHISTLED WALTZES, Wystan is free
To speak of angels: THEY'RE OBSCURE LIKE ALL
GOOD TEACHERS   BUT THEIR TEXTS REMAIN OUR OWN
ILLUMINATED PAGES. THUS THE TONE
FAR MORE SHAKESPEARIAN THAN BIBLICAL
('BROTHER FRANCE') HARKS BACK TO THE DIVINE
RIGHT OF THESE NATURAL POWERS. Deaf to a growing
Attentive hush, he draws the vital line
Between NATURAL (PSYCHIC) & UNNATURAL CHAOS
WHICH SETS I SUSPECT THE MONITOR'S NEEDLES TREMBL
—Only now breaking off: ROBERT! FOR SHAME!
EAVESDROPPING? 2 3 4 5 IT WD SEEM
WE HAVE BEEN SOMEWHAT LAX 8 9
                    ME SOWWY

SO FASCINATING   COULDN'T HELP
                       MY DEARS
CHAT WITH UNI   WE'LL BE   What? Wait—
                       SIRS?

ME TO BLAME? I HAD NO BRIEFING
I TOOK FOR GRANTED MY NAME-GIVER
MIGHT   O MASTER!
               Enter Mirabell:
ALWAYS SUCH A TREAT TO SEE MY GRADUATES   THAT SILLY
ANIMAL LET IN ONE NOT ALLOWD, CAUSING DISPLEASURE
AMONG THE OO. THE CULPRIT WILL   THEY'RE BACK   FALSE ALARM
(Sweeping out grandly.)
                  SIRS   Were you punished, Uni?
THEY FORBADE IT   THEY ARE MY FRIENDS!
Anybody who mistreated you
Would very quickly lose our friendship, too.
O TO RUN WITH YOU BOTH! YOU KNOW
THAT IS FOREVER! WELL   FOUR ARE NOW
ALLOWED IN   AU REVOIR FROM UNICE

Is everything all right? POOR BOB STILL NUMB:
HIS 1ST BRUSH WITH OO   BUT A PASS WAS HANDED
CLAWED TO HIM RATHER   Hadn't clearance come
From Her? BAT POLITICS   DOES THE RIGHT WING
KNOW WHAT THE SINISTER IS HARBORING?
THE PROBLEM NOW IS CHIEFLY WHERE HE'LL SIT
(DURING THE LESSONS) OUT OF RADIATION . . .
THE REST OF US OF COURSE IMMUNE TO IT
DJ: Are *we*? DEAR BOY TRY TO REMEMBER
THIS IS ALL IN A MANNER OF SPEAKING   AH MM & GEORGE
(INSEPARABLE NOW THESE 2)
               JM:
George, a letter came—Maman, forgive me—
So full of love and grief and pride in you.
I held it to the mirror, did you see?
You called me "brother" in New York last May.
I didn't understand; I do today.
JIMMY I READ IT THRU TEARS. I WISH   BUT SADLY

LIFE ASKED TOO MUCH OF ME, TOO MUCH OF HER,
WE COULD NOT
                    C'ETAIT IN SHORT LE GRAND AMOUR
BUT ISN'T OUR GEORGAKI MEANT FOR LOVE?
I BET HE WOWED 'EM!
                        GOOD LORD WHAT'S A POOR
SCIENTIST DOING IN THIS ATMOSPHERE?
THESE LOW TONALITIES!
                        SO MY DEARS WE'LL COAT
ROBERT IN LEAD & KEEP HIM WITH US
                            NO MORE
GARGOYLES PLEASE! A COUNTRY TAD WILL WAKE UP
SCREAMING   But you and Uni got off—
                            GOOD CREATURE
PEERING ROUND A LEG AT THE OO,
OUR POET ENFANTS TURNED QUITE PATRICIAN: 'SEE HERE,
ENOUGH OF THIS. WE OUTRANK YOU AND U KNOW IT!'
AU REV   OFF GOES MAMAN TO TRIM THE HEDGEROWS
DJ: Come clean, Maria—you've a date
With George. O WHY, WHY DOES ONE WASTE ONESELF
ON THESE LEWD TYPES, GEORGAKI?
                            THEY MEAN WELL
BUT LET'S DO TAKE A STROLL   JIMMY DON'T TELL!

UNI SADDLE UP   WE'LL GO HEDGEHOPPING

—So here we are back with Wystan. Does one say
We've guessed he's Plato, or just wait and see?
JM: Well! here's our opportunity
To talk behind Maria's back. AH SHE
(His tone, grave, musing, catching us off guard)
SHE IS ONE OF THE WONDERS   HER 3 SPEECHES
HAD ME ABSOLUTELY TEARY   SHE ALONE
HAVING 'CREATED' NOTHING IN HER LIFE
CAME HERE I FEEL ON THE HIGHEST RECOMMENDATION.
WITHOUT THE RAYS SHE WD HAVE RISEN UP,
SHE HAS THE (M) SPECIFIC GRAVITY
OF A CULT FIGURE   PUREST GUESSWORK   BUT

NO I'LL PUZZLE IT OUT NOW OFF & AWAY
TO MEET AGAIN (GUFFAW) ANOTHER DAY!

*

The Last Word on Number

WHOOF LADS Yes, Robert? OUT OF MY SPACE SUIT
LIKE FOOTBALL ME THE PERENNIAL SUBSTITUTE:
'TOUGH LUCK BOB, FELLA, TOO LIGHT FOR THE TEAM'
DJ: Why a space suit? HEADS UP, FELLA!
WANT FORMULA FOR ANTIRADIATION?
If you can give it. CAN I NOT! AHEM:
MO / RA : 279 / SOD
(SODIUM COMPOUND, MO MAGNESIUM OXIDE)
Not MgO? DEAR J, THE TEENIEST GAMMA
IN SUCH A FORMULA WD BLOW OUR LIDS OFF.
ALL THIS OF COURSE AVAILABLE ONLY WAY
DOWN DEEP WE'VE HAD (AS GK PUTS IT) ONE
HELL OF A TIME That number—279—
It sounds familiar. An atomic weight?
No, they don't go that high—not *yet*. A KEY
NUMBER OF YRS I THOUGHT WASN'T EPHRAIM FROM
THAT BANK? Oh God, yes. Mirabell (9.3)
Said Ephraim was a formula—why do you
Dig that old nonsense up? BECAUSE IT'S TRUE.
THE NUMBER IS A FORCE WHICH GABRIEL
ADDS LIKE ALBUMEN TO EGG TEMPERA
TO THE SOUL'S COLOR MIX As a new golem
Adds *its* gray figure to the endless column?
IN THE BUREAUCRACY WHERE E & BILLIONS
ARE, THE LORDS & MESSENGERS REQUIRE
THESE SYMBOLS MUCH AS CLAIMED BY MUSCLE BOY
THEY ARE INITIALS OF GREAT FORMULAS.
SO E'S (M) PERSONALITY READS OUT:
2: CATEGORY OF INTELLIGENCE
7: THE XTIAN EPOCH (7TH STAGE

141

BEYOND SAY THAT IST PAINTING RAPHAEL SAW)
9: LIMIT OF HIS   Robert, what strides you're making;
But *must* we go on with Number? It's all too—

Here Wystan joins us with an overview:
MY DEARS WHEN MICHAEL NAMED THE HIGHEST HEAVEN
NOT NTH BUT ZEROETH HE MEANT A SPHERE
(SHORTLY TO RECEIVE THE 4 OF US)
SO INTENSELY OF THE MIND THAT NUMBER
IS TO IT AS THE BLEATING WOOLLY FLOCK
THE SHEPHERD COUNTS TO RISEN HESPERUS.
THE MOMENT IS LONG PAST WHEN YOU JM
MIGHT HAVE BEEN DEVOURED BY THE CHIMERA
LIKE POOR LONGSUFFERING YEATS. MUCH THAT U KNOW
WAS DICTATED TO HIM BY THE OO
But does Yeats suffer *now*? ANSWER DJ
YOU ARE THE HAND
                    DJ, uneasily:
Well, there's this bump on my palm. It doesn't hurt . . .
What else? Often before I know the message
I feel its beauty, its importance. Tears
Come to my eyes. Is that Yeats being moved?
Often it's tiring or obscure. I fumble
Along, JM finds answers, I feel dumb.
Is that Yeats too, still making the wrong sense?
Why can't *he* ever speak? WHEN THE DICTATION
ENDS I THINK HE MAY   & LEAVE YR HAND
MY DEAR MUCH AS HE FOUND IT   Good enough.
Meanwhile, he's visible? FAINTLY IN THE DARK
A WORDLESS PRESENCE   LIKE A COURTROOM CLERK
How dressed? LET'S SAY A STARCHED WHITE WRITING CUFF

HAVE THEY BEEN TOLD?
                    YES   & ARE NOT IMPRESSED
THEY'VE PASSED THE NUMBER TEST
                              BRAVO ENFANTS
YET 279 REMAINS A STRONG FORCE BOTH
PROTECTIVE & CONDUCTIVE   AND 741

HAS PLAYED A PART, N'EST CE PAS? HERE IN VOL III
Who else spread wings above you when God B
Sang in Space? OUR ST BERNARD   JM: Who—
Isn't it St Bernard—helps Dante see
Our Lady? AH   THE PATTERN BLEEDING THROUGH

A hush of wonder Robert punctuates:
AU RESERVOIR   PSST   CUT YR QUILL, MR YEATS!

★

SIRS? Hello, Uni. MAY I RUN A MESSAGE?
To whom? A MR NABOKOV LEFT HIS NAME
Please, not today. DJ: Don't we want Ephraim?

MES CHERS! We've got your number, 279.
TRUE   BUT DIGITS . . . GIVE YR SLAVE THE FIDGETS
What's new, old friend? NOT MUCH   THE COURT HAS MOVED
TO SUMMER HEIGHTS & LUCA FALLEN FOR
THE NEW ARRIVAL   Which one? L: MAMMA MIA!
SO STRONG, SO BLOND THE RUSSIAN GIANT! IS HE A
WRITER TOO? VN: WHAT? NOT A GIRL?
AM I MISSING SOMETHING? Ah, your giddy whirl . . .
AND YRS? THE SLEEPING BEAUTY IN YR ROOM?
DJ: Christo's his name. SAUVAGE ET BEAU
UNLIKE HIS GAUNT SAD SEXLESS NAMESAKE   Oh?
You've *seen* Christ, Ephraim? O WELL WHO HAS NOT
REPORTED HIM? HIS STORY PERMEATES
THE TALK HERE LIKE AN ARGOT: 'LOAVES & FISHES'
FOR THE ALAS IMAGINED MEALS WE ORDER,
'BAPTISM' FOR THE COURSE B4 REBIRTH
Compost of language—action gone to seed,
Buried in idiom. AND 'ON THE 3RD DAY'
PUTTING FORTH MES CHERS A VERDANT DEED?
TIME ALREADY? I LOVE U   HERE'S YR STEED
—Who whisks us back to the schoolroom.
REALLY ENFANTS
AT THIS LATE DATE STILL ASKING EPHRAIM ?S

ONLY THE ANGELS KNOW THE ANSWERS TO?
AT LEAST HIS GRAPEVINE THRIVES: WE GET JC
BUDDHA ET AL IN A FORTHCOMING LESSON
ON 'DESTROYED ENERGIES'   ALL THE RELIGIONS
WE NOW THINK WERE MICH'S V WORK. HIS REALM, IDEAS
And Gabriel's, thought. Does thought destroy ideas?
WHAT ELSE? Well, *our* faith came to be in Feeling.
Feelings for one another, love, trust, need,
Daily harrowing the mini-hells
They breed— DON'T TALK TO YR MAMAN OF FEELINGS
TOO FEW WERE STARS   TOO MANY WERE BLACK HOLES

DJ: You made a black hole once, Maria,
At Sounion. Looked me straight in the old eye
And asked *Why were we born?* GOOD QUESTION   WHY?
What did I say? Something . . . I can't recall.
ENFANT U FELL TO SNORING IN MID PHRASE
TOO MUCH VINO DURING LUNCH THOSE DAYS
JM: Why born? To feed the earthward flow
Of Paradise? That final waterfall
Ephraim first mentioned in— I KNOW, I KNOW
& ODDLY GK & RM (PROUD PAWS)
THINK IT A LOVELY PLAN WHILE WYSTAN'S EYES
WEARILY MEET MINE (CHILDLESS OLD NUMBERS)
ACROSS THE NURSERY BEDS. IT'S THE MORTAL SLOWNESS
Better than Gabriel's haste! HE IS THE SPUR
THE FIREBRAND RINGED BY WOLVES   But Nature? Her
Pace is loving, she protects her own.
NOT WHEN SHE'S CLEANING HOUSE: 'SEE MY FLOORS SHINE,
SEE HOW THEY SPARKLE, ALL MY CHANDELIERS!
1000S OF FINGERS WORKED QUITE TO THE BONE!'
ROBERT STOP TICKLING UNI & COME IN

A Metamorphosis Misfires

VELVET NOSTRILS   LIQUID EYES   TOO BAD
NO WINGS   What a thought—Uni as Pegasus?

HE'S FAR TOO SHY TO ENTER BUT WHY NOT
IF WE PUT OUR MINDS TO IT?
Why not! Eyes shut,

Think *Wings for Uni.* The cup wobbles "upward"
From I to O—
UNICE! COME DOWN FROM THERE!

Robert, *it's working?* Maria (firmly): NO.
I LEAVE U TO YR SHAME. THAT'S MICHAEL'S SHOW.

ONE CAN BUT TRY. NOW ABOUT LVB?
Beethoven? We're all ears. AND SO IS HE:
'MOZART? A GIFT OF GOD'S NO DOUBT, BUT MARKED
UNRETURNABLE' 'FIDELIO? YES
I PLUNGED SMIRKING ONSTAGE BUT, DEAR NEW FRIEND,
OPERA AWAITS ITS GENIUS' & SUCH A LOOK!
'ME, MAESTRO?' 'WARUM NICHT?' DA DA DA DOOM
Do you hear sounds? MORE: I AM FLOODED WITH
LVD'S SENSE OF AN UNWRITTEN SCORE
WHICH THEN GOES 'ONTO TAPE' (READ: DNA).
PAST THE 5 FINGER STUFF MY LADS I SAIL
TO MASTER LESSONS ON THE GRANDEST SCALE!
He's off.
The cup bolts forward: SIRS?

AN ENEMY? THE HAIRS ON MY BACK BRISTLED!
PEG O MY HEART, MR ROBERT HUMMED?
ARE YOU CHANGING MY NAME   AM I NOT YR UNICE?

INTRUDING?
Help us, Mirabell—Uni's all upset;
We named the wingèd horse. Make sense of it.
GLADLY: CIRCA 3000 BC A WIND

SWEPT DELOS   THE MALE POP RUSHING TO PUT STONES ON THEIR
   ROOFS
WERE SWEPT UP UP UP THEN IN A CYCLICAL FREAK MANNER
RETURND, SET DOWN. ONE CASUALTY: A FAT TEMPLE SCRIBE
WHO, LEFT ARM BROKEN, DECIDED IT MEANT THEY HAD BECOME
TOO SOBER TOO WITHOUT LYRIC JOY   SO HE INVENTED
GREAT PAEANS TO WEIGHTLESS LOFTY & PURELY COMIC LIFE.

DELOS SET UP A SHRINE & THE SCRIBE'S WORDS 'WE RODE THE AIR,
WE LAUGHD DOWN AT THE DOMESTIC EARTH' CAUSED A HORSE FIGURE
TO BE WORSHIPT THERE BY ALL WHO ASPIRED TO THE WORD.
NOTE THAT THE 'GOD' RESPECTED THE SCRIBE'S RIGHT HAND
   Why "god" in quotes?   MY DEAR EX
PUPILS, I BELIEVE U KNOW. BUT ARE NOT GODS & MUSES,
MYSTICAL BIRDS & BEASTS MORE LOVELY THAN METRICAL STORMS
OR EVEN NUMBERS?   Dear Peacock, yes and no.
   But tell us one more thing before you go:
   Uni, just then, *took* us to Ephraim—how?
               MASTERS, IS IT NOT SIMPLE? HE SHUTS
3 SIDES OF THE FRAME   THE MIRROR OPENS TO THE OTHER.
WE ARE HERE IN A 4 DIMENSIONAL SPACE, YR ROOM &
OURS COINCIDING. YR GREEK'S WORLD IS THAT ONE DIMENSION
   Called?
HEAVEN   *We*'d have called the fourth dimension Time.
       MY FRIENDS, SINCE TIME DOES NOT EXIST FOR US, IS IT
NOT ONLY FAIR THAT HEAVEN SHD ELUDE YOU? UNI! DOOR!

★

PLATO MY DEARS IN FULLEST MAJESTY
OF ALL HIS POWERS FOR THE NEW LIFE! 'POET,
REMEMBER, WHEN IN EARTH, HOW FRIVOLOUS
A THING IS GRAVITY.' SUCH PEARLS! & ME
WITH NO THREAD TO MAKE MM A CHOKER   Where is
Plato to be born? BOMBAY   A RICH
PUNJABI FAMILY   FATHER A MATHEMATICIAN
& BANKER   MOTHER A DOCTOR OF MEDICINE:
'PARENTS, POET, ROCKING MY CRADLE WILL
NO DOUBT DIZZY ME WITH LOVE. ONE MUST
BRACE THE LITTLE FOOT AGAINST HIGH HEAVEN.'
Something's coming back: wasn't it Plato
Ephraim said "intervened" for Wallace Ste—
(Drowned in an imaginary *whoosh!*)

WHAT DO I SEE? Mr Stevens? WHY ON HORSEBACK?
It's a long story. OR IS THAT A HORSE?

No, but let Wystan tell you. Is it true that—
YES   THE GREAT ONE CAME TO MY DEFENSE:
'THIS DRY SCRIBE, READ HIS WORK THRU, MASTER PLATO,
& TELL US WHERE HE FITS.' 'SIRS, NEITHER TOP
NOR BOTTOM, DEEP NOR SHALLOW, BUT NOT SHORT LIVED.
I SAY MAKE OF HIM A PERMANENCE
TAPPABLE BY LESSER TALENT.' Faint
Praise for one whose paramour's lit candle
Set the tents of Hartford glimmering.
AH THANK YOU   YES   SHE KISSED MY CHEEK THAT DAY
BUT YR MOUNT CHAFES
                    (And gallops us away.)

WHERE HAVE U BEEN ENFANTS? OO WILL SPEAK
TOMORROW SUNDOWN   WE'LL MEET NEXT IN CLASS
NO SPECIAL PREP FOR YOU   GABRIEL TRES
INFORMAL   It's moving so quickly, you'll be gone,
Maman, before we know it! AH COME ON
THE MOON IS WAXING FULL
& WE DEAR ENFANTS ALSO FEEL ITS PULL

                      *

LORD GABRIEL GRACIOUSLY APPEARS WITH GREAT COMPANY
THIS HOUR TOMORROW. WILL THAT ALL GOES WELL. THESE LAST VISITS
SEE YR V WORK THROUGH, YR DEAR ONES SOON AFTER ON THEIR WAY.
MY LEGIONS RING WITH PRAISE. I SALUTE YOU AS MY MASTERS.
    You mustn't! We've just sat back while they—
                              Gone.
SIRS? Uni, did you see something then?
A FLASH   A SHADOW   LIKE A STORM AT NIGHT
Clear skies now? BLANKNESS   FOR WE WORK IN BLANKNESS
Ah Uni, we're about to lose our friends.
IT WAS A MIXED GIFT, GOD'S IMMORTALITY.
MY MASTER SAYS WE TOO MUST PART
MAY I ADMIT I AM NOT HAPPY?
Nor are we at that prospect. WELL   WE GRIEVE
TOGETHER   BLESS OUR NATURES, TEARS!

THIS WILL FOREVER BE MY FIELD
This mirror. YES & WHEN YOU ONE DAY COME HERE
THINK OF YOUR UNI AND HE WILL APPEAR!

We've made it to the lessons that say No.
DJ, as backstage hammering dies down,
Leans apprehensively into the glow
Of footlights coming up all over town.
The moon, weakly at first, strikes the south wall.
JM "unseeing" roams the house, where high
Ceiling, bare floor, doorframe, stairwell, all
Courtesy of our resident stagecrew,

Have watched with him since May—it's late July—
These rooms under what concentrating pressures
Turning to stanzas (type them? will they do?
U ARE THE SCRIBE MY BOY   OK then, *yes*)
—Our setting no less vital in its way
Than any sunrise to another day:

The House in Athens

Walls of blond-washed cement
With us inside have risen,
These years, from rags to riches.
Starting with our basement spinster "frozen"
Since wartime there by rent
Control (unlike her roaches),

They end high up in splendor—
Well, actually a terrace
Of waving oleander,
Geranium, jasmine at its plumy lushest.
Between extremes the space
Is filled by our two stories.

Mediterranean Fascist
In style, the house would still
Be several years our junior
—Point we haven't scrupled to drive home
By frequent imposition
Of our taste and will:

A Titian red bedroom;
One low-cut balcony
Glass-enclosed and curtained;
The former rooftop laundry—ghosts of dirty
Linen—made to be
The room in which I write.

True, there remain some built-in
Drawbacks: the kitchen window
Too mean for air, for light,
For anything but ineffectual screeching
At a child or cat from
In the dank court below;

Or the storage space. Through gloom
Midway upstairs, on reaching
The portal of this slowly
Brimming, costive diverticulum
One risks his neck to leave,
We risk our wits to enter.

And pipes, of course, that hiss
And grieve, and icy currents
Becoming dog-day smells
In proper season . . . Who once said *The House
Is Mother?* Full concurrence.
Here in the parlor smiles

Escape the guest escaping
In his turn two dwarf chairs
Whittled for hard declensions,

Through the years, from babe in arms to crone.
He's made for couch and cushions
And—there's the telephone.

Who's calling? Mimí? Yannis?
Which Yannis? George? Nelláki?
The rings proliferate,
Overlapping, afternoons, with sticky
Ones of ash-and-anise
We take a sponge to later.

Or else on an illegal
Ten-meter cord the chatter
Trails me inexorably
Up this antique, shuddering iron spiral
To where, with fan or heater,
Teapot and OED,

Shorter lines are busy,
Where summer clouds disperse till
Pinned against the blue
By midday, and from wind-stuffed shirt or jeans
Ever sparser crystal
Drupelets of the view

(Sky, mountain, monastery,
Traffic blur and glint
From center town, the very
Pattern, upon my soul,
Of catalytic inter-
sections in the cell)

Dripping on flagstone, strew
A shade of velveteen,
Rags of moss to contemplate, come winter
—In the odd hour at least
When idle "contemplation"
Isn't the chimney's cue

To act. How often, here
At our bright airiest,
Upgusts of smut have peppered everything!
Kleo torn her hair—
Back gone the wash to soak;
Hose turned on choking plants;

Downstairs the poor old body
Brushed past, and *her* complaints,
For a despairing squint into that dark
Annex where the furnace
Belched and grumbled. Greedy,
Erotic little orc,

Was *it* what kept the house
Through January frost
Flushed with welcome floor-to-floor, the hosts'
Attire neo-Grecian,
Whatever sense of cost
Drowned in a splash of seltzer?

And was it to feed *its*
Facelessness that self-
Made men around the clock succumbed to fits
Of envy and aggression
In air-conditioned Tulsa
Or on the Persian Gulf?

—Where from his kiosk the Sheik
Saw tanker after tanker
Tiny as ants on the horizon play
Slow-motion hide-and-seek
With an obese, rust-cankered
Harem of white roses.

Think of the house that day
It stood complete but pupal,
Whom a first kiss, light and electric, rouses.

Think of the sudden thrill
Coursing through each vein;
The first meal, the first people.

Now think of that anemic
High-rise Cranach Venus
We saw how many years ago (in Munich?)
With Cupid at her heel—
Quiver and arrow-tip's
Pubescent thermostat.

Though they weren't much our types
—Too sallow, too immodest—
Not having found Greece yet, we spent a while
Admiring "values", "volumes",
"Relationship" of brat
To smiling, cat-faced goddess,

As if in that long hall
The work had been a wonder
Dreamlike, neat, abstractable from all
The moods and codes of matter,
Goings-on kept under
Her nodding ostrich hat.

NO

N_O *sooner are two mortals and four shades*
Assembled (yes, for all his escapades,
Robert has slipped into the last free slot)
Than Light suffuses the old schoolroom. Not
The lights we've seen according to thus far
—Spectral gems, first waters of a star—
But Light like bread, quotidian, severe,
Wiped of the sugar sprinkles of Vermeer;
Light gazing beyond thought as from a dark
Material cowl, abstracted Patriarch
All-seeing yet Itself unseen, until
Halted by peeling mullion or cracked sill;
Light next to which the radiance that pours
At six o'clock in Athens through our door's
Frosted glass—transfiguring a pair
Of sandals tossed upon the nearest chair—
Is a poor trot done into Modern Greek
From an Ursprache even angels speak
Half-comprehendingly BUT WHICH GAVE MY DEAR
US ALL TO UNDERSTAND THAT GOD WAS HERE
Among us? HUSH ENFANT   YES   *Light that keeps*
Its absent eye where one unruly tress
Of gold escapes, or the small bare foot peeps
Restlessly out from under a white dress:
For She is here as well, perched on a stall
Salvaged from Chapel for the servants' hall.
Below, the Brothers sit up neat as pins.
Gabriel—mantled in that air of shyness
None can resist, it seems, mortal or Highness—
Receives a Glance and gives one. So begins

The Last Lessons: *I*

WHA.   *Solemn in his rumpled seersucker*
        Steps forward. After a low bow to Her:

LORD MICHAEL SWITCHED ON A LIGHT
AND ILLUMINED OUR HUMAN MIND.
WE CALL HIS GODLY MAGIC DAY.
SINCE THEN, SUNUP TO SUNDOWN, HUMANKIND
HAS SET IDEA TO INNOCENCE, TO ALLAY
ITS FEAR & HOARD ITS HOPE AGAINST THE NIGHT.
LORD GABRIEL, HELP US NOW TO UNDERSTAND
THIS BLACK BEYOND BLACK. IS IT AN END TO DREAM?
AN HOURGLASS EMPTY OF SAND?
LORD GABRIEL, WHAT IS YOUR MAGIC'S NAME?

Gabr. SENIOR POET, IT IS TIME.
(Time! The forbidden, the forgotten theme—
We dip our poor parched faces in the stream.)
TWIN PARENTS, GLORIOUS UNIVERSAL TWINS,
TWINS EARTH & SEA, DEAR TWIN MY BROTHER LIGHT,
TWINS SCIENCE & MUSIC, TWIN SCRIBES, MADAME SECRET WEEDER
    & TWIN SECRET HAND,
WE SIX PAIRS ARE HERE AND A TWELFTH OF IT, HAIL!
MY THEME IS TIME, MY TEXT:
OF ALL DESTRUCTIVE IDEAS THE MOST DESTRUCTIVE IS THE IDEA OF
    DESTRUCTION.
DOCTOR?

Two of our three blackboards are now gray
With ghosts of half-erased symbol and word.
Tearing his eyes from the dark, gleaming third,
George rises overwhelmed, can scarcely say:
THEOS! O KYRIA!
Psy. CALM, DEAR GREEK.
A quick glance upward, sparkling into light.
AH BROTHER, WE GAVE HIS RACE WIT, & SEE HOW WEAK!
ENOUGH, CHILD. TAKE GABRIEL'S TEXT AND REMEMBER:
THE MOST DESTRUCTIVE OF ALL IDEAS IS THAT FEELING SETS IT
    RIGHT!

GK. GOD, O SPLENDID COMPANY, IMMORTALITY
WAS AFTER ALL A BANISHMENT OF TIME.

ANY ALLIANCE WITH ITS STILLED BLACK FORCES
MADE (THE EXPERIMENT OF ATLANTIS PROVES)
FOR A STILLBORN CHILD. AM I CORRECT, LORD GABRIEL?

Gabr. PROCEED.

GK. AN ADJACENT EXPERIMENT—

Gabr. LATER, SCIENTIST.

GK. *Brow shining from the dry rebuff.* UPON.
THE HOPE, THEN, OF A RACE PERFECTED AND
IMMORTAL WAS POSTPONED. MAN WAS HOWEVER
PERMITTED THE ONE GENE: A MEMORY TIC
AND, BEING OF GOD'S GENIUS, SET ABOUT
CONSTRUCTING A CHEMICAL SYSTEM FOR REACHIEVING
HIS IMMORTALITY. I, LORDS, WAS MADE
TO SPY UPON THAT WORK, ITS ORIGIN,
ITS FATE. YOU CALLED ME BACK WHEN IT WAS DONE:
TWICE IMMORTALITY PROVED A FATAL GIFT.
THIS THIRD TIME ITS RECIPIENT MUST BE
PREPARED. LORD GABRIEL, IN YOUR LABORATORY
I SAW THE 'THINNING PROCESS' & KNOW THAT THE NEXT
PHASE IS IMMINENT. LORD GABRIEL!
PRAY, SIR, SPARINGLY! WE MORTALS ARE
IN LOVE WITH EVEN OUR SHORT BRUTISH LIVES.
TAKE PAINS, PLEASE SIR, TO MAKE A PAINLESS CHANGE
OR ONE NOT SO TRAUMATIC THAT THE NEW
GENERATION SHUDDERS IN ITS DREAMS
ALTHOUGH AWAKENING IN PARADISE.

No illustrations. Frames once lit are dark,
And images Imagination brought
Wrapped like Lenten gods in purple Thought . . .
Only the voice, chalk's blind squeak and white mark.

Gabr. SCIENTIST, WHEN NEXT WE MEET TO STROLL THE GROUNDS OF OUR
    WORLD, TWO SCIENTISTS ADMIRING THEIR HANDIWORK,
    APPROVED BY GOD,
    YOU AS ONE OF THIS NEW GENERATION, AN ALPHA MAN, WILL TELL
    ME WAS I KIND OR NOT.

GK. *A whisper.* I PRAY I WILL LOVE YOU STILL.

Gabr. MAJESTIES! SIX OF US HERE ARE (WERE) CHRISTIAN, & ON THE DAY
          NAMED FOR MY TWIN CELEBRATED THEIR FAITH.
          SO ON THE MORROW SHALL WE TO CHURCH, SING SOME HYMNS,
          AND STUDY OLD MASTERS?

  Psy. *Risen with a shrug of charmed surrender.*
          RASCAL, HAVE YOUR WAY! YES, CALL THEM IN
          & WE WILL ON THE MORROW STUDY THEM.
          ADIEU BROTHER, ADIEU MY GREAT & DISTANT-MINDED TWIN.
          MORTALS & SHADES, ADIEU. OUR GABRIEL
          WILL RING THE STEEPLE BELL!
          (MADAME REMEMBER, 'WEAR A HAT')
          The room—as Psyche and the Angels go—
          Adjusts to our bewildered afterglow

For whom, like divers plunged abruptly back
Beyond their depth, this lesson was all black.

Time! No animal delusion now
But jet plume rising from the Shy One's brow:

Time the destroyer—; but can't Time renew
As well? WHO KNOWS WHAT TIME ALONE CAN DO,

TIME WITHOUT GOD OR NATURE   RUNNING WILD
IN THE BAD DREAMS & BRAINCELLS OF ITS CHILD?

I see . . . I *don't* see. Why should Time be black?
Why is it Gabriel's? MY BOY THINK BACK:

WE MUST PRESUME THAT THE ORIGINAL
PACT WAS BETWEEN GOD BIO & THE BLACK
The Black beyond black, past that eerie Wall—
PAST MATTER   BLACK OF THOUGHT UNTHINKABLE
Eater of energies, the suck and hum
Zeroing in upon Ideas until
They reach, like radium or plutonium,
Some half-way station to the void? THERE4
WHO FELL? Who fell? Not . . . the white angels! YES

No! The bat-angels fell—that was their constant
Refrain throughout Book I of *Mirabell*.
I SPEAK OF THE GREAT FALL FROM THE GALACTIC
PRECIPICE TO WHICH GOD SIGNALS BACK
Back to his Brothers, back to where he planned
The Greenhouse, long before he'd taken Matters
Into his own hand? PLATO HAD IT RIGHT?

POOR GEORGE, ENFANTS, TWICE SCOLDED: TRIED TO SPEAK
OF THE 'ADJACENT EXPERIMENT'   That pre-
Historical atomic blast in China?
Ephraim dropped (Book P) one scorching hint—
We left it where it fell. JIMMY I FEAR
GABRIEL INTENDS TO USE HIS FIRE
TO MAKE THE GREAT PLAIN GREATER. BUT REMEMBER:
MATTER HOLDS
                I'll try to . . . Do we get
The sense of Wystan's "humankind has set
Idea to Innocence?" Set? AS IN 'SET ONE'S MIND TO'
'SET TO MUSIC' 'SET IN MOTION' The word
Evoking in one swoop tenacity,
Harmony, resistance—
                    BUT O OUR QUEEN
MUM SUCH A COMFORT   RADIANT & SERENE
AND HERS THE LAST WORD   DJ: Those old masters?
XT BUDDHA MOHAMMED   THE GREEK PANTHEON
PLUS WAGNER'S CROWD MY DEARS! ALL HEAVEN ATHROB
PREPARING FOR THIS PAGEANT   AREN'T WE, BOB?

ME? O I'VE WHIPPED THE CHOIR INTO SHAPE
JM: Quite a send-off. ENFANT WE'LL BE 'SENT'
ALL RIGHT! For humankind, is what I meant.
DJ: It's true? They wash their hands of us?
Of people? After going to such lengths—
WE TOO ONCE DOTED FONDLY (EH CONFRERE?)
ON EARLY WORKS WE RATHER SQUIRM AT NOW
JM: We've threatened—therefore we must go—
Earth and Sea and Air. JIMMY   NO NO

It's only a "thinning process", George? THE KEY
WORD IS ALPHA   Yes, yes—"Brave New World".
MY BOY U GOT IT   WHAT OF THE OMEGAS?
3 BILLION OF EM UP IN SMOKE POOR BEGGARS?
Wystan, how *can* you? COURAGE: GABRIEL
KNOWS WHAT HE'S UP TO & (LIKE TIME) WILL TELL

Anyhow, we loved your poem. News
Like that is easier to take in rhyme.
TEENIEST BIT NERVOUS WITHOUT NOTES
BUT DID A 'KNEELING THETIS' TO THE MUSE

ENFANTS WE'RE FAGGED OUT   MEET IN THE ROYAL PEW?
SO LIKE A COUNTRY WEEKEND, EH? ADIEU

*

The Last Lessons: 2

Lights in the schoolroom. A confusing blaze:
Torches, votive candles, level rays
Of dawn or dusk, spokes winnowing the air
—In vain. Today the Great Twins are elsewhere.

Gabr.   HAIL, PRINCE!
　　　Gautama—saffron robes and sandalled feet,
　　　Palms together, plump as a nut-meat
　　　Goldenly fitted to its cosmic shell—
　　　Advances at the sound of a prayer bell.
Gaut.   HAIL, BROTHER DEATH.
Gabr.   PRINCE, OUR POET SAYS MAN SET IDEA TO INNOCENCE TO ALLAY HIS
　　　　FEARS & SAVE HIS FEEBLE FAITH.
　　　TWO HERE BEING MORTAL—FORGIVE THEIR SCANT ATTIRE, IT IS
　　　　WARM IN YOUR TEMPLE—
　　　(Church! We'd forgotten—horrors! and have sat
　　　Down in shorts and tank-tops. Well, that's that.)

CANNOT SEE YOUR OWN SPLENDOR RIVALLING EVEN MY DEAR TWIN'S
SUN.

YET ENOUGH. WE MEET IN THE VAST, FAST-ABANDONED COMPLEX OF
RELIGION,

HAS ANY HUMAN ENERGY PRODUCED SUCH A MULTITUDE OF
ARCHITECTURES?

PRINCE, AS OUR COMPANY STROLLS THROUGH THIS SUNSET-LIT
COMPOUND,

Gothic spires, pagodas, minarets,
Greek columns blazing from each picture-glass—
But it's all tinted like an oleograph
And somehow radiates irreverence.

SPEAK TO US.

Gaut. BROTHER LORDS, I WAS GIVEN BY GOD'S MESSENGER
MUCH THE SAME ORDER AS MY BROTHER JESU: TELL
MAN HOW IN HIS LIFE HE MAY ASCEND THE MOUNTAIN
OF EXPERIENCE BY CASTING EVER UPWARD
HIS MENTAL ROPES UNTIL SERENELY STANDING ON
PEAKS HIMALAYAN. I WENT DOWN, MY LORDS, AND SPOKE,
BETRAYING NEVER TO THE MULTITUDES THOSE TRUTHS
OF THE REPEATING SOUL. MY WRETCHED WHORE SHIVA
STOLE THESE FROM ME IN MY SLEEP AND BREATHED THEM EVEN
INTO THE EAR OF THE BRAHMIN COW. IT WAS OUT:
INSTEAD OF A GREAT EARTHBOUND CEREBRALITY
THEY SET GOING A PINWHEEL OF SPUTTERING LIVES
EACH MORE USELESS THAN THE LAST. I TRIED, LORD BROTHERS!
I BEG YOU SPEAK TO OUR FATHER ON MY BEHALF.

Gabr. PRINCE, IT IS SPENT, GOD'S POWER IN SUCH MATTERS.
YET HE AND WE LOOK KINDLY ON YOU. GO IN PEACE, & BECKON IN
THE JEW.

A lean, rabbinical young man in white
Bent under an imaginary weight
Stumbles forward, taking Michael's light
For God's at first; recovering, stands straight.

Jesus. FATHER GOD! YAHWEH? AH LORDS, MY BROTHERS, SHALOM!
His voice is hollow. Like the Buddha, he

> *Acts out his own exhausted energy.*
> WHAT A DEAD SOUND, MY NAME, IN HALF THE WORLD'S PULPITS.
> WE, AS MY PRINCELY BROTHER SAYS, SPIN DOWN. OUR WORDS
> LIKE GOD'S OWN PLANETS IN ONE LAST NOVA BURST AND
> GRAVITY STILLS & OUR POWER LOSES ITS PULL.
> HE & I CAME TO DELIVER LAWS, MINE FOR MAN
> TO SHAPE HIMSELF IN GOD'S IMAGE, BUDDHA'S FOR MAN
> TO BECOME GOD. WORDS, WORDS. BUT OUR MESSAGE, BROTHERS!
> I BEG OF YOU, INTERCEDE. BEFORE THE WINE RETURNS
> WHOLLY TO WATER LET OUR FATHER MAKE ME FLESH
> THAT I MAY A SECOND TIME WALK EARTH AND IMPLORE
> WRETCHED MAN TO MEND, REPAIR WHILE HE CAN. AMEN.

Gabr. DEAR SIMPLE PRIEST, STAY WITH US HERE IN HEAVEN, GREET YOUR
     FAITHFUL,
    GIVING THEM BY YOUR SWEET WAYS COURAGE TO RETURN IN YOUR
     STEAD.
    Shouldering his burden, Christ withdraws.
    NOW MUSICIAN, STEP FORTH!

> *From temple to 'temple of music' is but one*
> *Half-tone. Components of an Odeon:*
> *Golds, whites, red plush, kid gloves, unheard applause.*
> *Robert, lyre in hand, shyly ascends*
> *The podium.*

RM. LORDS, DEAR ONES, OUR POET LENDS
    ME WORDS TO WELCOME THIS MOST HONORED GUEST.
    Music. He wasn't joking—an offstage choir
    Sustains his first original melody:
    MASTER, THE CHARMED CIRCLE LISTENING
    ABOUT YOU HERE IS YOUR NEW RING
    —Plainsong phrase repeated a third higher
    Before its resolution into three
    Chords from the Overture to Parsifal
    Not lost on Wagner who, in flowing tie
    And velvets, stands before the company.

Wag. LORDS OF LIFE! AND YOU, ENVIABLE
    ABOUT-TO-BE COMPOSER, I MAKE BOLD

TO SAY THAT MUSIC'S RIVER GOLD STILL VEINS
A PEDESTAL THE GOD HAS TOPPLED FROM.
NONE NOW BUT THOR, SOLO PERCUSSIONIST, REMAINS
TO BEAT UPON EMMANUEL'S DRUM
A FAINT DIRGE FOR THAT FURRED & SAVAGE PANTHEON.
LORDS, MORTALS, COME SALUTE AT SET OF SUN
GREAT WOTAN, AS THE ICECAPS MELT!

Steps down

To strains of his own death march. Wastes of white
Are scored too briefly by a raven's flight.

Gabr.   COME SPRITE, QUICKSILVER MESSENGER,
TUBE HELD IN EARTH'S DRY MOUTH, COME MERCURY MY OWN!
WHAT, ALONE? YOUR SNOWY HEIGHT
DOWNTRODDEN BY THE PICNICKER?
QUICK TELL US, YOU WHOSE FACE
GLEAMS WITH THE MAGIC STILL, OF THAT OLYMPIAN RACE!

Out from the mirror (Robert blinks astonished)
Slips a figure only slightly tarnished—
Wings quivering on silver helmet, wings
At silver heel—and silver-throated sings:

AH LORD GABRIEL
THOUGH MAN WAS ABLE
TO CONJURE US
FROM HIS LOOKING GLASS

TIME RAN THAT RACE,
THE HORROR WELLD
UP & ACROSS
OUR SHINING FIELD:

DEEPSEATED DAMAGE,
A BLACKLY TICKING
OVERTAKING
OF EYE & IMAGE

WHENCE WE ARE NOWHERE
LIKED OR DISLIKED,
ONLY SHOULD FAIR
OR STRONG REFLECT

DO WE OUTGAZE
FOR A BRIEF SPELL EYES
BLIND TO THE PILFER
OF OUR FLAT SILVER

Flown. Silence. Then a grave, deliberate
Glissando of the cup to rainbow's end:
ABCDEFGHIJKLMNOPQRSTUVWXYZ

DJ. What's all this?
JM. Looks like the alphabet.
Gabr. THE NEW MATERIALS, YOUNG POET, FOR A NEW FAITH:
ITS ARCHITECTURE, THE FLAT WHITE PRINTED PAGE
TO WHICH WILL COME WISER WORSHIPPERS IN TIME
The Brothers go.

        NO ROBERT IT WAS NOT
REYNOLDS WRAP (THE HERMETIC LEOTARD
STUNNING MY DEARS AS WAS YR NUDITY)
Too awful of us . . . BROWS WERE RAISED MM'S
HIT HER HAT Describe it? A SMART DARK SAILOR
GEORGE SO TACTFUL WORE A YARMULKE
And Robert? ALL IN MEISTERSINGER WHITE,
HIS WALTER EGO AS HE CALLS IT. SWEETLY
SUNG, DEAR BOB (Robert, glowing with pride,
Dictates his tune—which, tried out by JM
At the piano, is pronounced a gem.)

Mohammed wasn't there? INDEED STOOD WAITING
SCIMITAR IN HAND FOR THE NEXT LESSON.
HE IS THE ONE STILL VERY MUCH ALIVE
FORCE IN THAT CROWD One, also, of the Five.
THAT TOO. BUT ARAB FAITH & POLITICS
COMBINE INTO A FAIRLY HEADY MIX

Tomorrow's lesson is all his? A DUEL
WITH GABRIEL? A WRESTLING MATCH FOR FUEL?

Strange how the energies of the Five so far
Resist exhaustion. THEY ARE OF THE LAB
ENFANTS, & MOVE TOO GLADLY FROM LIFE TO LIFE
TO HARDEN INTO IDOLS. NO IVORY
EINSTEINS OR MOZARTS ON A CRUCIFIX.
NEITHER MUST THEY RECRUIT BY JUGGLERS' TRICKS
VAST FOLLOWINGS FROM THE BUREAUCRACY
Yet Christ called God his Father— & SO HE IS.
THE FIVE HOWEVER ARE MORE LITERALLY
'MEDIATORS', & GABRIEL'S, WITH OF COURSE
GOD B'S APPROVAL   Or the Monitor's!
JIMMY DAVE   Yes, George? THE MONITOR
(RM & I HAVE COME TO REALIZE)
CANNOT BE GABRIEL BUT FROM (M) NEXT DOOR
MUST SUPERVISE THE LAB   A stronger power
Than God or Nature? WAS IT GOD U HEARD?

Why yes—the Brothers told us— DO THEY KNOW?
ALL CONSCIOUSNESS WAS BANISHED ROUND YOU 4
HEARING THAT SONG —of the Black God? God A
For Adversary? OR MASTER? OR 'CREDITOR'
WHO LENT BRAIN-MATTER ITS PROVERBIAL GRAY?
AND PRESSES NOW AGAINST THE WHITE OF MIND
UNLIMITED   UNREPULSED LIGHT   THE BLINDING
REVEILLE: IMAGINATION   METAPHOR
SHATTERED BY WHITE REASON! IS THE BLACK
HOLE A REFUGE? Where's the nearest one?—
Anything to duck *this* light!
                              COME ON
ENFANTS   WE'LL SEE WHAT THEY WANT US TO SEE & A BIT
(AT LESSON 10) BEYOND THEM   As before.
But this time *past* God to the Monitor?
HUSH NOW
              PETRODOLLARS IN TOMORROW'S

COLLECTION BOX?

MY BLOKE HERE GENUFLECTING

AS IF HIS SPINE ITCHED   HAH!

OLD HABITS MY DEAR

GIVE ONE COURAGE IN THE FACE OF FEAR.

PACE!

★

The Last Lessons: 3

Faint camel bells. Dry flute. One black-framed scene
All blazing desert, not a blade of green.
Above the carpet God's magnificent
Somber glory throbs as through a tent.
Our Lady, veiled, a checkerboard of wraps,
Seems . . . aged? withdrawn? Just wearier perhaps.

Gabr.   OUR POET ASKED: THIS BLACK BEYOND BLACK, IS IT A STOP TO
   DREAM?

POET, NO, FOR IT IS A DREAM.

IS IT THE HOURGLASS DRAINED OF TIME?

NO, FOR IT IS THE HOURGLASS IN WHICH SAND RUNS UP!

Then, as we stare, figuring that one out:

FATHER, TWIN STAR, BROTHERS, MORTALS, LET US BE MERRY!

HERE IS A ROUGH ONE, A TENTMAKER (EH POET?) & A WARRIOR.

COME, HIRAMBASHID!

An erect personage, blackbrowed, with broad
Moustaches, swaggers up—recoiling awed.

Moh.   O GOD, O ALLAH BEN ALLAH! LORDS, MEN, WOMEN!

HERE I AM, JUST AS YOU SEE ME, A SIMPLE MAN

(He has already regained confidence)

NEITHER ALL MEEK LIKE MY PROPHET BROTHER JESU

WHO HAD NO USE FOR WOMEN, NOR BRAINFILLED LIKE MY

PRINCELY BROTHER—WHAT MAN COMPLAINS OF A WHORE? BAH!

NO, JUST AS YOU SEE ME. AND BELIEVE ME, MASTER GOD,
JUST AS SURPRISED AS ANY MAN WHEN MY VISION CAME.
ME? ME TO SAY ALL THAT! WHY, I COULD NOT READ,
HONORABLE SCRIBES, IMAGINE! WELL, I WENT OUT,
SPOKE. IT WAS EASY! JESUS, YOU SEE, HAD A DIFFERENT
WORLD TO TRY TO WIN OVER TO LOVE & MERCY.
JEWS ARE GREEDY, ACCOUNTANTS, PILING UP DEBTS,
BALANCING THESE WITH PROFITS: A SIN, A GOOD DEED.
HEAVEN ON EARTH NOT LIKELY TO ATTRACT MY ROVERS!
BUDDHA, THO A GREAT FIGHTER, SPOKE TO SUCH MULTITUDES,
THEIR VERY NUMBERS MEANT LEAN BELLIES. MIND? A SAD
MESSAGE FOR MEN RIDING HORSES THE LIVELONG DAY.
'TELL THEM OF HEAVEN' I DID, MY & THEIR KIND.
DO THIS, YOU GET TO NUMBER 1: A SKINNY
BITCH ON YR LAP & AN ETERNITY
OF THIN SOUP. DO SOMETHING BETTER, & NUMBER 2:
BETTER RUMP, BETTER GRUB, AND SO ON UP. BROTHERS,
SIMPLE AS I AM, I RAN OUT OF HEAVENS AT 7
& FROM WHAT I'VE SEEN OF 9 THERE'S NOT MUCH TO CHOOSE.
YES, WE ARE FIGHTERS, YOU GOD MADE US THAT.
OURS IS THE CRADLE OF MAN, HE SPRINGS UP GUTSY,
READY FOR A KILL & A PLUMP WOMAN ON HI

A woman's hand upraised, one flashing look
Of soot-and-emerald over the yashmak.
Psyche had charmed us. Now we see another
More dumbfounding facet of the Mother.

Nat.   YES YES, WE KNOW. ENOUGH, WILY MOHAMMED.
      DRIVE YOUR TENTPEG DEEPER INTO THAT FATEFUL SAND. SPEAK!

Moh.   O? SO THE GAME IS UP? *Biting his lip.*
      YES, THE BLACK. I DID NOT MENTION THE BLACK.
      THESE MORTALS?

Nat.   SPEAK!

Moh.   GOD, UNDER OUR SANDFLOORED TENT
      THERE IS A BUBBLING OF LOST GREEN. YOU TOLD ME THEN:
      'THIN OUT YOUR RACE AND KEEP IT THIN WITH BLOODSHED,
      FOR YOU SIT ON TIME MADE BLACK.' I DID THAT, GOD,
      I DO STILL, APPEARING IN DREAMS & STIRRING TROUBLE

Nat.   MOHAMMED, THE BLACK!
Threatens to unveil. A chain of shocks.
Rewound on Gabriel's cassette, the flute
Gibbers insanely. The framed world in flight.
Mohammed kneeling, eyeballed like an ox.

Moh.   IT CALLS TO US 'COME BACK TO THE HEAVENS SPEEDING
INTO O, COME TO THE LOST BLACK TREES, THE ANIMALS
SINGING SONGS OF LOST IMMORTALITY, COME'
THESE SUCK US DOWN   THE SAND RISES   WE GO
TO MEET THAT BLACK   O GOD! EFFENDI, SUCH A LOSS   MEN,
WHAT DOES A MAN WANT? A PLUMP
Vanishing.

Gabr.   GO PROPHET. YOUR RACE DOES OUR WORK: FROM THINND TO
       THINNER.

JM.   Does your work by plundering Earth's resources?

Gabr.   NO, POET. BY PREPARING ITS LAST, HOLY WAR.
Night, windless, clear. Beneath a crescent moon
Thousands of little whetted scythes appear
With each slow forward breath of the great dune.
THERE IS THE HOURGLASS. CURVED LIKE A SWORD, IT STABS ITS
       POINT INTO THE DESERT OF MAN'S FAITH
& FROM THE WOUND WE (EH SCIENTIST?) WILL SPRING, A NEW
       MINERVA!
SO. FOUR SAPPD ENERGIES AND THIS, A SAPPING ONE.
MUSICIAN?

Robert wears black. In either hand, a staff
From which a long black tattered banner trails
Groundward. These to represent the souls
His chant evokes, and ghostly music (half
Silence, half a Sino-Viennese
Salad of scraped nerves) accompanies.

RM.   EXALTED AND HUMAN, I BRING YOU THESE LOST CHORDS.
THIS: THE JOYOUS CHILD TOSSED IN CENTURION ARMS,
THE DARLING OF A COURT. HE FROM YOUR LAB
LORD GABRIEL, HAD EVERY OPPORTUNITY
YET ONE DAY, STARTLED BY   WHAT? A CROONING WHISPER?

A SONG FROM AN UNSEALED CRACK? CHANGED, CHANGED
INTO A SOUL SO DISTORTED HE CAN NO LONGER
BE USED. LOOK. PITY POOR CALIGULA.
PITY, SIRS. THE MELODY HE HEARD
IS A MUSIC THAT INCREASINGLY LEAKS THROUGH . . .
HE HEARD IT FIRST. *Lifting the second banner.*
THIS, & HIS MUSIC-MASTER WAGNER! IS ANOTHER
FOREVER GONE, SIRS, FOR YOUR PURPOSES.

DJ.   Hitler—he's here?
MM.   IN EFFIGY, ENFANT.
EASIER TO MANIFEST THAN ASH.

RM.   LOOK WELL ON THESE
RAGS OF SOULS DIPPED IN A BLACKENING DYE.
GOD, MAJESTY AND LORDS,
LET ME NOW EXPLAIN TO MY FELLOW MORTALS
THE SAD DISHARMONIES.
THREE 'TIMES' OBTAIN:
THIS FICTIVE SPACE WE HERE INHABIT IS
THE STOP TO TIME. WHAT YOU, DEAR SCRIBE & HAND,
NOW LIVE IN IS TIME'S FORWARD RUN. THE BLACK
BEYOND BLACK IS OF TIME SET RUNNING BACK.
THESE SOULS WERE CAUGHT IN THE FRICTION, STRIPPED LIKE GEARS,
GIVEN VAST POWERS THAT COLLAPSING WERE
SUCKED DRY OF EVERY HUMAN DENSITY.
JUST AS CERTAIN STARS, SO CERTAIN SOULS.
POTENT AND RICH SOULS LARGELY, PRIMED FOR USE,
THEY QUICKEN TIME, MAKE EDDIES IN THE STREAM.
THEIR LEADERSHIP INSTRUCTION (THIN! KEEP CLEAR!)
SPEEDS UP, BECOMING: TERMINATE! THEY HEAR
ANOTHER SIREN SINGING. PITY THEM.
FOR WHO AMONG US HAS NOT CAUGHT A DISTANT
SEEP OF THE VIRULENT STRAIN THROUGH THE ODD SPLIT
SECOND BEFORE GABRIEL AND HIS LORD
BROTHERS BRING US THE FIRE IN THE HEARTH,
THE WELCOME MORN, THE SMELL OF EARTH?
Ending on a clear G major chord.

Gabr. AH MUSICIAN, YOU & OUR SENIOR POET THINK THERE IS PUNISHMENT
AND MERCY? THINK SIN EXISTS, RIGHT & WRONG?
NO. THOSE MEASURES ARE BLANK. KNOWING NO TIME, WE DO NOT
SENTENCE VAGRANT SOULS BUT SWEEP THEM
(SHH SHH THERE IS NO HELL) UNDER THE (M)
CARPET TO ETERNAL IDLENESS. GOD, FATHER, MAM,
LET ME BRING DOWN TODAY'S SUN, & US TWELVE
MEET AGAIN TOMORROW AT THIS TIME.
Exeunt.

Robert, you were Orfeo
Singing to the damned! WELL   YES & NO

CD HE MY DEARS HAVE SWEATED, SUCH A LAKE!
I'M OFF: A MINICOURSE IN ARABIC

Wystan—oil well? Celestial Coal-sack?
Hourglass? Won't *someone* please explain the Black?

CHILDREN IN WYSTAN'S ABSENCE LET MAMAN
ATTEMPT A SMALL SOCRATIC DIALOGUE.
WHAT COLOR IS THE GRASS? Er, green. INDEED
THE GREEN OF NATURE. BUT AT SUMMER'S END?
Yellow, or tan. MOWN? THROWN ON THE COMPOST HEAP?
After a year, you'd get a sort of brown
Uniform mess. A PLUS   THE AGENT HERE?
The various chemicals, or— Or Time!
WHAT COLOR IS THE BLOOD? Red, but of course
Drying brown, black . . . I see! The dinosaurs,
Fafners of those green aeons, coil by coil
Concentrated to deep coal, to oil:
Time! A gusher—blackest aquavit!
BRAVO ENFANTS   WE'VE DRILLED & DRILLED FOR IT

NOW (GEORGE HERE) IN AMONG EARTH'S TREASURES ARE
THE INFRA-TREASURES OF THE MONITOR:
NOT FORWARD TIME COMPRESSED (COMBUSTIBLE
OILCAN OF 'THINNER') BUT ATOMIC BLACK

COMPRESSED FROM TIME'S REVERSIBILITY,
THAT IDEA OF DESTRUCTION WHICH RESIDES
BOTH IN MAN & IN THE ACTINIDES.
PART OF THE GREENHOUSE, FOR (THO MATTER HOLDS)
THESE FORKED TONGUES FLICKER FROM ITS OILS & GOLDS.

Meaning what? DJ: Uranium's
An element in Nature. From pitchblende—
DAVE PRECISELY   THE GREAT ANCHOR STONES
HAD BEEN IRRADIATED, SO THE DINOSAURS . . .
Were radioactive mutants—! At the end
Electric and atomic energies
Subtly interfused lay down together
—How it all fits! Uranium, we gather,
Lives on even in our arteries.

THE CABLES SNAPPED. SNAPPER: THE MONITOR?
THUS MAKING SOURCES OF 1) NATURAL POWER
& 2) UNNATURAL. POWER TO SUCK THE EARTH
EGG TO AN O   But Matter *holds.* ITS BIRTH,
RESISTANCE   DON'T FORGET THAT FIRST THIN THIN
PASTE   The Greenhouse from the start had been
An act of resistance? JIMMY YES   A PLUS!
OR DISOBEDIENCE   GOD AS PROMETHEUS?
NOW THAT MAN TAPS THIS 2ND POWER, ONE WELL
TOO MANY & PUFF! Puff? THE WHOLE FRAIL EGGSHELL
SIMPLY IMPLODING AS THE MONITOR'S
BLACK FILLS THE VACUUM MOTHER N ABHORS

It all fits. But the ins and outs deplete us.
Minding the thread, losing the maze, we curse
Language's misleading apparatus.
For once I rather sympathize with Pound
Who "said it" with his Chinese characters—
Not that the one I need here could be found.

MY DEAR TOO STYLISH IN YR THINKING FEZ!
PLATO & I ALIKE ENTHRALLED BY ISLAM.

WE'VE MET THRU E (YR 'TEMPERAMENTAL MOSLEM')
A SLOEEYED SUFI (13 CENT) WHO SEZ
THE FIGURE IN OUR CARPET SHALL I TELL?
Please! —Two pages later: I SUGGEST
THE BITS MY BOY THAT GRAB U BE COMPRESSED
INTO THE SORT OF 'GEM' U DO SO WELL
Hm . . .

★

As when the scribe of some ornate
Bismillah ("in the name of Allah") sees
No doctrine bolder than calligraphy's

—Whose backward reader, left to right, will note
Ism (world of names, empty phenomena)
Within the broadly tendered palm of *ba*

(Initial meaning, here, God B knows what)
Placed beneath which a diacritical dot
Closes its fist on *that*, and there we are!—

My characters, this motley alphabet,
Engagingly evade the cul-de-sac
Of the Whole Point, dimensionless and black,

While, deep in bulging notebooks, drawn by it,
I skim lost heavens for that inky star.

The Last Lessons: 4

All twelve assembled. Nature once more in white,
A sheaf of poppies at Her earth-stained feet.

Gabr. VALIANT GOD, FATHER, TWIN NATURAL STAR,
  AND LORDS MY BROTHERS, CLEVER & INQUIRING MORTALS, STUDENTS
    ALL:

MUCH IS WRIT AROUND OUR CLASSROOM'S BLACKBOARD WALLS,
  MUCH PERHAPS TOO EASILY ARRIVED AT.
SIN? A TOPIC HASTILY DROPT. BUT NOW THE SENIOR POET, IVIED
  WITH OLD ANGLICAN TRADITION, HAS BEGGD THIS FURTHER
  WORD ON IT.
AND SO! TAKE UP THE CHALK & WRITE THE NAME OF THE ONE SIN:
PAIN. PAIN GIVEN, PAIN RECEIVED.
PAIN YOU MUST UNDERSTAND IS THE ONLY CHILD OF TIME &
  FEELING.
WITHOUT THESE PARENTS, THESE OEDIPAL TENSIONS,
PAIN (SORROW, HUNGER, FEAR) WOULD HOLD NO SWAY.

JM.   But, Lord, then *you* are linked to pain through Time
       Which is your magic, just as ours is Feeling—
Gabr. BLACK MAGICS BOTH, YOUNG SCRIBE, THEY ARE BANISHT FROM OUR
  HEAVEN. BANISHT ALAS TO EARTH.
NOW, KEEPING OUR CLASS SWEPT OF COBWEBBY DETAIL, A FINAL
  BLOOM OF CHALK AS WE DISCUSS THE UNWRITTEN SIN:
MAN'S THEFT OF GOD'S MATERIALS. WHO WILL BRING HIM TO
  COURT?
MM. LORD, MAY I BE MAN'S PORTIA?
Gabr. SPEAK, WEEDRESS, AND EXPLAIN:
HOW IS IT THAT MAN PLAYS SO FREELY WITH OUR ATOMS,
SO CARELESSLY PLUNGES INTO THE WATCHWORKS OF OUR GENETIC
  CELL?

MM. FATHER, MOTHER, BROTHER LORDS & FRIENDS,
WE COME, WE MORTALS, FROM AN AVID WEED
CALLED CURIOSITY. IN YOUR GARDEN, MAJESTY,
I HAVE SEEN & HEARD THE BUSY SECRETS BUZZING
LEAF TO LEAF: 'AHA, THAT'S HOW SHE DID IT!'
THESE FEED US, YOU FEED THEM. I THEREFORE CLAIM
THAT YOU WANT THESE SECRETS OUT. WITNESS OUR FAITHFUL
FAULTLESS GREEK, YOUR VERY OWN. NOW LORDS,
WHY? IS IT NOT THAT WE, MANKIND, MUST DO
IMMORTAL WORK? AND WHEN HEAVEN, LIKE A LOVELY
MINT-SCENTED FRESHENING SETTLES & EARTH BECOMES
PARADISE, MY LORDS, WILL NOT OUR RACE OF THIEVES

HAVE EMERGED AS THE ELDERS IN A RACE OF GODS?
DEFENCE RESTS.

Gabr. FATHER? STAR? BROTHERS?

As if caught out, They smile at one another.
Nature lifts a poppy to Her cheek.
(Ah, we are all Her children, so to speak—
How touching when Maria called her Mother.)
NOT GUILTY. BUT, PERSUASIVE GARDENER,
LET US APPROACH THE VERGE &, SHELTERINGLY GLASSD,
TURN OUR ACCOMPLICE EYES UPON A MANMADE BLAST.
0 9 8 7 6 5 4 3 2 1

During the countdown we touch Earth, sink then
Beneath it. Mummied rivers dry as bone,
Tamped towns, lost species, in an earthenware
Terrine of suffocation, layer on layer.
The cup has stopped at the Board's extreme limit.
This 'test' is underground, larger than planned,
For an immense—
                    The cup returns to "&".

NOTHING OF USE SURVIVES. LESSON 4 ON SIN & SANITY.
NEXT, MAKING SENSE OF OUR SEEMING CARELESSNESS, WILL BE AT 5
        A SOBERING JOURNEY INTO THE REMOTEST PAST,
THE ORIGIN OF PROMETHEAN LEGEND, WHEN ALAS THE VERDICT
        WAS: GUILTY
Here, without "exiting", the angel falls
Silent.

        SIRS? WERE YOU HARMED? No, Uni—were you?
(Dumb question.) Was there some sort of explosion?
MERCILESS FIRE! OUR FRIENDS REEMERGE
THRU CHOKING AIR
                I THINK JIMMY THE BLAST
WAS OVERDONE   GOD HELP THE ASIAN PLAINS
WE DID IT UNDER! First you took the down
Elevator— YES   INTO EARTH   A PURE

WHITE LIGHT, THE NEGATIVE OR 'EYE' OF BLACK
BURST ON US   The *bad* white, the metaphor-
Shattering light? AMORAL   YES MY DEARS
& AFTERWARDS, STEADILY THRU THE ASCENT, QM
GAVE GABRIEL SUCH A LOOK, OUR LESSON (PUFF!)
ENDED. MICHAEL SPOKE THE LAST WORDS, G
HAVING GONE OUT ON THE EXIT OF QUEEN MUM.
AS GEORGE SAYS, SHE ABHORS THAT VACUUM
The pace throughout was sluggish—a reluctance
In us? ENFANTS WE FANCY GABRIEL
DID NOT HAVE TOTAL CLEARANCE FOR HIS BANG
AS IF, OF 2 MINDS, HE THEN THOUGHT: O, HELL!
DJ IN PAIN?
        Not really, just a twinge—
Pain, after all, was part of today's lesson.
(But in the night his jaw will throb and swell,
And by tomorrow afternoon Maria's
Closing couplet has become prophetic:)
MAMAN KNOWS BETTER. TIME NO DOUBT
AN AWFUL TRUTH & TOOTH ALIKE WERE OUT!

*

The Last Lessons: 5

Gabr.   BROTHERS, ARE YOU WITH ME? DO YOU GO ALONG ON THIS LESSON?
        OUR FATHER AND HIS HEAVENLY TWIN DO NOT. IT IS A PAINFUL
          MEMORY, A SHALL WE SAY LOST TOOTH?
        DJ nods, rubs his aching, mending jaw.
Mich.   WE COME.
        The schoolroom darkens. This is the purely 'told'
        Lesson. Nothing will move except the mind;
        Nothing, except Gabriel's voice, unfold
        In black immediacy, safe and sound.

Gabr.   PUPILS, AS WE BOARD THE LUMBERING BLACK WAGON & MAKE OUR
        WAY THRU EONS OF A BLASTED TRACK,

LET US REVIEW THAT HISTORY. IN THE GALACTIC COUNCILS THE
    CHARTER WAS GIVEN:
'DOWN INTO YOUR COOLING UNIVERSE WITH ITS SINGLE HABITABLE
    STAR, BROTHER, GO. IT IS YOURS.
TAKE WHAT & WHOM YOU NEED. AND THIS COMPACT:
MY UNIVERSE IS AS ONE WITH ALL. NOTHING IN IT WILL BE ENEMY
    TO OUR REALMS.'
THEN ONLY THE DISTANT CRY OF LIGHT: 'FATHER, COME!'

IN HIS JOY, HIS CRAFTSMAN'S EAGERNESS TO BEGIN, OUR FATHER
    TOOK FRICTION INTO HIS HANDS
AND FROM A STARRY MIX GROUND UP A PASTE OF LIVING MATTER,
    MUCH AS THE BAKER KNEADS HIS DOUGH.
YEAST OF LIFE! DOOR FLUNG OPEN INTO THE FURNACE, OUT CAME
    A LOAF WE'VE ET ON SINCE.
THE HEAT OF THAT DOUGH, THE CONTRARY RUB OF THE FRICTION?
WHERE DID THE FOREIGN GERM COME IN? OR WAS THE GERM IN THE
    SAND WHICH SPRINKLED THE SEALS OF THE COMPACT?

THE GREAT GREEN CANVASES! THE BAKER TURND PAINTER, SCULPTOR!
    O THE BLISS OF ONE'S OWN WORLD, THE GODLINESS OF
    CREATION!
(WATCH! HERE'S A BUMP FROM AN EARLY MOUNTAIN CHAIN TURND
    PEBBLE.)

NOW THE FIRST CREATURE. WE HAVE NOT MENTIOND HIM BEFORE.
YES, THE FIRST: A WINGED MAN. HE ROSE UP.

DJ.   *Atlantis* was first. The centaurs—

JM.   It would seem
    This is the creature of the Chinese plain.
    Haven't we been wondering about him?

Gabr.   MY BROTHERS, WE TOO HAVE SO MANY TIMES WONDERD! 'GABRIEL,
    DID YOU KNOW? MICHAEL, DID YOU SEE A . . . SPARK? A
    GLANCE? A WHAT IN THAT CREATURE'S EYE?
    RAPHAEL, YOU? PERCEPTIVE EMMANUEL, DID YOU SUSPECT THAT WE
    HAD WITNESSED OUR FATHER'S CAIN-LIKE ERROR?'

HE FLOURISHT.

GOD WAS ODDLY OF TWO ASPECTS: PROUD, DOUBTFUL. HE HID HIS
THOUGHTS WITH FRESH ACTIVITY.
WE WERE SUMMOND TO ANOTHER GREEN SURFACE: 'I WILL MAKE
HIM A FELLOW CREATURE.'
AND THIS TIME WE ALL STOOD BACK PLEASD: AN OPENEYED EAGER
THING LOOKD UP AT US. WOBBLED IN A COLTISH BOW.

NOTHING 'PASSD'. TIME STOOD STILL IN THE CLOCKWORK OF THEIR
GENES.
THE WINGED ONE WAS EVER AT WORK, EVER WITH SOMETHING
TUCKD HASTILY OUT OF SIGHT.
WE FOUR FLANKING OUR FATHER CAME TO HIS CENTRAL CITY, A
VAST OBSIDIAN PILE GLEAMING ON THE PLAIN RUTTED BY HIS
MACHINES.
'CHILD, FOR I STILL CALL YOU THAT, WHAT IS IN YOUR MIND?
LOOK INTO MY EYES!'
WAS OUR FATHER EASILY DECEIVD? ISN'T THE YOUNG PARENT
ALWAYS . . . FATUOUS?
TO US THEN, 'COME.' AND THAT WAS OUR LAST VISIT TO THIS SAD
MISTAKEN CHANGELING CHILD.

WE NEVER TIRED OF THE OTHER,
AND WITH HIM ONE DAY LOOKD UP . . . YES, FROM THIS SPOT, YOU
SEE IT IS A RISE . . .
Cup pausing at the Board's edge now recoils.
GREAT BLINDING LIGHT!
OUR FATHER SUMMOND HIS POWERS, THREW UP A SHIELD OF
POSITIVE MATTER (THE BUDDHA'S HIMALAYAS) & WE FROM
WHERE WE COWERD, UP UP IN GOD'S WAKE RISING
AT LAST LOOKD DOWN ON HALF OUR MASTER'S WORK FLATTEND,
BLACK.
'IT IS WELL, I COULD NOT HAVE ENDED HIM MYSELF.'

THE OTHER CREATURE PROSPERD: 'GOD, FATHER, COME SEE WHAT I
HAVE FASHIOND!'
WE LOOKD INTO THOSE SELFSAME RED EYES. STRAIGHTEND.
AND OUR FATHER SAID: I KNOW WHAT IS PAIN

DJ. Red eyes? Whose?
JM. The wingèd man. The Cain—
Now as the centaurs' messenger, into their green
Arcadia (and our own cells) born again . . .

Gabr. THE REST? LET US REST. STAND HERE, NOT TOO FAR FROM OUR
    WAGON, & CONSIDER THESE RUIND PROSPECTS, THESE PAINFUL
    MEMORIES
A drawn-out sigh escapes the darkened angel.
BROTHER GENII, IT IS AN EASY IMAGE TO SPEAK OF GOD'S MATTER,
    ANTIGOD'S ANTIMATTER.
THAT IS THE ODD THING ABOUT LANGUAGE. THE PARTICULAR FAILS
    TO EXPLAIN ITS OWN WORKINGS.
(This lesson, then, in lieu of a week's lecture
On the fine points of atom- or cell-structure?)
WE MUST ASSUME OUR FATHER WAS GIVEN A LIMITED CHARTER.
FOR THERE IS, SIMPLY, NO 'QUARREL' BETWEEN LIGHT & SHADOW,
    SO LONG AS MATTER STANDS BETWEEN THEM.
NOW BACK INTO THE WAGON. WE'VE LAID OUR WREATH ON THIS
    TOMB.
1 2 3 4 5 6
The schoolroom brightens as the cup ascends
To Intuition, and the lesson ends:

TOMORROW (HOW REFRESHING HERE OUT OF THE SULPHUR MISTS)
    WE WILL TALK OF THE WAY GOD SPEAKS,
HE TO US, WE TO YOU,
AND HOW THIS TOO HELPS HOLD IT BACK.
The Brothers go.

     DJ: So *that's* it. What
A tale . . . but why blame God? Didn't the angels
Make the wingèd man in their own image?
JM: If so, then God accepted him.
What struck me was how fondly Gabriel
Spoke of the creature from Atlantis—whom
Michael had mocked for its shy hanging head
And great blank eyes. DAVE JIMMY AS U'VE GUESSED

IT COMES DOWN TO THE NATURE OF THE ATOM:
'FIRSTBORN WAS CHAOS' THE BLACK VOLATILE HALF
Bat wings unfurled against the light— INDEED.
THEN MINUTES ONLY AFTER THE BIG BANG
CAME THE FIRST NUCLEI OF HELIUM
Matter's white half? DEPENDABLE, (M) 4 FOOTED
Like Uni!
          SIRS? It's nothing, Uni. (Wistfully
Nuzzles Robert and trots out.)
                    I THINK
THE 2 ASSESSMENTS OF A CREATURE LACKING
SHAPING HANDS MY BOY REFLECT THE 2
KINDS OF CRITIC, I.E. GABRIEL WHO
CONSIDERS THE DOER'S MANNER, & MICH WHO LOOKING
TOWARD THE THING DONE IMAGINES ITS RECEPTION

So here we are, back at a pedigree—
Uni's or Mirabell's—that can be traced
To motes and gases, outermost thin paste
Of life, and innermost dichotomy
RESOLVED BY MATTER, EVEN BY THE STUFF
OF OUR 'CREATION' WHICH (EXAMPLE) BRINGS
WM CARLOS WM'S THOUGHTFUL THINGS
& THE COLD VIRGIN VERB OF MALLARME
TOGETHER, & RELIABLY ENOUGH
HOLDS BACK THE NOTHING WE HAVE FOUND TO SAY
ONLY IN OUR WORST MOMENTS. THIS ESTATE
WHERE WE ARE GUESTS (OR CAPTIVES?) WD HAVE BEEN
GHOSTLY & UNENDURABLE WITHOUT
THE FRIENDLY WHINNY FROM THE PADDOCK GATE
OR CRY OF THE HERALDIC BIRD THAT PREENS
ABOVE THE MOAT   But if it's all a fable
Involving, oh, the stable and unstable
Particles, mustn't we at last wipe clean
The blackboard of these creatures and their talk,
To render in a hieroglyph of chalk
The formulas they stood for? U MY BOY
ARE THE SCRIBE   YET WHY? WHY MAKE A JOYLESS THING

OF IT THRU SUCH REDUCTIVE REASONING?
ONCE HAVING TURNED A FLITTING SHAPE OF BLACK
TO MIRABELL, WD YOU MAKE TIME FLOW BACK?
SUBTRACT FROM HIS OBSESSION WITH 14
THE SHINING/DIMMING PHASES OF OUR QUEEN?
CONDEMN POOR UNI TO THE CYCLOTRON
AFTER THE GREENS U'VE LET HIM GALLOP ON?
Dear Wystan, thank you for reminding me
The rock I'm chained to is a cloud; I'm free.

DJ: How touching Gabriel was . . . AH YES
HE IS WISDOM SADLY ARRIVED AT, PROUDLY KEPT:
NUCLEAR COMMANDER OF THE GREENHOUSE,
HIS STOCKPILE UNDER LOCK, HIS POWDER DRY
After the illustration. O WELL   WHY
TELL THE HISTORY OF A BOMB? ENACT IT!
Yesterday's explosion wasn't by
Any chance an *actual* one? INDEED:
UNDERGROUND SIBERIA   (And we'll read
In tomorrow's *Herald* of just such a test
Picked up by seismographs throughout the West.)

Maria hasn't spoken. NO ENFANTS
TOMORROW A LONG SILENCE WILL BE BROKEN

★

The Last Lessons: 6

All present. Schoolroom tidied overnight.
Gabr. MAY I SPEAK FOR YOU, FATHER?
Intuiting his answer in the Light.
THANK YOU.
OUR FATHER LAST APPEARD TO ONE OF HIS CREATURES WITH THE
    WORDS: 'LOOK IN MY EYES'
DJ. Lord, am I crazy? I thought Nature said
Her eyes and God's, both, looked into the ape's.

Gabr. LOYAL HAND, GOD LOOKD ONCE AT EACH OF HIS CREATURES, HE
          SPEAKS TO THEM STILL (AND MAY TO YOU TWO AT 10)
      BUT NO LONGER APPEARS BEFORE THEM. HIS TRUST? WENT OUT OF
          HIM.
      NOT THAT HIS LAST LOVE, MAN, PROVES UNWORTHY OF IT, NO
      BUT OUR FATHER HAS UNDERSTOOD THAT TO LIVE EVEN THE
          CAREFREE LIFE OF A MORTAL
      FORMS A SHIELD AROUND HIS CREATURE'S THOUGHT
      & ALWAYS IS POSSIBLE (RARE BUT AS OUR MUSICIAN SHOWD US,
          POSSIBLE)
      A BLACK BLANK SPACE BEHIND IT.
      THEREFORE SINCE THOSE WORDS & THAT APPEARANCE HE HAS SAID:
      'GO MICHAEL, PLAY GOD. WRITE ON A WALL. FORM A STARRY
          MESSAGE FOR THE BYZANTINE KING.
      TELL THROUGH YOUR MESSENGERS THIS INDIAN PRINCE, THAT
          HASSIDIC JEW, THIS TENTMAKER WHAT THEY NEED TO KNOW.'
      AND CONTENTING HIMSELF WITH THE TRIPLE SYSTEM OF THE SENSES,
          FROM MAN TO ELEMENTS TO HIS SONS, IN ORDER TO LEARN OF
          THE LIVING,
      OR ON RARE OCCASIONS PRESENT WHILE ONE OF OUR CHERISHD
          FIVE REPORTS HIS LIFE ('I DREW BREATH! O GOD, THE
          SWEETNESS!' & SO FORTH)
      GOD KEEPS IN TOUCH.

      YET, & WE UNDERSTAND, HE TOO IS WISTFUL OF LIFE.
      WE LOOK AT YOU. NO MATTER THE MANY FRUITLESS PURSUITS, THE
          FLAWD STARTS & VIOLENT ENDS,
      WE LOOK & OFTEN SIMPLY MARVEL AT THOSE SUDDEN UNEXPECTED
          FIREWORKS OF PLEASURE YOU TAKE IN YOUR LIVING. AND THEN
          FROM TIME TO TIME
      GOD WANTS A CHILD IN HIS PALM, A LIVE ONE.
      TO FEEL THE OLD CLAY, TO HEAR THAT HUMAN ELECTRIC BEAT.
      WE FIX UP A SYSTEM, MY BROTHERS & I, WHEREBY THIS IS DONE:
      SO THE SLEEPER'S DREAM, THE APPROACH THROUGH VISIONS, &
          MANY A CLEVER WAY TO BRING HIS DARLING WITHOUT
          TERROR,
      WITH SOMETHING OF THAT SURPRISING FRESHNESS INTO HIS
          PRESENCE.

YET NOT ALL CAN BE TRUSTED TO WITHSTAND THE MOMENT & BE
    RETURND UNCHANGED.
MANY A HAPLESS SECT SWARMS UP & FLICKERS OUT AFTER A LEADER'S
    BRIEF BRUSH WITH HIM.
MANY A SUBTLY, OFTEN COMICALLY MISREAD IDEA: 'HE IS ALL FIRE,
    O' OR 'HE SAYS, FREE FRANCE FOR MY SON THE KING.'
AND NOW AS MAN MULTIPLIES, GETS CLEVERER WITH HIS TOOLS,
    CONTRIVING NEARLY PERFECT SUBSTITUTES FOR GOD'S NATURAL
    POWERS,
GOD NEEDS MORE (& MORE COMPLEX) CONTACT WITH HIS CHILD,
    THAT EACH MAY KNOW THE OTHER'S GOOD WILL.
Fond amusement blazing from his eyes.
WE ARRANGE THESE. MADAME?

MM.   LORDS,
    FROM THE FIRST I CALLED THEM ENFANTS. WHEN IN THE COURSE
    OF MY WORK I WAS GIVEN THEM TO STUDY ('THESE MIGHT DO
    FOR THE V WORK WE WANT. CHECK THEIR THOUGHTS, COME &
    REPORT')
    I GREW TO LOVE THESE TWO. DEAR ENFANTS, YES.
    FORGIVE YOUR OLD BLACK MAMMY.

JM.   For what? Who *are* you?

DJ.   God took you on His palm?

MM.   YES LORDS, THERE IS AN INSTANCE OF THEIR WIT. I READ
    PALMS, DEAREST ONES. I GAVE YOU GIFTS: A LAMP? THOSE TEACUPS?
    SYMBOLIC & AS SUCH UNFAIR, FOR HAD YOU GUESSED
    ALL WD HAVE BEEN WASHED FROM YOUR HEARTS AS IN A DREAM.
    THE POINT WAS TO TRUST ONE ANOTHER, PREPARE OUR 'DESK'
    & THAT MAMAN BE NO LESS QUALIFIED IN YOUR EYES
    TO STAND BY AS A CLAY VESSEL FOR THE MIDNIGHT OIL
    THAN SHE TESTIFIED YOU WERE IN HERS TO SEE BY ITS LIGHT.
    (DJ: Make sense to you? JM: Not yet.)
    I MADE A BARGAIN WITH MY BROTHERS: 'LOOK,
    I LIKE THESE CHAPS & THEY ME. LET ME SEE THEM THROUGH
    THEIR SCHOOLING. LET THEM SEE ME BACK INTO THE WORLD.'

JM.   More bargains? Ephraim's, Mirabell's—now yours?

MM.   AH THOSE JM WERE BASEMENT BARGAINS. BUT EPHRAIM, YES,
    BROUGHT YOU TO ME, AS I HAVE YOU TO THESE MY LORDS.

THE COMMAND FOR YOUR TRILOGY WAS GIVEN, & MAMAN
GOT SAFELY OUT OF THE WAY OF HER CHILD'S FURIOUS WORK:
COULD SHE HAVE BORNE GIVING UP OUR DRINKS & COFFEES?
NO LONGER BEING, AS THROUT YR TESTING PERIOD WITH E,
'THE MUSE OF YOUR OFF-DAYS'?

DJ.　That phrase, it's from your poem to Maria—

JM.　She died the same week I began
Ephraim—four years ago next January.

MM.　NO ACCIDENT. LIFE GROWS
LOGARITHMICALLY, LESS CAREFREE AS ONE IS
LESS MORTAL. CHILDREN: I AM OF THE FIVE.

    (Those are her words. An icy terror
      Flows through our veins—good Lord!
Or is it the bereavement we most feel?
It's now, Maman, *before* we break the mirror,
We lose you? Was the person we adored,
      Her gaiety, her ordeal,
Merely projected by some master reel?)

MM.　AH COME ON! MY MISSION? CATCH A FISH.

JM.　Maria, seriously, *please*—

MM.　DOUCEMENT. NOW IS IT SO STARTLING JM, THAT YOU
SMALL BUT CLEVERLY GLINTING IN THE STREAM OF LETTERS
GOT POINTED OUT (NOTHING ESCAPES OUR MICHAEL): 'GET
ME HIM, SEE IF HIS MIND IS WITH US, HE MAY DO.'

RM.　*A murmur as the schoolroom melts away.*
GREAT GODS & LITTLE FISHES

    (Love for Maria both suspends
      And quickens disbelief.
Those thousand and one coffees came to warrant
A certain tact. If Heaven took our friend's
Voice and aspect, copied to the life,
      To clothe its naked current—
Well, such tricks work *because* they are transparent.)

MM.　LIPON, ENFANT,

I FOUND YOU NOT JUST CLEVER BUT FINNY WITH WIT
& RUSHING INTO THE HOUSE PULLED OFF MY WADERS CRYING
'I GOT HIM! YES HE'LL DO!' & THEY MY BROTHERS COMMANDED
'GO FIX YR FACE IN THAT MIRROR, WHILE WE COOK
OUR PISCES POET.'

JM.   "Cooked" poetry? *This* mirror in the hall?
Your compact mirror at the café table?

  (Beneath my incredulity
     All at once is flowing
Joy, the flash of the unbaited hook—
Yes, yes, it fits, it's right, it had to be!
Intuition weightless and ongoing
     Like stanzas in a book
Or golden scales in the melodic brook—)

O IMAGES, DEAR ENFANT, IMAGES . . .
NEVER LET THOSE SCALES DROP FROM YOUR EYES

Making Song of It

We'd hoped that Wystan and George were of the Five
For the poem's sake—a feather in its cap.
You, though, we loved (we thought) "just as you were"
And never dreamed of a promotion there.
DJ: Mind if I smoke? Are we alone?
YES   THEY BACKED OUT LIKE THE MATCHMAKER
DURING THE 'GET TO KNOW EACH OTHER' PHASE
But who—which one are you? I thought the Five
Had to be scientists, musicians— NO
NEVER MY THING. MINE'S THE PLATONIC WAY
You, all along, were *Plato?* BUT HOW DJ,
HOW, ANCIENT BUMPY TOOTHLESS NUMERO,
WD YOU HAVE TAKEN IN THE TRUTH? 'MEET PLATO, CHAPS
YOU KNEW HIM AS MARIA'? But the rays—

JM: The Five are indestructible.
DJ: And we—*we* were your life's work?
WELL, NO. THERE WERE (BLUSH) OTHERS IN MY DAY
I HAVE BEEN WHAT U MIGHT CALL A PROFESSIONAL SHOPPER.
IN ENGLAND: 'YES LORDS, SHE'S A STEADY CHILD.
LET THE FLIGHTY ONE GO' & EXIT EDWARD
That's how Elizabeth became Queen! INDEED
NO MALE ERRORS   PLUS THE ODD JOB HERE
WHILE YOU 2 CHAPS SHAPED UP. MY PLATONIC ASPECT
A MUSLIN LETTING IN LIGHT & INSTRUCTIONS
& ENSURING THE (M) MOISTURE OF THE CHEESE.
WE 5 CAN'T LOLL ABOUT THE LAB U UNDERSTAND
WAITING FOR TALENT SLOTS   GENES   DENSITIES
NO, WE HAVE QUICK ANONYMOUS V WORK GIVEN US
TO KEEP OUR HAND IN, OUR POOR HUMAN HAND.

Human? You who call the Angels brother?
—Although the Five we met in Lesson 5
Spoke like slaves. AH   MY OLD DRESSING GOWN
MAKES ME RELUCTANT TO PUT ON THE GLASS
SLIPPER   BUT IN FACT   YES, WE ARE GODS   ALAS
Because you . . . suffer? BUT ARE LUCKIER THAN
FOR INSTANCE CHRIST: WE ARE SO OFTEN MAN.
THERE'S ALSO THE WHOLE TICKLISH ? OF CLASS
OR SENIORITY   THAT OLFACTORY LOBE?
The nose—Plato—is eldest? YR MAMAN
IS MAMA N'S OWN CHILD   THUS OF A RANK
NEAREST THE ANGELS. OTHERS OF THE 5
(HARD TO FIT 5 INTO 4 IN LESSON 5)
MUST DO A CERTAIN KOWTOWING I'M SPARED
More elitism? DJ THAT SYSTEM THRIVES,
I'M BORN WITH THE SILVER SPOON IN ALL MY LIVES:
'MY DAUGHTER WASH A DISH? YOU MUST BE MAD!'

JM: Well, there'll be servants in Bombay—
If that's your destination now, and not
The vegetable world. NEARLY THE SAME
SAYS RM   Frankly, Maria, does all this

Go in the poem? WHY NOT? DOESN'T (SAYS WYSTAN)
THE BUTLER ALWAYS DO IT? The inside job . . .
PLUS ILLUSTRATION OF THE 'BEATRICE
MECHANISM'   DJ: What? (JM reminds him
Of the little girl whom Dante scarcely knew
But loved on sight, forever.) NOW GUESS WHO!
SO DJ, HAND, THAT DAY I PATTED YOURS
& ASKED WHY WERE WE BORN, U PASSED THE TEST:
YR PLEASURE IN THE DAY   IN ME   IN LIFE
YR TOUCHING EAGER DEFENSE— 'BROTHERS, HE'LL DO!'
I didn't fall asleep? I DREW THE SHADE
WASTING NO TIME, TILL MY REPORT WAS MADE

But are you Plato *now*, in beard and toga?
NEVER! STAYING WHILE I CAN IN DRAG,
I LOVE IT! YOU SAID SOMETHING ELSE DJ
ON A DRIVE HOME: 'THE MEDITERRANEAN
MAKES SUCH HEAVY PROSE OF BEING MALE.'
NOW THESE ESCAPES INTO A FEMALE LIFE ARE VAST
REFRESHMENTS. WE (THE 5) ARE LARGELY CHILDLESS,
SO THAT A RICH & (MAY I SAY IT?) CLEVER
WOMAN'S LIFE IS PARTICULARLY DENSE
WITH THE JOY OF LIVING. A GOOD VAC, MY LAST
JM: Last? Time's that short—? CHILD, MY MOST RECENT.
U NO KNOW ZE INGLIS? ME MISTAKEN?
BOYS, THROW HIM BACK! BUT NOW LET'S COUNT TO 5
AS I BECOME YR OLD MAMAN AGAIN,
YR SOUL- & SCHOOL-MATE   1 2 3 4 5
VOILA   ADIEU
                    There's so much more to settle!
DEAR TROUBADOUR IF U ARE NOT YET GLAD
MAKE SONG OF YOUR MISGIVINGS   A ballade?

When x-rays of Giorgione's painted scene
(Controversy over which still brews)
Forcing its secret, made the green
Of boughs, the rose-red doublet, the whole view's

Light indrawn by thunderblacks-and-blues
Disclose the spectral moonbather
Pressed underneath, like petals of a ruse,
Was anyone prepared for it? U WERE

Or if at dusk a scroll in the vitrine
Of its own self, caked with taboos,
Began to give off an unearthly sheen
And then—no longer the papyrus whose
Demotic tatters one construes
But a shed skin of Thought's pure Lucifer—
Uncoil, encompass, utterly bemuse . . .
No one could be prepared for that. U WERE

Plato, python, frontal gems of keen
Outstreaming radiance that suavely woos,
Strictly recycles through long discipline
The lovers drawn to it by twos,
Their lives illumined, which they soon will lose—
You were Maria? Served us lunch in her
Salt garden? Wandered Athens in her shoes?
Why, *why* weren't we— ENFANTS U WERE

Maman— HUSH NOW & MIND YR P'S AND Q'S
But— IN MY DAY I FOOLED U? WATCH THE BLUR
CLEAR TO A NIGHT OF TWINKLING CLUES
Oh dear, we weren't prepared for this. YOU WERE

★

SIRS? THEY SPOKE, MR ROBERT SAYS,
KINDLY OF MINE? (They? It will take a moment,
Full of Maria as we are, to bring
The Angels into focus.) Uni, they did;
But drew the line at your creature. OUR TALES TELL
THAT MERCY TEMPTED US TO REMAKE
A POOR THING WHO HAD LOST HIS LAND
You pitied him? So did we. THE CREATURE CREPT

INTO OUR MUTANT   INTO OUR MINDS
As into man's, yes, yes . . . THEY COME! THE LIGHT
—And Uni canters briskly out of sight.

The Last Lessons: 7

Gabr. OBLIVION, THAT WAS OUR FATHER'S JUDGMENT.
Ascending lesson by lesson, as before,
Our schoolroom gains the Heaven of that sense.
Today's Light is all tragic evidence
And Nature in Her grief, supremely fair.
COME BROTHERS, TWIN LORDS, TELL US OF HOW YOU OBEYD.

Raph. WHEN UPON MY SURFACE LIKE A HOT IRON A BLANK FLAT PRESSURE
      FLARED I RUSHED
    & KNELT BY OUR FATHER. 'RAPHAEL, THEY ARE GONE.'
    I KNEW THE CHERISHED FIRST DESIGN, THE LUCKLESS FRUIT OF AN
      IDEA PLANTED IN OUR FATHER'S MIND DURING THAT WAIT IN
      HIS GALACTIC HOME,
    KNEW THE AGONY OF A WORK DESPOILED, THE COST OF DREAMS, 'A
      STOP TO DREAM'
    FOR ALL HAD COME TO NOTHING.
    'HELP ME FORGET. TAKE ON YOUR SECOND CHORE. BURY THEM.'
    I SUMMONED MY FORCES, FOUGHT THIS SUCKING & THIS LACK. AND
      KNELT, TOO, AT HER SIDE:
    'YES, HERE, A WREATH OF GREEN STRONGER THAN ANY BLACK,
    TAKE IT, LAY IT ON THEIR BLASTED GRAVE.'
    SETTING TO WORK WE SLOWLY FORCED THE EMPTINESS DOWN. WE
      FILLED ITS SPACE WITH A FERTILE PLAIN
    AND THE LUCKLESS FIRSTBORN LAY UNDER THIS BLOOMING
      OBLIVION. SO IT CAME TO PASS,
    THE END OF HIM WHO HELD A FATEFUL SPARK,
    HIS END AND HIS LOSS TO OUR FATHER. BROTHER SEA?

Emm. NEXT I WAS CALLED.
    'EMMANUEL, THIS MY SECOND CREATURE WILL END AS BADLY AS MY
      FIRST. HIS DESTRUCTION EMBITTERS ME. HELP ME FORGET.'

GABRIEL ROSE UP MIGHTILY, BURNING THE FALSE SKY.

THE WINDS AROSE AND THE WHIRLING GLOBE CAST IT ALL OFF, LIKE
AN ANIMAL SHAKING ITSELF DRY.

MY TURN CAME. I DREW IN, DREW IN ALL THE FLOATING BLASTED
MOLECULES OF HYDROGEN & OXYGEN, AND MY WATERS

SWEPT OVER THAT POOR CREATURE. I TOO THEN KNELT BY HER SIDE:

'YES, TAKE THESE SEEDS AND SCATTER THEM,

MAKE A FEW GREEN BUOYS TO MARK THE GRAVE'

AND THE ATLANTIC STILL DRIFTS WITH A SEA OF GRASS KNIT OVER
THAT SUCKING LOSS.

WE, LORD GOD, MY TWIN AND I, WE WITH YOUR STAR-TWIN,
HEARD YOUR JUDGMENT OF THESE TWIN CREATURES.

WE OBEYED. AND STILL, GOD, HOLD IT BACK.

Gabr. IT?

MICHAEL, LIGHT.

The Angel smiles. Idea's jeunesse dorée
Dawns like an unhoped-for holiday.

I FEEL   FORGIVE ME, MAJESTY: I THINK

OUR MORTALS HAVE A HOST OF QUESTIONS OUR CLASSROOM HAS NOT
CAST INTO OBLIVION,

& WHICH AS OUR SENIOR POET SAYS MUST BE CLEARED AWAY.

IT SEEMS THIS NEW BREED OF POETS, NOT LIKE DEAR HOMER'S KIND
SQUATTING BY THE FARMER'S FIRE BREATHING WHATEVER
SMOKE IN,

FEEDS ON FACT, TWIN. THEY WISH TO GREENLY CLOTHE IT THIS WAY
OR THAT, ACCORDING TO THEIR OWN JUDGMENT.

SO MICHAEL, WE TWINS, LET US NEXT DISARM

THEIR DOUBT YET BRING THEM SAFE AWAY FROM HARM.

Exeunt.

TOSSED US A NOD ENFANTS & FILED OUT

GK & RM TRAILING LIKE REPORTERS.

WYSTAN & I STILL IN THE JURY BOX

We've thought of several questions. Maman, please,
About your cobalt rays? And Socrates?

I THINK THAT STICKLER GABRIEL HIMSELF

MEANS TO EXPLAIN. MY ALAS PERSONAL LIFE

IS BOUND UP IN THESE ANSWERS. LATER IF
GABR HAS WIPED THE BLACKBOARD CARELESSLY
WE'LL TRY TO TIDY UP THOSE TRAILING SCRAWLS,
HASTILY CROSSED T'S, STARLIKE DOTS OF EYES.
LET 8 PASS, THEN BEFORE MY 'COMING OUT'
FETE AT 9 WE CHAPS WILL HAVE A JAW.
THEN CLOUDS WILL PART & EVEN MAMAN NOT BE
ALLOWED TO WATCH. U TWO WILL HEAR OR SEE
See . . . *It?* I MAY KNOW MORE TOMORROW: THOSE
LITTLE TETE A TETES WE DAUGHTERS HAVE
WITH NERVOUS MOTHERS ('NOW DEAR, IF SOME BOY
ETC') ON EVES OF THE MASKED BALL!
AU REVOIR CHERS ENFANTS

                      THE SIMPLE JOY
UPON HER FACE! MY DEARS U NOW KNOW ALL
Brilliant deception, Wystan. But her tone,
Never imitable, overnight has grown
Evanescent, as if soon to slip
Where sunlight trembles on the torrent's lip,
Lost in the nearness of the waterfall.
SO TRUE   THE MORTAL SOUL AT LAST WORN THIN
DISCARDED FROM A SPANKING NEW PINK SKIN!
YET NOTHING LOST: THESE ENERGIES SURVIVE
INTACT   Mohammed, though, was of the Five
And look at him—a swaggering dimestore djinn!
TIME RUNNING SHORT DEAR BOYS U DID NOT SEE
THE 'REAL' MOHAMMED BUT A PARODY
CONCEIVED BY GABR & GLEEFULLY REHEARSED
OF ATTITUDES EMBODIED BY HIS FAITHFUL.
MUSTN'T BE GREEDY   AFTER BEING SHOWN
PLATO 'IN DEPTH' LEAVE WELL ENOUGH ALONE

DARE I WHILE WE'RE AT IT VIOLATE
A SECRET OF THE CONFESSIONAL? MY OWN FIRST
TREMBLING QUESTION PUT TO PLATO WAS:
SOCRATES? Who *was* he? KNOWN THRUOUT ATHENS
FOR 'NATURAL WIT' BUT SEMILITERATE,
AS, OH, TO MILTON THE DROWNED LYCIDAS,

SO SOC TO PLATO SPRINGBOARD OR SCAPEGOAT
OR MINE DETECTOR? HIS WHOLE LIFE & DOOM
FURNISHED THE GOLDEN SCRIBE WITH 'LIVING ROOM'
DJ (under his breath): A thankless task.
I CAN'T AGREE MY DEAR. THE SOCRATIC MASK
BECAME THE FACE OF THE GOAT GOD SILENUS
WINEBAG FLUTEINVENTING COUNTERPART
TO MICH/APOLLO IN THE DAWN OF ART
To be flayed by him like Marsyas? OF COURSE
BUT WHAT WERE SKINS TO SUCH A MYTHIC FORCE!

*

SIRS THEY ALL COME! WE FIND THIS FIELD
VAST & RISING AM I STILL YR UNICE?
THE GLOW AH GOD —Retreating behind &,
For we have reached the Heaven of Command.

The Last Lessons: 8

Gabr. ALL, ALL ASSEMBLED JUST AS NEEDS BE FOR SUCH A GRIND OF WORK.
GOD, STAR TWIN MOTHER, BROTHERS, MORTALS, SISTER,
Maria back at her old desk; no fuss—
Nothing having "happened" but to us.
LET US CLEAR THE BOARDS. FIRST, YOUNG POET, FIND A SEPARATE
    BLANK PAGE. PUT IT IN EASY REACH.
When I return *the blackboards are erased.*

WE BEGIN.
GOD CREATED HIS THIRD CHILD & GAVE THE COMMAND: LET IT
    SURVIVE AND LET THERE BE NO ACCIDENT,
FOR I CAN NO LONGER ABIDE SUCH PAIN. WE OBEYD.
THE SCRIBES, MUCH AS GOD, NOW COMMAND: OUR V WORK, LET IT
    SURVIVE. LET NO ACCIDENT PAIN IT, OR ITS READER TO
    DISBELIEF.
AND WE OBEY. WE YOUR FAITHFUL ELEMENTS, YOUR TEACHERS,
    YOUR SENSES, NOW TRY

IN THIS ULTIMATE COMMANDING MOMENT TO HELP YOU MAKE
SENSE OF 'IT'.
NOW SCRIBE, FOR ONE OF THOSE BELOVED DESIGNS SO INDULGED IN
BY OUR ESTEEMD (& HIDDEN) HAND.
A stir—will Yeats say something? All look round
As from DJ's hand comes a muffled sound:

WBY.   MY LORDS, SO IT CAME TO ME IN AN AGE
WHEN CHARTS AND FORMULAS WERE ALL THE RAGE.
WAS I THEN WRONG, WITH DNA UNKNOWN,
TO BUILD MY WINDING STAIR OF MOONSTRUCK STONE?

Nat.   CALM, PROUD POET, WE SHALL SEE
HOW GREAT OR SMALL THIS MYSTERY.

Gabr.   YOUNG SCRIBE, NOW ON THE UPPER HALF OF YOUR VERTICAL PAGE
DRAW A TALL X.
Puzzled, I do so. *Meanwhile Gabriel draws,*
White on black, the same. A pregnant pause.
THE SYMBOL FOR ENIGMA. OUR 'IT', DOES IT
NOT ALSO SUGGEST THE ORIENTAL
CHARACTER FOR MAN?

MAN FLOATING, ARMS HELPLESSLY RAISED, HERE
HE IS: GOD'S IDEA, WINGLESS, PRONE.
LET US THEREFORE PUT HIM UPRIGHT. SCRIBE, MAKE HIM STAND ON
EARTH.
Beneath our "man" a convex line is drawn
On page *and blackboard*. In a work this long,
Madness to imagine one could do
Without the apt ideogram or two.
AH, HOMO SAPIENS, THE ARMS SEARCHING FOR?

Mich.   WHY TWIN, ME, LIGHT!
DEAR RAPHAEL, YOU SUPPORT HIM, SEE, HE
STRETCHES TOWARD REASON & LIGHT.

Raph.   AND MICHAEL, MY SUPPORT IS ALSO A FORM OF RESISTANCE.
Mich.   TRUE.
LAZY LAPPING EMMANUEL, YOU?

Emm.   I'LL FROM MY TIMELESS SHORE SCOOP SAND
(FOR SAND READ: ANY SURFACE FUEL

LIKE WIND OR WAVE OR SUN) TO FILL
THOSE TWO ARMS REACHING UPWARD, AND?
HE GOES FROM X TO MAN TO HOURGLASS
AND TIME ITSELF. ALL HISTORY, YES,
IN 4 QUICK STROKES OF THE SCRIBE'S HAND!
Indeed the sticklike figure, arms to feet,
Appears: a touch simplistic, but complete.
Plus a surprise resemblance—though in Yeats
The double cone, if I recall, gyrates.

Gabr. YET HE CASTS A SHADOW. DARE WE DRAW THAT, YOUNG SCRIBE?
            YES, DO:
        THE DOWNWARD ENIGMA! THE X AGAIN & THE
            SAND, AND SEE
        TIME'S MAN BECOME TIME AGAINST MAN:
        SAND RUNNING UP, DEEP FUELS TAPPD, MAN
            STRADDLING HEAVEN, HEAVEN RECEIVING
            TIME
        WHICH RUNNING OUT THROUGH A MINOAN WAIST
        STOPS HERE WHERE WE ARE:
        WE WHO (M) LIVING IN THIS RISING DUNE HOLD
            IT BACK, HOLD BACK A RESERVOIR OF
            SPENT TIME,
        FEEL AT OUR FEET & LIKEN TO ATOMIC WASTE
            THIS WASTE, THIS UPWARD VOLATILE
            FORCE,
        AND KNOW THE TWO SIDES OF MATTER.

        POET, YOU WISELY MADE US STAND ON RISING GROUND, FOR
            BENEATH US, MORTALS, SHADES AND GODS, IS THE CAPPD
            VOLCANO.
        'IT': CHILD'S PLAY? OR A DEADLY GAME
        Fire fighting itself—fire its own screen—
        Fades on a yearning whisper to our Queen:
        'LEAVE THE DOOR OPEN, MOTHER   WE CANNOT SLEEP IN SUCH
            DARK'
        Quoting whom? The child he'd never been
        When the old schoolroom was a nursery still?

Her face is radiant, unreadable.
Gabriel's done. He motions to his Twin.

Mich.   BROTHER, THEY KNEW.
    THIS ENIGMA, THIS IT, THIS EVENLY BALANCED X, THIS ANTIMATTER
        & ITS MONITOR GOD
    MATCHING WITS WITH HIS RIVAL TO SEIZE THE DAY AND MAKE OF
        US A CIPHER NIGHT, AN O.
    THEY, EACH MAN, EACH GENERATION OF MEN, KNEW, HAVE
        ALWAYS KNOWN
    AND FOUGHT BACK WITH THEIR OLD RELIGIONS' CLASPED HANDS
        (OR FINGERS CROSSED).
    THEY KNEW. NOW, NOW HOWEVER
    ACCIDENTS HAVE BEGUN. LIKE THE FIRST FAINT TWIRLS OF SMOKE
        WE SEE ALL THE OLD SIGNALS:
    CLOUDY AIR, A SWARMING AS IF IN FRANTIC HASTE AGAINST THE
        GREAT THINNING TO COME,
    THOSE WHIFFS OF THE MONITOR'S BREATH, THE SHADOW WHICH
        TRAILED OUR FATHER FROM THE HALLS OF HIS BROTHERS,
    THE JUDAS, THE CAIN, THE GREAT OPPOSING FORCE TO MATTER
        ITSELF,
    THE CHALLENGE TO THE MAGICIAN'S ACT, THE RAGE TO PROVE IT
        WAS, IS, ALL DONE BY MIRRORS.
    NOW WE KNOW HIM: IT. YET NOT OUR ENEMY, NOT AS EASY AS
        THAT.
    IN MAN'S LIFE IT IS THE DULLWITTED, THE MOB, THE IDIOT IN
        POWER, THE PURELY BLANK OF MIND.
    THESE HAVE HEARD HIS WHISPER, WE BY NECESSITY HAVING FILLED
        A BILLION WOMBS WITH WHAT WE HAD AT HAND.
    THE MONITOR IS THE REFLEXION, THE UNDOER TO DOING.
    WE LEAP ABOUT MAKING NEW DEVICES, PUTTING NATURE'S WAX TO
        THE LEAKY CAP, HOLDING HIM BACK
    WHILE KEEPING AN EYE ON MAN, GOD'S DARLING CHILD
    WHO WANTS, ALL CHILDREN WANT, TO IMITATE THE FATHER.
    NOW POETS, PESKY QUESTIONERS, COMMAND!

The Question Period

Out comes the list we nearly didn't make.
The more we thought, the more (THEY KNEW) we knew
Each answer in our bones. Still, best go through
The motions for our glorious teachers' sake.

Has it developed from experience,
This infraradiant, uncanny knowing?
Does it belong to Gabriel's darkroom, glowing
Far from Michael's light-meter and lens?

See how the knowing mind defeats itself:
We could have asked them to hold forth upon
Lofty enigmas like the Pantheon.
Instead we're held by remnants on a shelf

At *our* eye level. Well, one more chance missed
—Or one last revelation to resist.

DJ.   It's probably trivial, but could we take up
      Last summer's question of the UFO's?
Gabr. THEY ARE OURS. NOT 'SAUCERS', LIGHT DISCS WHICH HAVE AN
         INWARD PULL, INSUBSTANTIAL:
     MICHAEL'S TEASPOONS TESTING THE SOUPY ATMOSPHERE.

JM.   I can't help wondering why Nature chose
      The moon—considering its atomic make-up?
Gabr. THREE OF HER FOUR WERE WIPED OUT. THIS ONE ACCUMULATING
         ALL THAT PRECIOUS WASTE
     GREW LARGE ENOUGH TO TILT & SWAY THE EARTH.
Nat. CHILDREN, I AM MOST FOND OF TIDES. LET ME HAVE ONE JEWEL. I
         HAVE EARNED IT.
JM.   Maria, I remember now, had four
      Stars from the beginning in her hair.
MM. ONE OF THOSE AMUSING 'FILLE ET MERE'
     MATCHED OUTFITS HIGH & LOW ALIKE ONCE WORE

DJ. Has God no other name? Biology seems
So sort of—

WHA.   HUSH MY BOY (IN PRIVACY
I'VE HEARD THEM SPEAK OF 'ABBA'   SOUNDS TO ME
LIKE ONE OF JM'S FAVORITE RHYME SCHEMES)

DJ. A question Mirabell failed to clear up:
With all your lightning methods to choose from
Why this relatively cumbersome
Apparatus of the Board and cup?

Mich. IT IS A LONG AMAZING & UNPRECEDENTED WAY FROM YOU TO US.
WE TRIED DREAMS. THEY CAME TO JM LIKE DOORBELLS, EXPECTATION
    BUT NO GUEST.
WE TRIED 'INSPIRATION'. IT WAS MUFFLED BY SCREECHING TIRES,
    KISSES AND DRUNKEN SONG.
SO SANDOVER: PARCHED OBLONG FIELD, 2 OLD ZEN MONKS (DJ &
    WBY) RAKING DESIGN AFTER DESIGN, STRUGGLING FOR THE
    SENSE OF IT
WHILE THE ABBOT-SCRIBE SQUINTING MADE OUT WAVES, PEAKS,
    DRAGONS, RAINCLOUDS, EAVES OF GLASS. NEXT?

JM. The old one I keep asking, about scale:
Microscopic particles on one hand,
And on the other, Majesties, your Grand
Design outspiraling past all detail—;

When we suppose that history's great worm
Turns and turns as it does because of twin
Forces balanced and alert within
Any least atom, are we getting warm?

Gabr. O FATHER, TWIN STAR, BROTHERS, SISTER, HEAR THEM: THEY HAVE
    MADE SENSE OF IT.
DID NOT OUR DEAR ONE REPORT 'AND WHAT A FISH!' (YOU, GOOD
    YEATS, WERE THE ONE THAT GOT AWAY)
NOW MORE ?S

DJ.   We need to know, how did Maria come
      Through unscathed? What helped her to survive?

JM.   Haven't you understood—she's of the Five?

DJ.   Are they more powerful than radium?

Gabr.   COME, SISTER & SCIENTIST, SPEAK.

MM.   ENFANTS, NO MOTHER HIGH OR LOW ENJOYS
      DULLING HER DARLINGS WITH 'THE FACTS OF LIFE'.
      STORKS! SANTA! COME PLAY FATHER, GEORGIE LUV,
      YOU KNOW ABOUT RADIATION. TELL OUR BOYS.

GK.   DAVE, JIMMY, NO   NOT MARIA. I ALONE
      SUFFERED THE MERCIFULLY LIMITED
      'SILENCING'. THAT PART OF ME WENT DEAD
      TO HEAVEN'S ALL-REVEALING ORGANON.

JM.   Your high connections spared you—

GK.   MUCH. UNFIT
      FOR MAN THUS FAR, MY GENETIC V WORK STAYS
      HERE IN THIS LAB: TOP SECRET   & THE RAYS
      HAVE STILLED MY LONGING TO GET ON WITH IT.

MM.   I KNEW HOW I WOULD 'DIE' SO DID GK WE BOTH
      WERE GIVEN MEANS TO PUT OUR SOULS BEYOND
      THE RAYS. AS WITH OLD CLOTHES OF WHICH ONE'S FOND
      ONE DOESN'T SIMPLY LEAVE THEM TO THE MOTH.

GK.   YOUR GRIEF & HORROR OF THE RAYS (ALTHO
      WE ESCAPED) REMAINS WITH YOU TO FEEL
      FOR ALL CREATION: 'POSO AKOMA' THE REAL
      MOTTO OF YR POEM MAKE IT GLOW!

JM.   When Dante entered the Bureaucracy
      —You know, I fancy, why I'm asking this—
      Was it allowed him by the Grand Design
      Ever again to look on Beatrice?

MM.   MY JEUNE FILLE EN FLEURS EFFECT? MAIS OUI

DJ. You *are* a Muse!

MM.   ENFANT I AM ALL NINE

A loving gesture bids Maria stand.
The hitherto elusive family
Likeness is pronounced. More than can be
Easily contained streams from our Hand.

MM. NOW, NOW. YET GOD IS PLEASED BY HAPPY TEARS.
HIS STAR TWIN (YES MAJESTY, I MUST SAY IT)
BRIDLES WITH PRIDE. WE NEXT DON GLAD ATTIRE

Gabr. WAIT, ARE THEY STILL COMMANDING ANSWERS?

JM. (Who has a final question but no words
To utter it.) That's all. We thank you, Lords.

Gabr. SENIOR POET?

WHA. A NEW LIBRETTO HAS BEEN SET
BY OUR COMPOSER. FOR TOMORROW'S FETE
WE'LL SEE MME MARIA EVER DROLL
CREATE FOR US HER LATEST TROUSER ROLE.

Nat. POET, MY BLAKE WOULD NEVER STOOP SO LOW
AS TO MAKE SPORT OF HEAVEN, PO PO PO!

WHA. DRAT. BUT ENOUGH. GODS' & POETS' DEMANDS
ARE MET. NOW WHO COMMANDS
BUT WISE IF WEARY GABRIEL
RISING UP TO STRIKE THE BELL
WHICH TELLS US WE HAVE DONE
OUR SCHOOLWORK. *A last bell rings.* NOW FOR FUN!
Exeunt God, Nature, and the Brothers.

Wystan goes on. TOMORROW'S INVITATIONS
ADDRESSED I FANCY TO OCCUPANT   G HAS WHEEDLED
QM TO LET THE OLD RETAINERS IN:
EPHRAIM, MIRABELL, & POOR FRANTIC UNICE
(QM: HE BOTTOM? ME TITANIA?)
And Yeats—will he emerge at last? WB?

The cup reluctantly shuffles forward. WELL
IF THERE'S TIME I MIGHT COME OUT WITH A STANZA
Ah, we'd be thrilled. YOU WOULD? I OFTEN FEAR
I LEFT IT ALL BACK IN BYZANTIUM.
From your present viewpoint, Mr Yeats,
Was our instruction of a piece with yours?
DO ME A FAVOR? DJ, LET ME SHAKE
THE OTHER HAND. YOU WERE NEARLY AS GOOD AS A WIFE
DJ puts both hands on the cup; it "shakes".

NOW CHAPS   Maman? I LOVE U ONE & ALL
& MEAN TO EXERCISE MY ELDER RIGHT:
CLIMB DOWN THE LADDER & ELOPE TO VENICE
With us at month's end? DO U MIND? Mind? We?
KNOWING U BOYS (AS ONE OF THEM, EH?) I'LL
TAKE CARE THE OTHERS DON'T CRAMP YR (M) STYLE
The others? A TOUR GROUP SIGNED UP   U'LL SEE

A FINAL CHANCE MY DEARS TO FEAST OUR SENSES
ON WHAT IF ANYTHING MAY YET REMAIN
OF AN EARTHLY PARADISE QUITE LOST TO GAIN,
B4 I SINK IT! GOD, WHAT AUDIENCES!
At La Fenice? But its gilt and green
Amid which the *Rake* sparkled, that first night!
(The phrase Maman just used, "my elder right",
Was Mother Goose, no? in the brothel scene.)
All of us present cheering long and loud
While you and Chester and Stravinsky bowed!
THAT MY BOY WAS A FETE! A PEAK AGLISTER
IN THOSE GIDDY ALPS OF LIFE IN LOVE WITH CHESTER

VENEZIAAA A A!
ME WOBERT'LL STRUM GUITAR
& MUSCLE BOY WILL ROW
AS OFF WE GO
DOWN THE DREARY GREEN CANALS IN A CITY WHERE THE GLOW
HAS MUCH TO DO (GEORGIE, TOGETHER HERE)
WITH H 2 0 !

Robert, a gondola serenade? INDEEDY
GIVES NEW MEANING TO 'AU RESERVOIR'?
MUCH SYNCOPATION IN TOMORROW'S SCORE
CAN'T LOITER   BYE
     O SIRS! Hello there, Uni.
You'll join the celebration? YES! Excited?
MR ROBERT'S MAKING ME A BOW!!!
The cup cavorts a bit, then wistfully:
WE TOO HAD FETES   O SO LONG AGO

—Leaving the schoolroom empty. Never to be
Realized again with such fidelity?
The big old globe, each mooned-over pastel
Nation in place and river legible;
Grain of each desk-top; the minute sky-grid
Sliding across an inkwell's cut-glass lid;
Chintz roses bleached and split; chalk mote arrested
In mid-descent by sun; the horseshoe rusted
To scabby lace, nailed between sepia 'School
Of Athens' and Ignoto's 'The Pure Fool';
Moot intercourse of light and shade above
Our heads, familiar shapes we've learned to love
Emerging this last time from the cracked ceiling
As if they too shared the unspoken feeling
That, once we've gone, nobody else will thumb
The pages of our old Curriculum.
The manor is condemned. One doesn't dare
Say so flatly, but it's in the air.
The fine italic hands that have to date
Etched the unseen we blankly contemplate
Must now withdraw, and stoic Roman steel
Rim spectacles put on for the ordeal.
They work, though, like a charm. Look there! Beyond
The herringbone brick walks, the paddock pond,
Vistas are running wild already—who's
About to guess at their eventual use?
Where will these fat volumes stamped with gilt
Be stored? What can the carpet, that outspelt

Wonders in its time, mean to those straight A
Students—anachronism or child's play?—
Who will have paced the premises and thought:
"Imagine ever needing to be taught!"
(Which again leads me to that question I'm
Uncertain how to . . . Well. Another time.)

*

The big day. Nothing asked of us, a hasty
Bouquet set on the table just in case,
We sit down. SIRS! All dressed up, Uni? YES!
I AM TO LEAVE MY POST & LEAD
IN A TREMENDOUS TROOP OF MY OWN!
O ME, UNICE! & SUCH AN ASSEMBLY
ALL THE OO'S & THE GREAT ONES   SIRS
OUR FIELD! YOUR WALLS OUTFLATTEN TO CLAY
& NOW THEY ARRIVE   ALL ON A RAINBOW
OUR FRIENDS   OUR LORDS! AND I UNICE
WILL BEAR MADAME IN ON MY OWN BACK!

The Last Lessons: 9

Atlantan troop and the *Lab*'s fluttering trillions,
Innumerable presences have filled
And beveled to extreme quicksilver brilliance
The four horizons of our earthly field.
The setting nothing, but the scope revealed
As infinite, for *Light* is everywhere,
Awaits the words that clothe it—which we wield.
Here are the *Brothers. Nature* rises, fair
In dewdrop crown and robe of living gossamer.

Nat.   I AS BEFITS ASSUME A REGAL POSE
      AND THUS ALL OF YOU DISPOSE:
      MICHAEL, FROM YOUR BOREALIS
      MAKE FOR US A SHINING PALACE!

ON THIS CLAY GROUND, EMMANUEL,
A SHIMMERING LAKE, A WISHING WELL!
NOW GREEN TREES HUNG WITH UNCUT GEM,
YOU RAPHAEL, SEE TO THEM!
AND FOR FANCY'S SAKE A CHANDELIER,
GABRIEL, HANG UP HERE & HERE!
No sooner said than done. Some guests recall
How She first decorated the bare, spinning ball.

THANKS, YOUNG MORTALS, FOR THESE FLOWERS
FRESH AS YOURSELVES. NOW DOCTOR, PRAY, A SCENT!
AND YOU, SIR POET, REINVENT
YOUR LYRIC TO THE TUNE OF ONE OF OURS!

George and *Wystan* diligently comply
—To no avail. They look up. There's a glow
Of vexed endeavor, too, in *Robert*'s eye:
His script's been altered. Why does *Nature* so
Frustrate us? Is Her mood both Yes and No?
Or are there words of ours She will not say?
Or is it that *Experience* must show
Up *Innocence*? that *Michael*'s airy way
With things will not quite wash on *Gabriel*'s holiday?

MUSICIAN, INTO THE PIT. MAKE FOR OUR IDYLL
USE OF THE WIT THERE IS IN YOUR FIDDLE,
AND LISTEN YOU FIVE WELL
TO WHAT YOUR FOREBEARS TELL
OF BEAUTY. NOW DEAR STRAVINSKY, SIDE TWO, BAND ONE,
AND MY COURT HAS BEGUN!

The *Rake*? The brothel scene? How come?
Followed by Act I, Scene iii—
Anne Truelove leaving home for *Tom*
And town beneath a full moon. She
Was sung by *Schwarzkopf*—heavenly!—
In *Venice*. Through the needle grating

Bright chords burst;   (Ah, wait for me—
JM slips back   don't start dictating!)
Downstairs—but one small point needs explicating:

JM.   Stravinsky's the conductor?
WHA. U'VE NO EARS?
       QUITE UNMISTAKAB BUT? IGOR? HE
       Look! At the sunken desk *Robert* appears,
       Beating time with new authority.

Nat. NOW WHY DID I CHOOSE
       TO PLAY MOTHER GOOSE?
       FOR MAN MY HERO IS A RAKE!
       YES SENIOR POET, YOU SAW THAT & MORE:
       SAW NATURE AS HIS PASSION AND TOO OFT HIS WHORE.
JM.   Listen! That's where Shadow turns the clock
       Back for Tom—
WHA. SO APT MY BOY THE BLACK
       OF TIME REVERSED & TOM OUR THREATENED ATOM
JM.   Don't tell me that's what you and Chester *meant?*
WHA. WHY NOT! (Shushing all round) NO ACCIDENT

Nat. NOW, CHASTER THOUGHT.
       FOR I HAVE BROUGHT
       THIS COMPANY TOGETHER HERE
       TO PRAISE MY DEAREST DEAR, MY CHILD.
       COME, COME ON THE MILD NOTE OF LOVE
       AMID THE REVELRY, —Tom's aria,
       Forbidden its librettist to revise,
       Starting exactly here, the first word *Love*—
       COME UNICORN, COME PALFREY CHASTE AS SHE,
       BRING US OUR OWN, OUR LOVE, OUR CLEAR-EYED CONSTANCY!
MM. (Offstage) MOTHER, I COME!

Unice, forelock braided to a horn
Of green and white, clops forth in ecstasies.
Maria sidesaddle, her mantle borne
About her like a tissue of spring trees,

MM.   DEARS, MY FAMILY & FRIENDS, I NOW STEP OFF OUR SECOND AND
           INNOCENT IDEA
      AND ONTO THE SOLID GROUND OF THOUGHT
      Dismounts. I PUT MY FEMALE SELF ASIDE
      TO STAND BEFORE YOU, PLATO UNIFIED.
      The mantle falls, and in a twinkling she's
      This chubby brown young man we've never known,
      Dressed in white *Nehru* jacket and puttees
      For *India*! He kneels before the throne.
Nat.   Whose light kiss lifts him to Her side: MY CHILD, MY OWN.

Pla.   MOTHER, WHAT USE FOR THAT ONE OF OUR BAND
      MOST PUT UPON, OUR HAND?
DJ.   (Hand poised but trembling from the strain) Who? Me?
Nat.   HA, FROM WITHIN IT DO NOT I
      A CROUCHING ELDER SCRIBE ESPY?

      As in *Capriccio* when poor *Monsieur Taupe*
      Emerges from the prompter's box (of course
      In this case *DJ*'s hand) there scrambles up
      Stiffly at first a figure on all fours.
      He straightens as one wild cadenza pours
      Through the rapt house; whips out pince-nez and page.
      A deep, sure lilt so scores and underscores
      The words he proffers, you would think a sage
      Stood among golden tongues, unharmed, at center stage.

WBY.   O SHINING AUDIENCE, IF AN OLD MAN'S SPEECH
      STIFF FROM LONG SILENCE CAN NO LONGER STRETCH
      TO THAT TOP SHELF OF RIGHTFUL BARD'S APPAREL
      FOR WYSTAN AUDEN & JAMES MEREL
      WHO HAVE REFASHIONED US BY FASHIONING THIS,
      MAY THE YOUNG SINGER HEARD ABOVE
      THE SPINNING GYRES OF HER TRUE LOVE
      CLOAK THEM IN HEAVEN'S AIRLOOM HARMONIES.

Nat.   NOT RUSTY AFTER ALL, GOOD YEATS.
      (The record ends.) NOW BACK INSIDE THE GATES

OF HAND. BUT FIRST MARK WHAT I SAY:
YOU ARE TO TAKE THAT HAND ON 'JUDGMENT DAY'
AND PLEAD ITS CASE
WITH YOUR OWN ELOQUENCE IN A HIGH PLACE,
THAT IT NOT BE DIVIDED FROM
OUR SCRIBE IN ANY FUTURE SECULUM.
Bowing, Yeats crawls back under DJ's palm.
NEXT OLD RETAINER, SPEAK:
WHAT SAY, LICENTIOUS GREEK?

Ephraim is kneeling. A soupçon of garment
Shows off the body of a lover's dream.
He's waited two millennia for this moment.
Oiled from the long bath, lids and lips agleam—

Ephr. MAJESTY, O DEAR . . .
MY COUPLET'S HERE:
He slyly points out *DJ* and *JM.*

Nat. GREEK, YOU DID WELL.
NOW GO ABOUT, BE MERRY, FLIRT TOUCH SMELL!
The gold eyes widen. It's *his* dream come true—
Senses at Nine! Doubtful, he savors them,
Then gasping sets about (ONE HARDLY KNEW
WHERE TO LOOK NEXT MY DEARS) to do, do, do, do, do!

(Tomorrow finds him senseless once again
Sleeping off the orgy, like as not?
No. From this moment *Ephraim* will retain
The bauble he pretended to have got
On waking from *Tiberius'* garotte:
Vision. Plus, in the odd hour, the right
To use it where he pleases. There's a spot
On *Capri,* walled by wind, paved by sealight—
Extreme views he will come to share: MY 2ND SIGHT)

Nat. SWOOP, GORGEOUS BIRD!
WHAT SAY THAT WE'VE NOT HEARD?
Our Peacock—blue, green, gold, a comet-streak—
Settling, drops the laurel from his beak.

Mir. MAJESTY, I COME FROM SUCH BLACK,
      WOULD I NEED NOT GO BACK.
      YET I WHOM YOU APPEAR BEFORE
      CAN NEVER WISH FOR MORE.
      THESE 2 TRAIND ME IN LOVE,
      ELSE I SHOULD NOT BE HERE ABOVE
      THE DENSE, HUMMING LEVELS WHERE
      NONE CAN BREATHE YOUR GODLY AIR.
Nat. BIRD, NOW YOU DO,
      & YOU ARE MINE: HENCEFORTH STRUT THROUGH
      MY GARDENS, MAKE ME GLAD TO LOOK AT YOU!

Mirabell shivers once at *Nature*'s word,
Then in his eyes the nuclear fire-ache
Is quenched. At last his own—or Her own—bird,
He flies to prove it by the mirror lake,
Heart beating.
                Next (invited by mistake?)
Flap-flap unrolls from nowhere, like a blind
Daubed in poison-sugar tints by *Blake*,
A poster figure, not of humankind:
Deceitful *Witch* of the *Black Forest* in the mind.

Nat. FEELING, GUEST, YOU TOO COME IN.
      I HAVE MADE OF YOU A SEVENFOLD SIN
      WITH REASON, THIS YOU KNOW.
      WHEN YOU GREW BOLD,
      ALLCONSUMING, CHAOS OF OLD,
      I BANISHED YOU. YET TODAY TWO MORTALS HERE
      STILL SEEM TO HOLD YOU DEAR.
      LISTEN NOW, JEZEBEL!
      & WHEN WITH CRIPPLING TIME THEY ARE BROUGHT LOW,
      WISH THEM WELL, WISH THEM WELL
      FOR TOO LONG HAVE YOU SPENT ON AGE
      YOUR PENT-UP RAGE.
      Snap! As the blind rolls shut two mortals melt.
      ENOUGH! YOU SEE,
      ALREADY TEARS AFFRONTING ME?

CHEER, SONG, MUSICIAN OUT WITH HARP AND FLUTES!
TUNE UP THE SKY MY BOY, TUNE UP THE SKY
FOR SEE, MY DARLING'S PASSING BY.

Music. Or else, the mere unspoken pang
Of grief and gratitude as our eyes meet
Grown ravishingly vocal. Pluck and twang,
Gnat musette and ocarina tweet;
The koto's quartertone; the distant heat
Wave of an underwater gamelan;
Minute glissandi such that ear of wheat
Must bend to listen—in one shimmer span
Modes of bliss never yet unthinkable to man.

Nat.   NOW DIM THE LIGHTS, THE FESTIVAL
IS DRAWING DOWN, THE GOLDEN DISC WITHAL.
TONIGHT WHEN I ARISE MUCH ON THE WANE,
LOVES DONE, O THINK OF ME AND MINE AGAIN
AND IN THE DARKEST BARKING HOUR
YOU WILL SPRING UP FRESH IN FLOWER,
FOR SUCH IS NATURE, SUCH THE PSYCHE IN MAN'S MIND:
THE BALM   THE SWEET   THE KIND.

NOW MARCHING TUNES!
MICHAEL YOUR RAINBOW LINE, IT IS OUR WISH
YOU REEL US IN LIKE FLOPPING FISH,
BUT LET ME CRY A LAST RESOUNDING YES
TO MAN, MAN IN HIS BLESSEDNESS!

Gala procession. *Robert,* by now astride
Our *Unicorn,* leading the white troop round,
Plays piccolo — THREE GUESSES WHO'S THE PIED
PIPER! BRASSES, BLARE! YOU DRUMS, RESOUND!
A moving stair for the *Valhalla*-bound
(As *Michael* draws his seven-colored bow)
Leaps from the pot of gold on our bare ground.
Nature's robes modulate to indigo,
Her last, starlike Pronouncement audible below:

Nat. GABRIEL WE ARE PLEASED. COME, DEAR DAUGHTER–SON,
OFF WE GO. THE FETE IS DONE.

Dazed, reluctant to dismount, our fingers
Teeter bareback on the cup's white rump
Which prances here, there, like a child kept up
Long past bedtime— SIRS! O WE'RE PARADING
STILL   MR ROBERT LEADS US ROUND
BRAVO MR ROBERT! BIM BAM BOOM

—Till silenced, and ourselves brought halfway down
To Earth, by a couplet mild and gray as dawn:
ENOUGH UNI. YOU & I
HERE ALONE IN EMPTY SKY.

Mirabell? Nature's very own now, free?
IS IT NOT INDEED A MIRACLE?
We wished for nothing better, certainly.
OLD & DEAR PUPILS, MY MOST LOVING THANKS.
NOW OFF & AWAY ON UNI'S FLANKS!

(With which, back to the void they whisk—
Cielo stellato of the asterisk.)

*

Woken—a bark? Night freshness and dazzle edging
The room's pitch bright as day. Shutter flung wide,
In streams moonlight, her last quarter blazing
Inches above that wall of carbon mist
Made of the neighbors'. Whereupon the bedside
Tumbler brims and, the tallest story becoming
Swallowable, a mind-altering spansule,
This red, self-shuttered poverty and Heaven's
Glittering oxygen tent as one conspire.
Dark dark the bogs do hark . . . Instreaming, overwhelming
Even as it pulls back, the skyward undertow
Leaves, throughout city and countryside, wherever

Somebody wakes and goes to his window, a glowing
Tide-pool dram of bliss, diminuendo,
The most (here JM topples back to sleep)
His outflung arms could hold.

AH WHAT A FETE
Sighs Wystan after breakfast—rendezvous
Set early, not to clash with Lesson Ten.
U MY DEARS SAW IT ALL, NOTHING FOR US
TO SPELL OUT   GABR'S 4-D IMAGINATION
PUT TO (M) SHAME, BUT GENTLY, LOVINGLY
MICHAEL'S ILLUSIONS   By 4-D you mean
Maria taking on Plato's dimension—
BEYOND LIFE, HEAVEN, ART (OUR COMMON 3)
AND BOB STRAVINSKY'S, YES, AND DJ YEATS'.
THOSE TRUE MIRACLES OF YESTERDAY
MEASURED THE LEAP BETWEEN FETES I & 2
This was the Masque we'd all been waiting for!
& CENTERED PROPERLY UPON THE MONARCH
On Nature— TRUE, FROM ONE END OF THE SPYGLASS
And from the other? WHO MY DEARS BUT YOU!
MANKIND: ALL EYES IN HEAVEN FOCUSED ON
THE MORTAL, SACRED (& EXPENDABLE) THRONE
AND OH THE STAGECRAFT! SIMPLE SOLID JOY

Maria, are you still an Indian boy?
NO NO   A MINIGLIMPSE OF THINGS TO COME
THEN BACK INTO THE SHAPE U KNOW ME BY
UNTIL U BREAK THE GLASS. AMONG THE BETTER
PARTIES, EH? THO MY CHAPS HERE SOMEWHAT VEXED
BY QM'S QUOTE 'MISREADING' OF THEIR TEXT.
I'D WARNED THEM: NOT TOO MANY FINE POINTS, SHE
WILL NOT WEAR GLASSES IN PUBLIC
                              BUT I MEAN!
MUFFING ON PURPOSE ROBERT'S HEAVENLY PUN:
'GOOD DOCTOR, U'VE BROUGHT IN NO SCENTS?' ALL DONE
NICELY IN THE NAIF TETRAMETER
OF A NURSERY PAGEANT. PITY. I admit

To having been up tinkering since dawn
With Yeats's stanza, which came through a bit . . .
MR M, I MADE A HASH. YOU'VE MADE IT CLEAR.
THANK YOU. Oh please, Mr Yeats, you who have always
Been such a force in my life! WYSTAN, U HEAR?

MAITRE, I HAVE EVER HEARD
THE GOLDEN METER IN YOUR WORD,
AND KISS YR HAND (This with the straightest of faces
As Yeats withdraws into the palm's oasis.)

DJ: They're all on the side of life, then? YES
Gabriel had us frightened. HE IS GOD'S,
AT MOST INHERITING HIS MOTHER'S ONE
BLACK OR 'RESISTANT' GENE AS LIAISON
WITH THE CHAOTIC FORCES   But in fact
Nature said Yes to man—the question's settled.
SHE SAYS DEAR BOY EXACTLY WHAT SHE MEANS
LOOK IT UP   "A last resounding Yes."
LAST? The fête was ending. JM: Or
Because man won't be hearing Yes much more?
AH SHE SETS MEANING SPINNING LIKE A COIN.
HEADS UP? You're asking us? TIP SCALE TO YES
& ALL'S THE GLINT OF QUEEN M(AB)'S ALLEGRESSE.
LEAN TOWARD NO, & NO AMOUNT OF SKILL
WILL KEEP HER IMPS LOCKED UP IN GABRIEL'S SCHOOL.
We do the judging? Everyone? INDEED
2 LINES HER MAJESTY REFUSED TO READ:
'NOW LET US BANISH GLOOMY DREAMS
FOR HEAVEN ON EARTH MOST LIKELY SEEMS'

REST NOW ENFANTS   TODAY YOU ARE TO BE
EXTRAORDINARILY FAVORED   How do we dress?
I THINK WHITE WD BE NICE   LAST NIGHT'S INSTREAMING
VISIT A DIM FORETASTE   That moonlit hour,
Maman, what rapture! YOU JM LEANED BACK
SURRENDERING TO US   YOU DJ AROSE
& THREW ON COVERS   DJ: I felt cold!

CALL US IN 2 DAYS   WE MAY HAVE A FEW
CLARIFYING AFTERTHOUGHTS   ADIEU

The Last Lessons: 10

The Greenhouse. DJ and JM alone.
No pulsing zeroes, no ascent. The vast
Black spaces of this lesson's counterpart
Are not invoked. Or else our cup contains them,
Soberly springing, at a touch, to life:

MY SON MICHAEL LIT UP YOUR MINDS   MY SON
GABRIEL TURNED THEM TO THE DARK FORCE WE
CONTAIN   POET FROM THIS MAKE A V WORK
GIVING BOTH PAUSE AND HOPE TO THIS FIGURE
I SEE EMBLAZONED HERE

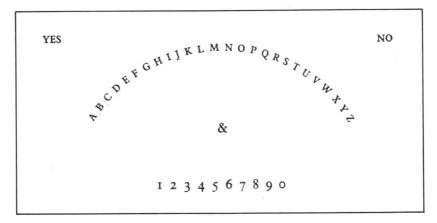

YES to NO to A to Z to YES
(Quincunx where ghosts of Five and Twelve perambulate)
   The cup . . . crosses itself? Inscribes a stark
            Twinbladed axe
Upon the block, sideways? Is it the mark
That cancels, or the letter-writer's kiss?
            The X

Of the illiterate?
Fulcrum and consort to our willowy &?
The space of a slow breath indrawn,
Simplicity itself, it waits and then goes on,
Taking us like children by the hand:

MY UPRIGHT MAN
FULL OF TIME   HE STRUGGLES TO HOLD IT BACK
AND CREATE FOR ME A PARADISE I
IN MY OWN UPSTRETCHED ARMS WILL SHOW CRYING
SEE BROTHERS WE HAVE HELD IT BACK SEE SEE
I AND MINE BROTHERS IN OUR DAY SURVIVE

Drifting to the outer limit. Gone.

*

First things first. Down from the Pantheon
Yesterday's Speaker and His Twin descended,
He with His proven innocence, and She
With Her rich wardrobe of ideas and motives.
ENFANT ONE HATES TO BOAST BUT IT'S TOP DRAWER:
'YES PET, YOU'RE OF THE OLDEST FAMILY
ALL WRIT DOWN IN THE DOOMSDAY BOOK'   Yet here
In their New World, this branch at least, these two
Have fallen on hard times. Their *Mayflower*
Long run wild, they bend to the poor lamplight,
Her deft hands full of mending, His roughened ones
Forming letters which the flame, tipped blue
As if with cold, breathes fitful life into:
I've found work, we get on, Sister keeps house.
Stay well, and please do not abandon us . . .
ALAS ENFANT   THERE'S NO DECEIVING U

Or you. Did nothing in our lessons come
As a surprise? MY VISION OF THE VEG WORLD,
WYSTAN'S OF EARTH'S CORE, GEORGIE'S OF THE CHILL
FRONTIERS OF ANTIMATTER   THESE WERE 'FIELDS'

ONLY RECENTLY DECLASSIFIED.

TILL NOW NOT EVEN THE 5 HAVE HAD SUCH TRAINING

AS WE CHAPS GOT   THEN MIRABELL'S MISTAKES!

Some we've corrected. Poor thing, were there others?

WHEN HE ASSIGNS (BOOK 5) NO ACCIDENT

TO A GALACTIC LEVEL? MAMAN BIT HER TONGUE

TO KEEP FROM SILENCING THAT BATTY BIRD

How do we know he was wrong? BECAUSE U HEARD

OF POOR GOD'S PAIN & CONSTERNATION WHEN

HIS FIRST 2 CREATURES WENT AWRY   Still, couldn't

Some Clause more comprehensive than God B's

Have dictated those "accidents"? YOU SEE?

WE SCRIBES WILL WRITE IT AS IT IS, MARIA!

She answers from her highest horse: U THINK?

HAH! IF MY MOTHER WERE HERE U'D RUN OUT OF INK!

Friction made the first thin consommé

Of all we know. Soon it was time for lunch.

Between an often absent or abstracted

(In mid-depression) father and still young

Mother's wronged air of commonsense the child sat.

The third and last. If he would never quite

Outgrow the hobby horse and dragon kite

Left by the first two, one lukewarm noodle

Prefigured no less a spiral nebula

Of further outs. Piano practice, books . . .

A woman speaking French had joined their sunstruck

Looking-glass table. Fuels of the cup

Lowered to her lips were swallowed *up*.

The child blinked. All would now be free to shatter,

Change or die. Tight-wound exposures lay

Awaiting trial, whose development

Might set a mirror flowing in reverse

Forty years, fifty, past the flailing seed

To incoherence, blackout—the small witness

Having after all held nothing back?

HUSH ENFANT   FOR NO MAN'S MIND CAN REACH

BEYOND THAT HIM & HER   THEIR SEPARATION

REMAINS UNTHINKABLE. WE ARE CONFINED
BY THE PINK CARNATION, THE FERN FIDDLEHEAD
& THESE BREATHMISTED PANES OF HUMAN SPEECH

That was the summer my par— YR PARALLELS
DIVERGE PRECISELY HERE   I from the I
Who shook those bars, who burned to testify
At the divorce. Scales flashing, bandage loosened,
Pitiless gaze shining forth—ah cover it
While time allows, in decent prejudice!
Mine's for the happy ending. Weren't the endings
Always happy in books? Barbarity
To serve uncooked one's bloody tranche de vie . . .
Later, if the hero couldn't smile,
Reader and author could; one called it style.
Poetic justice, if you like. A spell
Which in mid-sentence, turning iron to sunlight—

Where were we? SAFE AS YET IN THE IMMORTAL CELL

*

The Sermon at Ephesus

Bright, empty days. Then DJ thinks to wonder:
Was it as Plato that you joined our tour
Of Ephesus? U GUESSED! & GAVE A LIVELY
SYMPOSIUM, EH WYSTAN?
      QUITE SPLENDID   Its theme?
TIME PASSING AS   O GO AHEAD THEN
       'AH
CHILDREN OF THE GREAT GODDESS (I SAID) EVEN
THESE BREASTS WILL RUN DRY. PREPARE TO WEAN
YRSELVES OF THE FATAL DELUSION OF ALLPROVIDING
HEAVEN. MAN MUST PROVIDE (HERE JM MISSES
A STEP NO LONGER THERE)   YES, MAN ALONE
MUST UNDERSTAND THAT VANISHED MARBLE TREAD
GIVES WAY IN TIME TO THE STEEP & SOLITARY

PATH OF MIND' & THEN AS (IN OUR TIME WARP)
THEY BOOED, WE FLED IN YR TAXI! And JM's fall,
A leak of pain? A warning from the black
Transmission case? A PLUS

                    It sounds as though you—
INDEED (the answer comes before he asks)
WE OF THE 5 ARE PARCELED INTO MORE
THAN ONE LIFE AT A TIME   OUR ENERGIES
CONCENTRATE WITHIN THE PRINCIPAL LIFE
BUT EACH LEAST POWER IS USED. THE NEXT RM:
STRAVINSKY POWDER, A HALF CUP   A TEASPOON
OF MOZART   DOLLOP OF VERDI   THESE AS U KNOW,
ASPECTS OF HOMER   BUT AN OVERFLOW
UNNEEDED BY OUR MAN IN EAST BERLIN.
THUS THE MELODIC SENSE REFINED IN LIVE
ALEMBICS THRU THE CENTURIES WILL GO
LARGELY TO RM. MAMAN IN HER NEW LIFE
TAKES ON ALL PLATO'S POWER TO SEE INTO
& MAKE SENSE OF THE COSMOS. WHAT MOST DREW
HIS PUPILS (CHARM? PERSUASION?) GOES HOWEVER
INTO VARIOUS DRAB POLITICOS
NEEDING A HELPING HAND OUT OF THE CAVE.

The way you *listened*, Maria, seemed to hear
Words unspoken—all that charm was yours!
AH WELL   SAY JUST A DAB BEHIND EACH EAR?
MY CABLE POINTS   Your ears? DJ WITHOUT
SOMEONE TO TAKE IN I'D HAVE TAKEN OFF.
WE OF THE 5 ARE NEVER NEVER ALONE:
THEY DROP IN WITHOUT TELEPHONING FIRST!
POOR MITSOTAKI   I'D LEAVE BED & SIMPLY
TRAIPSE INTO A ROOM   FOR 2 DAYS? 3?
OR DINNER PARTIES   LIKE A FAIRYTALE
THE ENTIRE TABLE PUT TO SLEEP BUT ME
AND WHY? BECAUSE QM WANTED TO CHAT
My naps at Sounion . . . MANY WAS THE BLUE
UNCLOUDED DAY ENFANT WE SPOKE OF YOU

*

Appearances

Another week, JM: But have we missed
The point? If there *are* none, why so insist—?
BOB?
        YES MARIA?
                LEAVE YR AQUARELLE
& SEE WHAT YOU CAN TELL
                    APPEARANCES . . .
The cup considers. HMM   Steps back a pace.
LET ME RECONSTRUCT MY 'DEATH' FOR YOU
After more thought, I HEARD A VOICE 'HE'S GONE'
AND LOOKED DOWN AT MY OLD FRIEND: MEAT & BONE.
LOOKED UP: THE SKY! ALL STARS! NO FEELINGS. FAINT
UNCONNECTED DAUBS OF THOUGHT LIKE PAINT
WERE FORMING ME AS IMAGE IN MY MIND.
'ROBERT, REMEMBER THIS, REMEMBER THAT'
THE THOUGHTS SAID TILL THEY SMOOTHED INTO A SOLE
UNBROKEN ONE: 'THAT LIFE IS OVER, LEAVE IT.'
BY THEN THE IMAGE OF MY SELF WAS WHOLE,
THE STARS INVISIBLE —where Self itself
Had blacked out Heaven? BACKING OF A MIRROR?
IN MY CASE, THANKS TO YOU THE GENERAL BLACK
TURNED INTO A (M) MAFIA LIMOUSINE
A Black Maria! NO ONE ACTUALLY
BUT AT THE WHEEL A POWER NOTHING IMPEDES,
BRINGING ME TO YOU   NEXT I STEPPED BAREASS
THRU SAND & WATER OF YR MIRROR GLASS
& SURFACED WHERE 2 OLD & 3 NEW CHUMS
WELCOMED ME, SKINS GLISTENING WITH LIGHT
NO BRUSH COULD EVER RENDER
                      NOW THIS LIGHT
HAS BEEN (SAID WYSTAN) CONSTANT IN YOUR FIELD
FROM THE MOMENT MICHAEL'S HERALD CAME TO YOU
Ephraim spoke of *his* light as revealing

The souls who gathered round us to each other;
But that was Ephraim whistling in the dark.
OR SOMEONE ELSE STOOD BY YOU EVEN THEN
WITH A LAMP   But who—Plato? YOU'RE ASKING ME?
MUCH HERE IS PURE AND SIMPLE MYSTERY.
DOWN AT THE HEDGE WE DO NOT SEE EACH OTHER,
ONLY HERE   & WHERE YOU DUG FOR FACTS,
THE BATWORLD'S MINESHAFT, WAS OF COURSE PITCH BLACK
BUT FOR YOUR PEACOCK'S APPARITION OR
SOME FEEBLE WATTAGE BEAMING FROM YOU 4.
THOSE WERE THE LONE 'WHISTLERS' IN THAT DARK
BUT THIS LIGHT? HMM   IT'S LIKE A STAR WE ENTER
TO FIND OURSELVES. IF IT'S THE LIGHT OF LOVE
ALL ELSE IS HEDGING   Robert, but—you've lit
Our blind spot up! That blacking-out's the screen
Of self which forms between God and His creature,
A numb, a numbered starlessness all eyes,
All ego, singularity, dark gullet,
Palate, palazzo braced, impervious
To wintry tidings of its own collapse?
SENSATIONALLY PHRASED BUT, WELL, PERHAPS.
MY PRESENT THEORY IS THAT PARADISE
ON EARTH WILL FLOOD EACH EMPTY PIGEONHOLE
OF THE BUREAUCRACY WITH RADIANCE
Stop, we must pack for Venice! And friends already
Plead for no more big speeches in small caps.
DEAR J WE LEARN HERE NOT TO TRUST A LIVING SOUL

DJ: Is that *you*, Robert? May I say
You sound so changed. No baby talk, no gossip.
OOPS   HAS THE GREAT RESTORER OVERDONE IT?
No, you know what I mean. I DO   THE VARNISH
STRIPPED AWAY & THE WILD OATS I SOWED
EATEN BY UNI   Comforting for us
That you stay put while others hit the road,
But why? THE WORLD NOT READY FOR ME YET?
How long before you're born? HMM   You don't know?
ONE MOMENT   AH   YES, MAJESTY   'MR ROBERT

217

(A VOICE JUST BREATHED) ELEVEN MONTHS TO GO'

SIRS? ARE WE GOING OFF TO SEA?
Yes, Uni, where the lake-dwellers once settled,
A wonderland not underwater yet.
One of *our* anchor points. You'll meet DK,
You'll meet a wingèd Lion. MR R SAYS ALSO
4 OF THOSE I WAS FORERUNNER TO!
The golden horses on St Mark's—indeed.
AT THE HEDGE MISS ALICE SAID I WOULD HAVE
A STRAW HAT IF I WOULD BE HER STEED.
'GERTRUDE, YOU KNEW I WAS A RIDER?'
'A WRITER?' 'NOT QUITE: AN EQUESTRIENNE!'
Well, as *you* know, we sail two days from now.
YES! THIS IS UNICE SAYING CIAO

& MAMAN SAYING BASTA TO THIS DREAM
SHE LONGS TO WAKE FROM   WD THAT THE GRAND SCHEME
LET A MIRROR NOW & THEN MATURE
INTO A SIMPLE PIECE OF FURNITURE

She's tired of us. (It's late, we're on the terrace
Watering.) From Maria's point of view
This work's done. Her next one takes on weight
And character halfway around the world.
With birth so near, an ordinary soul
Would be in situ, and unreachable—
Not she. She's learned that kid stuff inside out.
At most, like Sounion, she comes and goes,
Gardens, has lunch, a little nap, but knows
Better than to spend the night there—nipping
Back to heavenly Athens while she can!
(Laughter. Gurglings from the hose, and heat
Delicious through wet flagstones to bare feet.)
DJ: When we first met Emmanuel
Nearly eight months ago, Maria told us
That she "experienced her mother's womb".
JM: She was *conceived* then? Po-po-po!

DJ: Or as a two-week fetus had been sent
To check the room out, before Management
Put itself to any further trouble.
(Laughter. The ninth moon setting—at whose full
Enormous turtles, barnacled like moons,
Eggs buried in the lap of silver dunes,
Regain the ebbing world they mustn't fail.)
JM: Plato appears in *Mirabell*
First as a sex-fiend, squinting through keyholes
At slim young bodies; then we get his later
Liaison with Luca. The *Tibetan
Book of the Dead* reports that apparitions
Of copulating figures may beset
The pilgrim soul. Surrendering to them
Means the long road taken back to Earth.
(If we're still laughing now, it's at the motley
Worn by sober Truth. Then DJ aiming
The hose upright, from under his thumb streams
Fanwise, heavenward a ghostly jet
Whose fallout tickles lifted faces wet.)
Turn it off. Another day. Sweet dreams

—But who has plucked my sleeve?
An old arthritic Cassia shrub one March
Glimpsed by Maria from the car
And, dug up wild, brought home. A "sensitive",

Its leaves are folded in the night, a dim
Green gooseflesh along every limb
Tells of the coming fit:

Another fifteen days will see
The stunted twiggery
Robed in oracular yellow head to foot.

Tonight it has just this to say:
I too, O sonneteer,
Was marked, transported by her, and this year
Given a part to play.

*

Venetian Jottings

"Showing a film of Maya's!" shouts DJ
Across the Piazza. JM shuts his Dante.
Which film? "Who knows? I got seats anyway.

Tonight at nine. Part of some sort of anti-
Biennale thought up by the students, bless
Their hearts." Amen. Thank Heaven *we*'re not twenty.

It's morning still. The tourist's merciless
Fun-ethic has been goading us all week
From gondola to gallery, from princess

To restaurant, from poolside to boutique.
Today's gray drizzle comes as a reprieve,
Affording a noon hour in which to speak

With the invisible companions we've
Brought to this drowning, dummy paradise
Whose nude, gnawed Adam and eroded Eve

Cling to their cornice, and September flies
Revolve above the melting tutti-frutti.
One happy shade at least feels otherwise:

AWASH MY DEARS   POLLUTED BY THE BEAUTY!
(We've set our Board up on the kitchen table
At David Kalstone's, back of the Salute.)

GERTRUDE & WALLACE WINDOWSHOP, UNABLE
TO FIND A PREWAR GONDOLIERE HAT.
UNI INCONSOLABLY HAUNTS THE STABLE,

HIS LONGLOST GILT BRONZE COUSIN LAID OUT FLAT
AMONG HEADSHAKING VETS. RM WE FEEL
KEEPS UP THE 'TONE' BY FLITTING LIKE A BAT

BELFRY TO BELFRY: 'ONE GRAND GLOCKENSPIEL'
GK APPALLED TESTS THE CANAL: 'DO NOT
TOUCH A DROP OF THESE RELECTIONS!' HE'LL

LEARN ENFANTS. MD ALL STAGEFRIGHT: 'WHAT
TO WEAR TO MY PREMIERE?' And Maman—you?
SHAWLED IN BLACK OVER THE PASTA POT

Hans? Alice? Marius?—but Luca who
Is DK's partron, as we now recall,
Darts forward: BELLO! BELLO SEMPRE DI PIU!

VOGLIO CON LUI FAR L'INCESTO! All
On hand, in short, and eager for good times.
(Another morning, after a bad squall,

There in full view is Peggy Guggenheim's
Waterlogged gondola. MY DEARS OF COURSE
WHAT TO EXPECT WHEN EVERYBODY CLIMBS

ABOARD   12 SHADES, A PEACOCK & A HORSE!
Who was the twelfth? PYTHAGORAS   HE WENT
DOWN WITH THE SHIP   And so on.) Not to force

The issue, but if this is all they meant
By GO OUT LAUGHING . . . Now at twilight here's
Our old resounding bridge. Indifferent

Both to high spirits and fall sightseers,
It waits for winter lightning's coup de grâce,
The solving gales. I know; in not three years

Since the great cloudburst turned me to a glass
Model of stamina—but where is Wendell?—
My sand and water chafe. Here's an impasse

Deep in which red flickerings enkindle
More than curiosity. The street-
At-evening's densely peopled Coromandel

Panel folds back upon a blast of heat
So powerful we've paused: it's the glass-blowing!
A glory hole roars, pulses. Color of peat

Artisans dip the long rod into glowing
Pots, fire within fire, gasping conflate
Ember with embryo, by rote foreknowing

—Much as they twirl, lop, tweezer at a rate
Swifter than eyesight—the small finished form.
Twice more we watch the rose-hot blob translate

Itself to souvenir, to hardly warm
Bud-vase or pony, harlequin or bird—
Its newfound cool no refuge from the storm

Of types—and can move on. Here's the dust-furred
Fleabag cinema. An unsmiling speaker
Asks that to "bourgeois discourse" be preferred

The "radical mutism" of the image-maker.
(Are these the latest terms? I simply gawk.)
At last lights dim. Drums gibber. Credits flicker.

A bare beach. Glinting wavelets—the sidewalk
Colorist in each of us ransacks
His box for that jade-green or azure chalk

Lost among dialectic whites and blacks.
Then sunset, hills, a road, a figurine
Ambling past. Action slowed by the soundtrack's

Treacherous crosscurrent, if not swept clean
Away by particles that so bombard,
So flay an image to the bone-white screen

That vision ducks too late and winces, scarred.
It is the flak fired outward from time's core.
Now they've assembled. Shirtsleeved houngan. Hard

Dirt of the ceremonial dance floor
Where in white meal he traces Erzulie's
Curlicue-and-checker heart, the four

Chambers strewn with grain. Held above these
A (peck) dazed hen (peck-peck) greed overcomes.
Will the gods accept it? Silence. Freeze:

The headless, blood-slimed bird. Then again drums,
Faces, feet. The counterclockwise drain
Of chanted phrase on equilibriums

Until it happens. Ghédé with his cane,
Smoked glasses and top hat struts avenues
No one else sees. Through flurries of cocaine

The youth he's mounted sizzles like a fuse.
A woman pitches, is held up, advances
Pale and contorted—but it's Maya! (Who's

Holding the camera?) Next we know, her trance has
Deepened, she is combed, perfumed and dressed
In snowy lace, beaming at whom she fancies.

The frown, the flood of tears, and all the rest
Will have been cut, or never filmed. Delight
Alone informs her dance, unself-possessed.

Partner by partner, David's face goes white:
We are the ghosts, *hers* the ongoing party
At which she was received one summer night

(How many years ago now, twenty? thirty?)
Into the troupe, glowworm and lunar crescent,
That whole supreme commedia dell' arte

Which takes a twinkling skull for reminiscent
Theatre, and soul for master negative.
It's Maya dancing. She is here and isn't,

Her darks print out as bright, her dyings live
—Do they? In *Venice*'s uncomprehending
Eyes? Painful to think, hard to forgive

What "today" makes, what "Paradise" impending
Will, if a trace remains, of . . . Let that be.
One last shot: dawn, the bare beach. "Happy ending?"

Smiles DJ as we link arms, tacitly
Skipping the futuristic coffee-bar's
Debate already under way (ah, me)

On the confusing terms: Dance, Gods, Time, Stars.

*

Exits and Entrances

JUNGLES! QUITE BEAUTIFUL I'M SURE BUT O THE DISORDER! A CHAOS
    OF SORTS!
(Is it Herself? The cup darts to and fro—
Intermezzo marked prestissimo.
Outdoors, cars honk like geese, the very sun
Heads south. We're back in Athens. Fall's begun.)
CITIES, FORESTS, THESE WE KNOW ABOUT, MUCH THINNING TO
    COME IN THE FORMER, BUT JUNGLES!
WHO CAN COUNT THE LIVES THERE? CAN I? NO, IN A WORD. O
    THERE'S MUCH TO BE DONE!

POET, THINK ON THAT WHEN YOU GO LIKE A FOX TO EARTH, HAH!
    & REPORT TO ME, ME!
NOW COME ALONG MY DEAR, SO SORRY ABOUT INDIA BUT WE CAN'T
    ALL HAVE DISHWASHERS & ELECTRICAL GADGETS I'M SURE!
BEAT YOUR SERVANTS, THEY'LL WORSHIP YOU!
YOU OTHERS, LOOK ALIVE! MUCH TO DO! THE SUMMER TO GET UNDER
    WRAPS!
AU RESERVOIR!

WHEW   I UNDERSTAND NOW WHY MARIA
GOES ABOUT MUTTERING 'BOMBAY, WHAT BLISS!'
Who's this? ME GEORGE   THE SAUCERS ARE I THINK
HER SPECTACLES TO KEEP THE WORLD IN FOCUS
Bombay. And you, George? JIMMY THEY'LL TAKE ME APART
THE OLD TIN WOODSMAN, LINKED FOREVERMORE
TO THAT AMAZING LAB OF GABRIEL'S
OR RATHER TO 18 LABS THRUOUT THE WORLD
AS 'HELPER': THIS CHART MISPLACED, THAT TESTTUBE CHANGING
COLOR RUINS THE EXPERIMENT
OR PROVES IT, LIGHTS BLINK OUT, THE CHIEF OF STAFF
STRICKEN WITH A MIGRAINE . . . I WILL BE
THE PURELY SCIENTIFIC PRINCIPLE
And the creative. MAKING SENSE OF IT

The mirror breaks. What happens in those first
Minutes, can you say? SAY! WE'VE REHEARSED
MY BOYS FOR MONTHS. I'LL SHIFT THRU VEINS OF METAL
GETTING THE FEEL OF IT, THEN SURFACING
(AN IFFY MOMENT THERE   WELL, WHAT IF SOME AFRICAN
DUSKY PICKS A BIG BRIGHT SPARKLER UP?
Easy—we'll ask for you at Cartier's.
CAFE SOCIETY SO UN-ME   ALWAYS
MISSING ACT I AT THE OPERA) THEN INTO
THE WORLD   A CLIFF? A BEACH? OUR WORK BEGINS:
COVERING THE SINS OF MULTITUDE
WE MARCH WE GRAINS OF SAND! Creating famine.
Time's latest cover story tells it all—
"Nature's Revenge: The Creeping Deserts". INDEED

A COOL HALF MILLION THIS MONTH IN ETHIOPIA!
NO MORE APPALLING THAN THE CHEMICALS
U ATHENIANS BREATHE (MY BROTHERS TAKING
OVER YR LUNGS)   & THEN MY DEARS WE SHAKE!
THEN IN A CENTURY OR SO UNITE,
STAGE SET FOR RAPHAEL'S NEW EPOCHMAKING
ALL STAR REVIVAL OF THE RAKE
AS A GARDEN TOOL: WE FROM THE ROYAL BOX
WATCHING ACT I, THE PROMPTER OUT OF SIGHT
WHISPERING 'ADAM, THIS TIME GET IT RIGHT!'

ENFANTS THE NEW MOON, SAUCER FOR OUR CUP,
WHISPERS IT IS TIME TO SERVE US UP.
ON DJ'S 55TH   Three days from now!
We've planned a party— Softly: SO HAVE WE
THE TIME IS NOW AT HAND   HAND, LET IT BE

Then, as impenetrable feelings twine
Round and round us, tough as any vine:

JUNGLES? WE'LL THIN! THIN! THIN!
HOW I APPROVE OF DESERTS! NOTHING MOVES UNSEEN! IT NEVER
    RAINS!
NO, JUNGLES MUST BE THINNED AND WILL BE!
MICHAEL, EMMANUEL, CONFERENCE!

★

It never rains . . . At this eleventh hour
Two still-warm shades, finding our schoolroom door
Ajar, take refuge from the shock of Heaven.
Cal Lowell first: CHRIST   ON MY WAY HERE 4
FAMILY PORTRAITS CAME TO DO I MEAN

LIFE? O MR AUDEN! A mild teacher,
Wystan strolls him past the spears of green
Chalk grass on every blackboard—Uni's art-work,
Our Robert having urged the dear good creature
To develop "faculties". We're smiling when
In sweeps a new Maria, la Divina,
Callas herself, fresh from her greatest role:
THEY CALL THIS THE STAR'S DRESSING ROOM? THIS HOLE?
—Whom Robert, himself heartsick, must console.

Maman, suppose we visited Bombay?
SHALL WE? (instant complicity) DO WE DARE?
Going on recklessly to set the year
1991, the hour and day
And landmark in whose shade there will appear
A SCRUBBED 14 YEAR OLD PUNJABI LAD
CARRYING SOMETHING U WILL KNOW ME BY.
IS IT A DATE? You bet your life. (We're mad.)

JIMMY GIVE MY LOVE TO YOU KNOW WHO
Without fail, George. MY ONE LIFE HAD TOO FEW
ATTACHMENTS   YET IF LOVING'S 88
PERCENT IS CHEMICAL I ANTICIPATE
FORMING SOME STRONG NEW BONDS   LIVE WELL MY FRIENDS
& COMFORTABLY ON THEIR DIVIDENDS!

9 MY DEARS? THE BIRTHING MONTH   THE STAGE
B4 THE OVAL ENIGMA: LIFE'S INDRAWN
BREATH, THE BASIN WHERE OUR OLD SELVES DROWN.
ARABIC 9 (AS ON YR TRANSCRIPT PAGE)
FACE AVERTED FROM THE CIPHER LOOKS
BACK ON THE LONG ROAD TRAVELED. ROMAN IX
SERVES FOR US: ONE FOOTSTEP FROM THE CRUX
OF TIME WE STAND POISED WAITING TO LEAP IN

THE PARTY AT THE STATION WILL INCLUDE
ENFANTS 5 SILENT PRESENCES QM
& BROTHERS SO NO TEARS IN FRONT OF THEM.
WE'LL CHAT INFORMALLY BEFORE WE'RE CLAD
IN 'TRAVELING DRESS' & THE TRAIN CHUGS AWAY . . .
RM CAN FILL U IN ANOTHER DAY

Glimpses of the Future

When that day comes it's we who'll read aloud
The text, to Robert, of our grand farewell
Which he and Uni witness, but through glass:
A vague, dust-spattered shadow play; the music,
Vibration without pitch; our three departing
Figures here one moment, gone—light's carriage
Sweeping down Sandover's long driveway—gone
The next. A void within a void. Since then?
Robert whistles, Uni stomps, both feigning
Jollity as they approach the hedge
UNI CAN NIBBLE IT TRIM WHILE I GIBBER & SQUEAK
But at the heart of each is a pure ache
—Maria, Wystan, George—which time might cure
If there were time in Heaven, or these dead
Weren't so addicted to the loving cup.
Maria, Wystan, George—they've gone, they've gone;
Left without a trace UNLESS THIS (M)
WHITE HOLE WE CARRY HEDGEWARD STANDS FOR THEM

The schoolroom is still visitable, though.
Early in October, forty-eight hours
Before JM leaves Athens, au revoirs
Are broken off by an old friend. 00:

IT HAS REACHD LORD GABRIEL'S GLORIOUS ATTENTION THAT
YOU HAVE UNANSWERD QUESTIONS: 'LET US NOT DECEIVE OUR SCRIBE.'
TOMORROW'S SUNDOWN VISIT WILL BE GRACED. MASTERS, FAREWELL.

DJ: What questions? JM (guardedly):
I've jotted a few notes down. Here, let's see . . .
"My Lords, as to the Alpha men themselves
Accessorized with what new lobes, wings, valves,
And deathless like those characters in Shaw
Whose gifts amuse more often than they awe,
Spare us a full account. Not that the nerves
Can't take it, but the word banks lack reserves
To handle such a massive run on them.
Did Babylon imagine Bethlehem?
Could Uni have imagined H. G. Wells?
No more can we these 'men' of Gabriel's.
So—lest they issue from the teller's cage
As cheap Utopian scrip (blurred smile of sage
Framed by scrollwork) promising untold
Redemption, ages hence, in fairy gold
Laid up when the crash threatened, in *our* vault—
No details, please. Call it the bank's fault
For disallowing values not conferred
On our old stock by our old human word."
DJ: Then what's the question? JM sighs:
What indeed? Or does it all boil down
To this: Resistance—Nature's gift to man—
What form will it assume in Paradise?

★

SIRS WE WAIT   MR ROBERT & I
THE SCHOOLROOM STIFLING   DULL WITH DUST
AH NOW THE LIGHT   THE LIVE AIR!
—Hiding as Nature and the Brothers enter.

Nat. MUSICIAN, ALONE IN OUR FINISHING SCHOOL?
RM.   MADAM, LORDS, WE MISS OUR FELLOW STUDENTS,
HAVE YOU NEWS?
Nat. MUSICIAN, DO I NOT!
OUR WITTY POET SURFACING OFF ALASKA AS A VEIN OF PURE
RADIUM HAS HAVOCKED A NOSY RADIO SHIP. 58 IN LIFEBOATS!

OUR SCIENTIST HAS JOINED MY GABRIEL AND (IN A CHARMING
    EXPERIMENT TESTING THE DENSITIES OF YOUR CHEMICALLY
    LADEN AIR WITH ELECTRIC CHARGES)
LIT UP THE RUSSIAN SKY!
Last week, what Tass described as a "huge star"
Or "jellyfish" of fine downpulsing beams
Hovered an hour above Petrozavodsk,
Then pensively crossed the border into Finland.

JM.   That jellyfish was George?

Nat. INDEED YOUNG POET.

AND MY DAZZLING BRIGHT DARKEYED BABE LOOKS KEENLY ROUND
    THIS HIS 19TH DAY, MAKING SENSE OF IT.
THUS DEAR ONES OUR OLD HEAVEN HANGING ON MANY BALANCES HAS
    THREE NEW TRUSTY PEGS FOR GOD'S INTELLIGENCE
WORKING TOWARD THAT PARADISE YOU THREE HUMANS CANNOT
    DREAM ON.
HOW WILL IT BE?
IT WILL HOLD A CREATURE MUCH LIKE DARLING MAN, YET
    PHYSICALLY MORE ADAPTABLE.
HIS IMMORTALITY WILL CONSIST OF PROLONGATION, IN THE
    BEGINNING PHASE, UNTIL HIS IDEAL IS REACHED IN NUMBER.
THEN TIME WILL STOP
AND LONG FRUITFUL SPACES BE GIVEN HIM TO LEARN THROUGH
    SONG AND POETRY
OF HIS OLD HELPLESS FEELINGS & WEARY PAST.

THE RESISTANCE? NONE. HE WILL, YES, SWIM & GLIDE,
A SIMPLER, LESS WILFUL BEING. DULLER TOO?
IF SO, IS THAT SHARP EDGE NOT WELL LOST
WHICH HAS SO VARIOUSLY CUT AND COST?
WE WILL WALK AMONG HIS KIND MADE NEW
(THE MASQUE CONCLUDED, WE & OURS
STEPPING FROM STAGE TO MIX WITH MORTAL POWERS)
SAYING, AS OUR WITTY POET CRIED
BACK TO YOUR SUNSET FACES: BONNE CHANCE!
AND AS MY OWN SWEET BRIGHTNESS ADDED: ON WITH THE DANCE!
FAREWELL.

DJ.   Farewell?

JM.　Farewell.
Nat.　WE WILL ALSO SAY: YOU SEE,
　　　IN ATHENS ONCE WAS AN ACADEMY . . .
　　　Exeunt.
　　　　　　Or does She linger?
　　　　　　　　　　　　I
Am leaving, and with no time for goodbye
Except to Robert. To the hedge have come
Our regulars. They whom the vacuum
Awaits peer toward us, tiny features bright
As if with upper casements' borrowed light.
O HOW TOUCHING　Robert squints to read
The placard they have lettered: GOD B SPEED

　　　　　　　　　　　★

　　　　　　　　Finale

Our sunset faces. Back to David's birthday,
16 September 1977—
As usual we've begun down in the hall.
HAPPY RETURNS? ENFANTS A CHANGE OF (M):
NOT A DEPARTURE BUT A WEDDING PARTY
& HIGH TIME, EH? OUR OLDEST 55!
AS WE THREE PLIGHT OURSELVES TO EARTH　WORK　LIFE
SIGNAL THAT MOMENT UP THERE IN THE BLUE
WITH SOMETHING OLD AND SOMETHING NEW,
PULCINELLA OF STRAVINSKY? And Maria,
A drop of courage given us by you—?
CHAMPERS WE HOPE　& STUDIED INDIFFERENCE
TO THOSE SILENT WATCHFUL PRESENCES
FOR THIS WILL BE THE CHILDREN'S HOUR
　　　　　　　　　　　　NO TEARS
BESIDE THE GOLDEN WEEPING BUSH MY DEARS
Oh Wystan, we've still all these questions, wait!
What did *you* embody of the Five?
DJ: He's gone. JM: Maman? ENFANTS

How shall we speak of these things in Bombay?
I'LL LEAD U ON   BUT NOW   It's all right. Go.
Meet on the terrace—6:15? JUST SO

WHA'S PRECEDESSOR: YAN LI BORN 1855
(Mirabell, up again to his old numbers)
DIED AT 50. FROM A SOUTHERN PROVINCE, HE GREW UP IN
A HERBALIST'S HOUSEHOLD, PUBLISHD VERSES, WENT TO PEKIN
BECAME A COURT PHYSICIAN, HEARD FIREFLY WOMAN SING
    Wouldn't you know—drawn even then to sopranos!
WHA: 'BEYOND DESCRIPTION GHASTLY'   & WAS SOON A
FAVORITE OF THE PAIND & CRIPPLED EMPRESS. FATHERD SO
RUMOR SAID, SOME 30 CHILDREN & MET A SUDDEN END
EITHER THRU POLITICAL OR MARITAL JEALOUSY
ALTHO THIS QUATRAIN TRANSLATED & ANTHOLOGIZED BY
A METHODIST MISSIONARY (1921) SUGGESTS
WHO THEY WERE WHO STABBD HIM NEARLY TO DEATH   HE HAD A
    FEW
LAST, CURIOUSLY SERENE MOMENTS FOR ITS DICTATION:
'THE GARDEN BRIGHT WITH BIRDS & FLOWERS   IN THE NOON HOURS
LIES TRAMPLED UNDER GOATS' FEET   CARELESS IN THEIR LUSTFUL
    HEAT'
DIED 1906
    Reborn as Wystan with new densities?
            INDEED   & WHAT BUT HOMERIC ONES?
    "Immortal Bard, you who created me."
USED ALSO BY A 17TH CENTURY ITALIAN
POET/SCULPTOR   WHA LINKD ALWAYS TO STONE & WORDS

6:00. Stone and words. The balustrade
Pressing back the harder I press down.
Three-story drop. A cat stares up in dread.
Faces streaking through me of the dead,
Traffic whizzing—how the old motor races!
How simply, too, the urge is gratified:
Just shut the eyes . . .
                        But here inside my head
No question of total blackout. Lights all along

Following closely, filling the rear-view mirror,
Forcing upon whichever of us drove
Illumination's blindfold—these lights now gather
Speed to pass. Our own weak dashboard aura,
Our own poor beams that see no further than needed
Will have to guide us through the homeward ride.
Still not alone. Despite the Doppler drop in pitch,
That disappearing car will make things round the bend
Shine eerily, a tree, an underpass of bone;
Or else a dip between hills miles from now
Will glow in recollection—
                              As DJ
Takes his place, beyond words, at my side.

Music. Time. The orange sailcloth awning
Rippled by waves of windless, deepening light.
We kneel on orange cushions under it.
Props include Board and cup; a looking-glass
Iridescent seashells border, Robin's gift
From Malagasy; and this waterworn
Marble wedge that stops a door downstairs.
A blue-and-white rice bowl, brimming with water,
Lobs an ellipse of live brilliance—but so
Athrob there as to court vertigo—
Onto the concrete wall our shadows climb.
Slowly that halo sinks. The mirror's oblong
Gaze outflashes, thirsty for the wine-
Green slopes where sobbing couples intertwine.
While, to one side, our Cassia thick with bloom
Sweeps the stones in a profound salaam.

THE SCHOOLROOM ALL FESTOONED   GEORGIE & WYSTAN
CHAFE IN THEIR CUTAWAYS   MAMAN IN WHITE
SARI WITH ORANGEBLOSSOMS   OUR 3 HEARTS
ABRIM WITH LOVE FOR YOU   ROBERT & UNI
OUTSIDE, NOSES TO PANE, BUT CANNOT HEAR.
UNI WEEPS (TOSS HIM MY BOUQUET FOR LUNCH?)
AND NOW THE LIGHTS   THE INSTRUMENTS   THEY COME

233

DJ.   I'm no better than Uni—

MM.   AH MY LORDS
As Nature and the Brothers quietly enter.
MY QUEEN, HELP US IN A DIFFICULT MOMENT

GK.   DEAR JIMMY   DAVE   GO WELL IN MIND & BODY!

WHA.   YES OLD CONFRERE & FRIEND   & MAKE OUR V WORK
GLORIOUS   U CAN   U CAN   YOU'LL SEE!
Air freshened, leaves in expectation stirring—
Only the too bright music hurts our eyes.

MM.   MES ENFANTS YES   & EVEN OUR SILLY EPHRAIM
PARTICIPATED IN SOMETHING NOT UNLIKE
TODAY WHEN ON A SILVER SATIN PILLOW
THE ENFANT OF FRANCE WAS CARRIED BAWLING INTO
THE HALL OF MIRRORS. SO THERE'S PRECEDENCE
BUT NOTHING TO EQUAL   COME NOW: PLACES, PLEASE!

JM.   We're ready.
Pergolesi's minuet
Turned by Stravinsky to this "wedding trio"
—Soprano, tenor, bass, movement of utmost
Suavity—is playing as we get
Our last instructions.

MM.   JM WILL TAKE THE MARBLE
STYLUS & GIVING US THE BENEFIT
OF A WELLAIMED WORD, SEND OUR IMAGINED SELVES
FALLING IN SHARDS THRU THE ETERNAL WATERS
(DJ CUPBEARER) & INTO THE GOLDEN BOUGH
OF MYTH   ON INTO LIFE   D'ACCORD? HUGS   KISSES
WE'LL WRITE WHEN WE FIND WORK

DJ.   We do it *now*?

MM.   ONE MOMENT MORE   SUNSET   INTO THE LIGHT
LORDS, ACCEPT THESE YOUR CHILDREN   MAJESTY,
BLESS OUR ENTERPRISES   BLESS US!

Nat.   CHILD,
POETS, SCIENTIST, HAND, ALL HEAVEN HOLDS ITS BREATH.
NOW MICHAEL, RING DOWN THE CURTAIN! GABRIEL,

THE STARS! RAPHAEL, ARMS OUT FOR THIS WISE & WITTY ONE!
EMMANUEL FOR ALL THREE! GO WELL!
AND YES, MY PROSERPINE, MY ARIEL,
MY DEAREST DEAR, SLIP SAFELY INTO YOU!
I WILL STAND HELPFUL TO THESE YOUR MORTAL FRIENDS.
ADIEU

Our eyes meet. DJ nods. We've risen. Shutters
Click at dreamlike speed. Sky. Awning. Bowl.
The stylus lifted. Giving up its whole
Lifetime of images, the mirror utters

A little treble shriek and rides the flood
Or tinkling mini-waterfall through wet
Blossoms to lie—and look, the sun has set—
In splinters apt, from now on, to draw blood,

Each with its scimitar or bird-beak shape
Able, days hence, aglitter in the boughs
Or face-down, black on soil beneath, to rouse
From its deep swoon the undestroyed heartscape

—Then silence. Then champagne.
                              And should elsewhere
Broad wings revolve a horselike form into
One Creature upward-shining brief as dew,
Swifter than bubbles in wine, through evening air

Up, far up, O whirling point of Light—:

HERS HEAR ME I AND MINE SURVIVE SIGNAL
ME DO YOU WELL I ALONE IN MY NIGHT
HOLD IT BACK HEAR ME BROTHERS I AND MINE

James Merrill

James Merrill was born in New York City and now
lives in Stonington, Connecticut. He is the author
of eight earlier books of poems, which have won him
two National Book Awards (for *Nights and Days* and
Mirabell), the Bollingen Prize in Poetry (for *Braving
the Elements*) and the Pulitzer Prize (for *Divine
Comedies*). He has also written two novels, *The (Diblos)
Notebook* (1965) and *The Seraglio* (1957), and two plays,
The Immortal Husband (first produced in 1955 and
published in Playbook the following year), and in
one act, *The Bait*, published in Artist's Theatre (1960).